# CONTEMPORARY GREEK FICTION IN A UNITED EUROPE
## FROM LOCAL HISTORY TO THE GLOBAL INDIVIDUAL

# THE EUROPEAN HUMANITIES RESEARCH CENTRE

## UNIVERSITY OF OXFORD

*Director:* Martin McLaughlin
Fiat-Serena Professor of Italian Studies

The European Humanities Research Centre of the University of Oxford organizes a range of academic activities, including conferences and workshops, and publishes scholarly works under its own imprint, LEGENDA. Within Oxford, the EHRC bridges, at the research level, the main humanities faculties: Modern Languages, English, Modern History, Classics and Philosophy, Music and Theology. The Centre stimulates interdisciplinary research collaboration throughout these subject areas and provides an Oxford base for advanced researchers in the humanities.

The Centre's publishing programme focuses on making available the results of advanced research in medieval and modern languages and related interdisciplinary areas. An Editorial Board, whose members are drawn from across the British university system, covers the principal European languages. Titles currently include works on Arabic, Catalan, Chinese, English, French, German, Italian, Portuguese, Russian, Spanish, Greek and Yiddish literature. In addition, the EHRC co-publishes with the Society for French Studies, the Modern Humanities Research Association and the British Comparative Literature Association. The Centre also publishes a Special Lecture Series under the LEGENDA imprint, and a journal, *Oxford German Studies*.

*Further information:*
Kareni Bannister, Senior Publications Officer
European Humanities Research Centre
University of Oxford
76 Woodstock Road, Oxford OX2 6HP
enquiries@ehrc.ox.ac.uk
www.ehrc.ox.ac.uk

# LEGENDA

EUROPEAN HUMANITIES RESEARCH CENTRE

*University of Oxford*

# Contemporary Greek Fiction in a United Europe

## From Local History to the Global Individual

❖

EDITED BY

PETER MACKRIDGE AND ELENI YANNAKAKIS

LEGENDA

European Humanities Research Centre
University of Oxford
2004

Published by the
European Humanities Research Centre
of the University of Oxford
76 Woodstock Road
Oxford OX2 6HP

LEGENDA is the publications imprint of the
European Humanities Research Centre

ISBN 1 900755 85 8

First published 2004

British Library Cataloguing in Publication Data
A CIP catalogue record for this book is available from the British Library

LEGENDA series designed by Cox Design Partnership, Witney, Oxon
Printed in Great Britain by
Information Press
Eynsham
Oxford OX8 1JJ

Copy-Editor: Dr Leofranc Holford-Strevens

# CONTENTS

❖

# ACKNOWLEDGEMENTS

❖

The editors would like to express their thanks to the following for their assistance in organizing the conference from which this volume developed:

Alexander S. Onassis Public Benefit Foundation
The A. G. Leventis Foundation
The Hellenic Foundation, London
The Hellenic Foundation for Culture, Athens
Dr Victoria Solomonidou, Culture Counsellor,
Greek Embassy, London
EasyJet

They would also like to thank Ms Christina Theochari, Greek National Book Centre, for her kind assistance with bibliographical details.

This volume has been produced with a generous grant from the J. C. Costopoulos Foundation.

The quotation from 'Annus Mirabilis', from Philip Larkin, *Collected Poems* (London: Faber and Faber, 1988), © Faber and Faber, is reproduced by kind permission of Faber and Faber.

The quotation from 'Poseidonians', from C. P. Cavafy, *Collected Poems*, trans. Edmund Keeley and Philip Sherrard (Princeton: Princeton University Press, 1992), © Edmund Keeley and Philip Sherrard (for the translation) and SNH/Cavafy Archive (for the original), is reproduced by kind permission of Professor Edmund Keeley, Mrs Denise Sherrard and Mr Manolis Savidis.

# NOTES ON CONTRIBUTORS

❖

*Venetia Apostolidou* is Assistant Professor of Modern Greek Literature in the Education Department at the Aristotle University of Thessaloniki. She has published books and articles on the history of Modern Greek literary criticism, on post-war fiction and on literature in education.

*Vangelis Athanassopoulos* is Professor of Modern Greek Literature at the University of Athens. He has published books and articles on Greek literature of the nineteenth and twentieth centuries.

*Vangelis Calotychos* is Assistant Professor of Comparative Literature and Hellenic Studies at New York University. He has published widely on modern Greek literature and culture in comparative contexts, including *Modern Greece: A Cultural Poetics* (Oxford: Berg, 2003).

*Vangelis Hatzivassiliou* is a literary critic on the Athens newspaper *Eleftherotypia*. He has published monographs, collections of essays, articles and anthologies relating to contemporary and older Greek poetry and fiction.

*Maria Kakavoulia* is a lecturer at Panteio University of Social and Political Sciences, Athens. She has published two books on the narrative analysis of modern Greek prose. She is currently doing research on language and communication, discourse analysis and literary and media narratives.

*Angela Kastrinaki* is Associate Professor of Modern Greek Literature at the University of Crete. She is also the author of short stories, a translator of literary theory, a book reviewer and an essayist.

*Konstantinos Kosmas* works for the Hellenic Foundation for Culture in Berlin. His Ph.D. dissertation for the Freie Universität Berlin, 'After History: History, Historical Novel and National Identities at the End of the Twentieth Century', is shortly to be published.

*Peter Mackridge* is Professor of Modern Greek at the University of Oxford and a Fellow of St Cross College. He has published numerous books and articles on Greek language and literature from medieval to modern times.

*Argiro Mantoglou* is a writer and a literary critic. She has published two collections of poetry and three novels. She works as a book reviewer for the Greek newspaper *Eleftherotypia*.

*Mary Mike* is Associate Professor of Modern Greek Literature at the Aristotle University of Thessaloniki. Her work on gender studies, ideology, thematics and technique of Greek prose writing during the nineteenth and twentieth centuries includes *Melpo Axioti: Critical Studies* (Athens: Kedros, 1996) and *Transvestism in Modern Greek Prose (19th–20th centuries)* (Athens: Kedros, 2001).

*Anastasia Natsina* is currently completing a D.Phil. in Modern Greek at the University of Oxford. Her research interests and publications focus on contemporary Greek fiction (mainly short stories) and postmodernism.

*Dimitris Païvanas* taught Modern Greek at Melbourne and La Trobe Universities between 1984 and 1997. He co-ordinates Modern Greek Language Courses at the Babel Language Centre in Athens and is writing his Ph.D. thesis on the prose fiction of Thanassis Valtinos at the University of Birmingham.

*Dimitris Tziovas* is Professor of Modern Greek Studies at the University of Birmingham. His publications include *The Other Self: Selfhood and Society in Modern Greek Fiction* (Lanham, MD: Lexington Books, 2003) and the edited volume *Greece and the Balkans: Identities, Perceptions and Cultural Encounters since the Enlightenment* (Aldershot: Ashgate, 2003).

*Eleni Yannakakis* holds degrees from the Universities of Athens and London (MA, Ph.D.). She has taught Modern Greek Literature at the Universities of Crete (1991–3) and Oxford (1997–2003). She has published widely on issues of twentieth-century Greek literature and is the author of the novel *On Taste and Other Horrors* (in Greek).

# NOTE ON TRANSLITERATION
# AND TRANSLATION

❖

In the main text of this volume, the titles of novels and collections of short stories are quoted in English translation. Where an English translation of the relevant volume has been published, we refer to the title used in the published translation; otherwise we use a literal translation of the title. The original Greek titles are given in the notes, while the bibliography gives both versions. Except where otherwise stated, the English translations of quotations from Greek fiction have been done by the authors or translators of the relevant chapters.

All Greek names, titles and other Greek words have been transliterated into Latin characters. A fairly straightforward and consistent convention has been used for this purpose, except that where authors are already known in English through translations published as separate volumes, we use the version of the name that appears on the translated work.

INTRODUCTION

❖

# Greek Fiction in the Age of Globalization

*Peter Mackridge and Eleni Yannakakis*

In 2003 a new Greek literary magazine for young or non-established writers appeared, called *Here's an Apple*. The editor's note in the first issue, labelled as a non-manifesto, had this to say:

Having been born or come of age in the period after the restoration of democracy, we feel neither the guilt of the Left nor the guilt of the Right. By 'politics' we mean chiefly international events. We have always had CNN at home and the international press at the newsagent's. The whole planet is our domain and we've walked practically all over it. Apart from CNN we have always had MTV. Since CDs come out on the same day all over the world, we listen to the same music in Athens as in Moscow and Seattle. We see the same films almost simultaneously and the same theatrical productions with a few months' delay. We have always had access to information. The internet is taken for granted as much as the coffee-machine and the lift. Technology has brought up-to-date information. The more information, the less knowledge, some claim. Perhaps they are wrong. *Apple* has contributors who, if nothing else, love reading—reading and writing. It is writing we would like to trace, and we suspect that we have much in common with Banana Yoshimoto, Ray Loriga and Niccolò Ammaniti. For the moment, no one equal to Flaubert has been found in our group, but we're not giving up.[1]

This very illuminating note seems to sum up the ideology of contemporary Greek literature, or at least a large part of it; even more importantly, it indicates a conscious and wholehearted acceptance of the methods and implications of globalization, to the extent that they are promoted as a positive value within a local cultural ideology. In the Greek context, this editorial marks a conscious alignment with the cultural ideology of the rest of the world—or at least a desire for such an alignment, since there would be no need for such a declaration if this were complete. Nevertheless, it points to a radical change that started discreetly soon after the restoration of democracy in 1974 and is still continuing to escalate. This turning-point implied that contemporary Greek literature and culture were moving away from collective ideals and the preoccupation with local politics and concentrating instead on issues of a private and personal nature—which are, in a sense, at the same time international. Contemporary Greek literature thus appears to be participating actively in the current process by which cultural borders are being abolished throughout the world.

The year 1974 was a turning-point for Greek literature and culture, but even more so for Greek history, for it witnessed the last in a long series of events that have marked the turbulent history of the Greek state since it was established in 1830. Once the Greek state had became independent from the Ottoman Empire, it offered a national identity and citizenship to those inhabiting the area enclosed within its geographical borders, who until then had possessed loosely defined ethnic or cultural identities.[2] However, the future of the young kingdom proved more precarious than expected, chiefly because of territorial disputes with its immediate neighbours (Turkey and Bulgaria), until her present borders were secured and solidified in 1923. Even after that, Greece was occupied by the Axis Powers in the Second World War, which was immediately followed by civil war (1945–9), and went through a very turbulent Cold War period, culminating in the imposition of the Colonels' dictatorship (1967–74). Since 1974, however, Greece has been enjoying its longest ever period of peace and democracy, while its entry into the European Union (1981) has been followed by a period of unprecedented affluence.

## Relations with Europe

Greece's relations with other European countries did not start with its entry into the European Union. The establishment of the Greek state was itself the work of Europe, that is of a group of the most powerful countries in the area at that time, namely Britain, France and Russia. More importantly, the ideological preparation for the Greek War of Independence in 1821 that led to the establishment of the Greek state can be credited to ideas that originated in Renaissance and Enlightenment Europe and were imported into Ottoman-dominated Greece by the Greek-speaking élite, who frequently travelled to Europe and in some cases resided there permanently. However, it was not only revolutionary ideas that were imported into Greece at that time; there was something more than that, namely the legitimation of the Greeks' cause and the construction of their cultural identity.

In spite of the uninterrupted continuity in the use of the Greek language from antiquity to the nineteenth century in the area of the Ottoman Empire that now belongs to Greece, the various Greek-, Vlach-, Slav- and Albanian-speaking communities that lived in this region lacked any established and homogeneous ethnic or cultural identity, mainly because of the high degree of mobility of these populations in the preceding centuries, starting from the Roman Empire and continuing through Byzantium to the period of Ottoman domination. Instead, religion was the main criterion of belonging for these populations. The construction of fixed identities and the requirement of allegiance to a particular national state was the ideological invention of the nineteenth century across Europe. The nations of western Europe were attempting to establish their own cultural identity and their own historical and cultural origins at that time. The rediscovery of Ancient Greece by Europeans in their effort to establish a cultural precedent and a continuity for themselves, the 'westernization' of the classical heritage,[3] as Constantine Tsoukalas calls it, greatly benefited the cause of the Orthodox Christian populations of the Greek peninsula, who acquired not only their independence from the Ottomans and a recognized national state within fixed geographical borders, but also an unquestionable cultural identity of their own: they were recognized as the rightful cultural—if not physical—descendants of the Ancient Greeks. In Tsoukalas's words,

it should be kept in mind that Greece largely owed its independence to an international military intervention, which if not motivated was at least facilitated by the omnipresent European romantic cult of antiquity. Once again, Greece was seen and saw itself as the 'geocultural' vanguard of a European civilization fighting against the barbarians.[4]

Thus both Greece and the rest of Europe ultimately drew their cultural identity from the same source.

However, if Europeans feel that part of their cultural past lies in Ancient Greece, how have Greeks felt about Europe? Local history again played an important role in Greeks' attitude towards Europe between 1830 and the end of the twentieth century. In spite of the fact that bonds with Europe continued to be tight on the political level after 1830 (Greece's royal family was even imported from Europe),[5] Greece was culturally and ideologically split between East and West, since for almost a century the country continued to be preoccupied with expanding its geographical borders towards the north and the east. This cultivated a Hellenocentric and irredentist mentality that favoured nationalistic ideals. The turning-point in this attitude was Greece's defeat in 1922 at the hands of the Turkish army in Asia Minor,[6] which put an end to Greece's irredentist and expansionist policy and led, with the Treaty of Lausanne in 1923, to the consolidation of Greece's geographical borders, which have remained approximately the same ever since. It is no coincidence that soon after this defeat there was a decisive turn towards Europe on the part of the intellectual élite. It was in 1929 that the first calls for a cultural convergence with Europe were made. In a seminal essay, entitled *Free Spirit* and later considered as the manifesto of literary Modernism in Greece, the novelist and playwright Yorgos Theotokas, who had spent some time in Europe, bravely urged the young generation of intellectuals to reject the introverted and Hellenocentric tradition of the past, not only in literature but also in culture as a whole, and to look outward towards Europe in terms of a relationship based on equality and the mutual exchange of ideas.

Indeed, the literary generation that is considered to have started in the 1930s—possibly the most important in the history of the literature of the modern Greek state—and which is commonly identified with the cultivation of Modernism in Greece, exhibited strong ties with Europe and European thought. Regardless of various differences that distinguish it from its European counterparts, Greek Modernism was primarily European as regards both the spirit and the letter. Its advocates were educated in Europe and were well read in European literature and aesthetics. However, Greek Modernism's alliances with Europe were more aesthetic than cultural; strictly speaking, these writers confined themselves to intertextual relations between literary works rather than broadening out to relations between similar life-styles and mentalities.[7] However, this pro-European attitude caused reactions from certain Greek intellectuals, who argued for a redefinition of Greek cultural identity towards a more Hellenocentric orientation. This ideological change led to an output of literature inspired by Hellenocentric ideas, especially towards the end of the decade, and more specifically after the imposition of the Metaxas dictatorship (1936–41), when nationalism as the dominant ideology was fast spreading across the whole of Europe.[8] This tendency continued and even strengthened during the 1940s.

After the Second World War, the attitude towards Europe was complex because of the specific socio-political conditions prevailing in Greece during the first phase of the Cold War (the Greek Civil War, the Greek-Cypriot struggle for liberation from British control and union with Greece, and an intense political instability leading to the imposition of the Colonels' dictatorship in 1967). Both ideologically and culturally, the pendulum swung between a pro-Western and a nationalistic attitude. The imposition of the dictatorship entailed first the isolation of Greece from Europe and an inward turn, secondly, the imposition of severe censorship and, thirdly, the escape of many democratic intellectuals to the West and particularly to France. It was these intellectuals who, after 1974, once more became the importers of European culture into Greece and who dominated Greek cultural and political life, through academia, literature, the media and even policy-making.[9]

Greek culture seems to have changed considerably since 1974. Greeks are currently enjoying being part of Europe in many respects. The two decades following Greece's official entry into the European Union have been marked by political stability and an unprecedented economic growth which to a great degree is the result of aid flows channelled into Greece through the Community Support Framework. This combination of political stability and affluence has resulted in a sense of well-being among Greeks, who have developed highly consumerist patterns of behaviour, manifested in the purchase of lifestyle goods, access to information from the internet and the international media, and the ability to travel extensively and to study abroad, both in Europe and further afield. These patterns in their turn reinforce Greeks' sense of feeling European through the adoption of a lifestyle that people in the West have or are assumed to have. It also reinforces their gradual move away from a traditional and typically Greek way of life in favour of more internationalized patterns of behaviour.[10] As Yorgos Chouliaras has put it,

in Greece, too [as well as in Western Europe] differences of dress, food, the built environment, furnishings, everyday behaviours, and, in general, various attributes of cultural distinction have been losing specificity. [...]. It can be demonstrated in general that loss of cultural specificity and homogenization in a globalizing environment is carried out by willing consumers in the expectation of improvement in their conditions of everyday life. [....] Greeks and Spaniards, Southern Europeans in general and others at the peripheries of Europe, can be expected, [...] to be enthusiastic Europeans. They associate a changing way of life that conforms to European patterns with a higher status and cultural recognition.[11]

As we shall see later in this introduction as well as in the chapters by individual contributors, fictional characters in contemporary Greek literature (and most probably writers too) feel entirely at home in Europe (and to some degree in the rest of the world), while they often claim that European culture is their own.[12] In the view of a contemporary critic, Dimosthenis Kourtovik, Greek writers have demonstrated in their work that they feel

quite Greek, quite European and quite cosmopolitan, without finding any contradiction in this threefold identity. It is not an ideological stance, but an expression of the reality they are experiencing. They don't 'go to Europe' as previous generations did, since they do not view Greece as something radically different from Europe and do not feel that they betray their Greekness when they place their characters within a cosmopolitan environment.[13]

However, the question we are faced with here is which culture they are gradually assimilating and feeling comfortable in. Is it a European culture—here meaning a mixture of attitudes, ways of life and thought encountered in the currently dominant European countries —or the globalized, chiefly American, culture, that is gradually eroding the individual cultures of Europe?

This is a very vexed question, as is the very issue of globalization itself. However, it has been argued that whatever diversion from traditional European values and culture is implied by globalization, it is basically and primarily of European origin. As well as the 'decentralization' of capital and power[14]—the creation of multiple political and financial centres around the world, pre-eminent among them being America—the apparent loss of Europe's dominant role in the globalizing process is false and misleading, in the sense that the capitalist ideology is exclusively the offspring of Europe. This explains why on economic issues, which are primary when we talk about globalization and the mobility of capital, despite the fact that Europe and even America may be gradually losing dominance, Euro-American cultural values still preserve their supremacy, since the world system keeps functioning on Euro-American political and sociological models.[15]

A significant problem lies in the chasm between European 'high culture' and American 'mass culture', with the latter tending to steal a march on the former.[16] This is due to the economic, technological and military supremacy of America over Europe and to the fact that America has access to many more markets around the globe than Europe does. For Greeks, however—and possibly for other Europeans too—it is not easy to distinguish what is American from what is European. For many Greeks, whatever is not traditionally Greek[17] is automatically classified as Western; this is an umbrella-like characterization accommodating American culture too. In this sense, Greeks are bound to follow a 'western' culture without really being in a position to detect either the mutations to which traditional forms of European culture have been subjected because of globalization or the non-western elements that this culture has absorbed during the globalizing process.

## Globalization and Culture

The phenomenon of globalization[18] has given rise to numerous debates and arguments about its true nature as well as its implications and prospects.[19] Without embarking here on a similar discussion concerning the multifarious definitions of globalization,[20] we can try to describe it in the light of its manifestations: globalization becomes obvious when people all over the world (at least social strata of an equivalent financial calibre) consume the same products, receive information about the world from similar sources, share similar criteria for the definition of happiness, have similar worries, are threatened by the same diseases, have similar nutrition and eating patterns, and choose similar ways of entertainment. Globalization has been blamed for the intervention in the lives of people on the other side of the planet in both practical and institutional terms, the impact on the environment, for instance through the establishment of dumps for industrial waste far away from the area where the industry is based, the inter-continental trade in human organs and the international sex industry.

Globalization is not the direct result of the 'imperialist' policy of a single country, such as America, though America is at the heart of the globalization process. The nation-state, the creation of the period of modernity and nationalism, started to outgrow its function and to lose power in 1945. During the Cold War it weakened even further through the establishment of transnational formations and alliances of countries on the pattern of the American and Soviet models. Geographically, if not ideologically, Europe was somewhere between these two different models. However, it was the flourishing of multinational corporations that seems to have delivered the *coup de grâce* to the autonomy of the nation-state and brought about the current globalization phenomenon in practice, in the time of post-modernity. National companies, whose production and delivery of goods or services took place within the national borders of one country, have been succeeded by multinational corporations whose capital is of international origin, and which have been transferring their production sites all over the world, including Third World countries where labour and raw material are cheap.

The result of all this is that, on the level of the companies, there emerged the so-called 'decentralization of capital', implying the lack of need for fixed sites of production and a fixed place of origin and disposition of capital. The promotion of multinational corporations into a powerful regulating factor, not only in financial matters but also in social and cultural areas, and the subsequent fragmentation of power, have sometimes led to the upgrading of certain areas that accommodate the production site or the corporation headquarters and the downgrading of others that are marginalized and condemned to poverty, all this taking place often without serious consultation with the national states involved, whose authority is thereby undermined.[21]

As we have seen, significant changes have followed on the level of society and culture. This has happened chiefly because a new cultural consensus was required, namely a homogenized code of conduct, lifestyle and entertainment patterns, so that mobile populations feel at home in each new environment where they are sent to work; this homogenization of culture concerns both the population of employees and the host society. The new culture is a mixture of all the heterogeneous or even 'exotic' features that the mobile populations around the world come across, which after being adjusted accordingly are commercialized and become popular and trendy goods and lifestyles that are now marketed all round the world.[22] Entertainment plays an important part in this new globalized culture: multinational corporations in the culture industry take up the task of producing cultural products (moving images, printing and publishing, audio, spectacle) aimed at entertaining the world's masses but also at homogenizing them even further. Technology, on the other hand, in the form of communication and transport, comes to 're-connect' those people with their places of origin and with the rest of world for personal or professional purposes. The development and use of technology is not limited to those who continually change their place of work; it is being used increasingly by millions of people around the globe,[23] who can communicate efficiently and quickly. However, this mode of communication through technology implies a loss of the physical contact that exists in traditional societies, and this may result not only in a sense of self-sufficiency and individuation but also in feelings of loneliness and alienation. These mobile populations are gradually losing their strong sense of national and cultural identity and becoming 'creolized'.[24]

A counter-effect of this relative homogenization of culture is the flourishing of the sense of locality. Historically, it is well known that when the nation-state was strong, as in the age of modernity, individual cultures were repressed in an effort to homogenize and assimilate the various different populations living within the borders of the state; the imposition of a single ideology and culture on all citizens was necessary for the preservation of the power of the state. By contrast, in the time of postmodernity and with the gradual weakening of the traditional notion of the nation-state, local differences in language, culture, religion, race and gender are tolerated and accepted, and ideological, cultural and religious polyphony prevails, since the power has now been transferred to centres outside the borders of nation-states. The revival of locality is even encouraged, so that the impression of freedom and democracy is given to the groups concerned, while at the same time these local cultural features are gradually incorporated and commercialized and become features of a global civilization, which apart from the financial profit they offer, will facilitate the globalization process even further, with people around the globe feeling that their own individual culture is part of this process.[25]

## The Metamorphosis of Greek Literature

There is no doubt that contemporary Greece is participating wholeheartedly in the culture of postmodernity[26] and whatever it implies, while the impact of globalization seems to be affecting all aspects of economic or cultural life. *Apple's* editorial, quoted at the beginning of this introduction, implies exactly that. According to Nikos Mouzelis, Greece's 'obvious indicators of a post-modern trend are [...] on the cultural level, the striking depoliticization of the younger generation, its orientation to individualistic consumerism, as well as its return to the Orthodox faith (whose apophatic approach to the divine has striking affinities with post-modern sensibilities)'.[27] The first two of these tendencies, which, according to Dimitris Tziovas, are due to the rise of individualism in Greece in recent years, constitute the dominant features of contemporary Greek literature (viewed here as reflecting as well as affecting prevalent cultural and societal tendencies). From being a society aspiring to collective ideals, Tziovas argues, Greek society is gradually becoming an individualistic one, where individual happiness and well-being are gaining the upper hand at the expense of public interest and the political; the fact that Greek society—which had hitherto not gone through the individuation process that other Western countries did after the Renaissance—has become increasingly individualistic in the last thirty years is, according to the same author, a consequence not only of the waning of the role of the nation-state in Greece and elsewhere, but also of the waning of the Greek Left, which had idealized collectivity and promoted 'a sense of duty toward it as the ultimate moral principle for ensuring social solidarity and ideological conformity'.[28] Under the auspices of a left-wing ideology and with memories of the Second World War and the Greek Civil War still fresh, the fiction of writers who first appeared in the 1940s and 1950s[29] was over-whelmingly political, whereas that of the writers of the 1960s[30] started including themes of a private nature. With the dictatorship and the imposition of censorship, literature became political again, but in order to do so it had to be allegorical or simply non-existent: many writers stopped publishing at that time as a resistance to the regime. The political continued to be dominant after 1974, but the writers of fiction who first appeared in the mid-1970s[31] start viewing the politics of the immediate past through a subjective perspective: the hostile political environment simply constitutes the canvas on which the evolving consciousnesses of the characters are prominently drawn. The erosion of the political by the private and subjective perspective is celebrated in a seminal novel by Aris Alexandrou, *Mission Box* (1975),[32] in which subjection to any (political) ideology is drastically questioned.[33]

In the last quarter of the twentieth century, faced by the gradual disappearance of a national readership that might share his/her fictional accounts of important historical and political events in terms of a political and cultural consensus, the writer addressed readers who had gradually become depoliticized, individualized and culturally, ethnically or religiously diversified, and his/her work was adjusted to take account of these new conditions.[34] The writers who made their first appearance from 1980 onwards (who include most of those whose work is discussed in the present volume) are now dealing exclusively with themes of a personal and everyday nature; politics has been ostracized from much of their fiction, especially during the 1990s;[35] when it exists, it is either an entirely decorative element (an indication of locality, for instance, among several others) or is viewed negatively.[36]

However, even in the past, there were periods in the history of Greek literature, such as the inter-war period, when there was a strong tendency towards themes of a private nature as a reaction to the failure of history to fulfil people's ideals. Yet that literature was still profoundly, albeit implicitly, imbued with the historical and political anxieties of its time. By contrast, the recent 'privatization' of literature implies the thematization of the everyday, the ephemeral and the intensely individualistic: the same anxieties are of an exclusively private nature, and they are the same anxieties as can be experienced anywhere in the world. As Elisavet Kotzia has rightly put it, the difference between the work of the writers of the inter-war generation and that of the post-dictatorship writers is that the former exhibit a sense of a moral responsibility in relation to society, or to God, or to primordial philosophical issues of good and evil, while in the work of the latter there is no 'sense of vision, duty or mission'.[37]

However, it is not only the lack of a sense of duty that differentiates the fiction of the inter-war period from that of the post-dictatorship period: there is also a significant difference in matters of technique and use of language. As we have already mentioned, inter-war writers introduced Modernism into Greece. Their formal experimentations were often radical enough to render some of their work so élitist and intellectual that they were not approachable by a wider readership. Though the use of modernist techniques returned in the 1960s in the work of such writers as Stratis Tsirkas and Melpo Axioti, the dominant mode of the more or less political fiction of the period between the war and the dictatorship was realism. Though realism still holds firm in post–1974 fiction, this writing appears increasingly multiform in the sense that Modernism is combined with techniques usually encountered in postmodernist fiction, such as the amalgamation of different genres[38] and discourses and the construction of parodies and fantasies.[39] Other significant changes in contemporary fiction include the predominant use of a first-person narrator (in keeping with fiction of a subjective, often autobiographical nature), the reduction in the distance between narrator and characters, the radical fragmentation of the linear sequence of time and the use of utopian location. There seems to be a radical change in the use of language too: from the ornate language of inter-war Modernism, we have moved to a representational, journalistic type of discourse[40] or to a discourse based on oral communication,[41] where everyday colloquialism combines with the idiolects of specific social groups or with various Greek dialects. Another interesting phenomenon is the use of English sentences or words (in Greek or in Latin characters) embedded in Greek fictional texts.

The settings of the stories have also changed, as we shall see in more detail later in this introduction and in the individual chapters: from a clearly Greek setting in the fiction of the post-war generations we move to a kind of cosmopolitanism, especially during the 1990s and after, which brings this literature superficially close to the cosmopolitan fiction of the inter-war period. However, this new cosmopolitanism is of a different kind from the superficial, undigested and rather decorative depiction of travel in the inter-war fiction of upper-class writers who could afford to travel and study abroad:[42] it is rather the result of the globalization of culture, where actual long-distance travel, together with virtual travelling on the super-highways of the web, is viewed as an ordinary activity for almost all social strata in Greece.

Finally, special reference should be made to the unprecedented rise in the number of women novelists in recent years. Because of the general boom in the Greek publishing industry, with the number of fiction titles appearing each year having increased tremendously since 1980, there is more space for women writers to secure a publisher; on the other hand, the majority of fiction readers nowadays are women.[43] In this respect, women writers are aware that they have a greater likelihood of being read by women than by men, and this is bound to affect the choice of theme: for instance, women readers might have a preference for fiction about family life or personal and love problems.[44] But, regardless of intention, women's writing all over the world tends to be more subjective and personal than that of men, and this, according to Tziovas, has contributed significantly to the rise of this type of fiction recently.[45]

Let us now investigate the various tendencies exhibited in the themes of contemporary Greek fiction in greater detail. These tendencies reflect preoccupations with (*a*) the private and the personal, (*b*) travel as an indication of cosmopolitanism and ideological flexibility and (*c*) the revival of an interest in the past.

### (a) The private sphere

By the private sphere we mean a broad and general tendency—also permeating some of the novels we examine under the other two headings—to weave the story of a novel around a personal issue, affair or idea of a private nature that has no large-scale collective ramifications. The collective and ideological ideals that characterized Greek fiction up to the end of the 70s have given way to those of happiness and well-being on a personal or family level.[46] Even if these texts are set in a particular locality and often depict local cultural particularities, the setting does not acquire ideological dimensions, but simply represents the familiar for both writer and reader. Even so, the degree of fidelity with which local culture is represented varies, especially in the fiction of younger writers, where, in spite of the local setting, the culture can be considered more international and cosmopolitan (through references to music, bar culture, general lifestyle, culinary habits, etc.) than typically Greek, at least as compared with the culture depicted in the novels of older writers. This tendency can be observed in most fiction of the 80s and 90s, including some of those works exhibiting the 'travel' tendency, such as those by Dimitris Nollas, Neni Efthymiadi and Alexis Stamatis, as well as some of those exhibiting the historical tendency, such as Zyranna Zateli's *And at Wolf-Light they Return* (1993) and Ioanna Karystiani's *Little England* (1997).[47] The majority of these novels orientated towards private life adopt a traditional mode of narration.

### (b) Geographical and ideological wanderings

In contrast to the mainly Greece-bound fiction of the 80s, the 90s have been marked by a significant tendency to broaden the geographical borders of fictional stories. Travel to Europe, the Balkans and the rest of the world (with a preference for the United States) and the encounter and interaction with the Other are the main features of this tendency. This latter feature seems to reflect a sincere desire to interact with non-Greeks in a non-discriminatory manner, either through journeys by Greeks beyond their national borders, or through the experiences of immigrants to Greece from the Balkans and the former Soviet Union.[48]

Travelling to the rest of the world here implies something more than a sterile cosmopolitanism aimed at impressing readers in Greece or appealing to the taste of those outside the country, since the experiences of the characters abroad usually seem to be the result of a profound rather than a touristic contact with the other place. Europe in particular, as we have extensively discussed, is viewed in most cases not as a geographical alternative to Greece but as a broader homeland where Greek characters feel physically, culturally and ideologically at home. In these works, they feel that they belong to Europe and know its culture, and that they themselves, as descendants of the Ancient Greeks, are connected with the people who made such a significant contribution to European civilization.

On the other hand, in the majority of cases, the Other, and particularly the one that comes from Eastern Europe and the former Soviet Union, is viewed in a non-stereotypical manner. Especially when it comes to those arriving in Greece as immigrants, the tendency is to share the point of view and the emotional world of these people during their interaction with native Greeks, who often treat them in a far from friendly way.

In general, this large group of novels shows Greeks being rather relaxed about their perceived Greekness. For reasons that include the ease with which Greeks travel abroad nowadays, the influence of the media and, as far as the European Union is concerned, the ideology that 'Greece belongs to the West', contemporary Greek fiction exhibits both a marked cosmopolitanism and a sense of being Greek that leaves some space for the inclusion of the Other.

### (c) The revival of the 'historical' novel

Together with an outward look beyond Greece's national borders, there has been a turn towards Greece's historical past. This turn tends to manifest itself in two kinds of novel. The first represents a whole period (when important historical events may or may not be occurring) as the socio-political background of the novel's plot and its fictional characters.[49] The second kind presents the fictional biography of more or less well-known historical figures.[50] What is interesting about this turn to the past is the fact that the past is now seen from a modern ideological perspective. At a time when history itself is increasingly viewed as historiography, that is as simply a matter of perspectives, and contemporary Greek society has almost entirely freed itself from the ideological polarizations that had shaken it until the 1970s, current representations of the past now appear to be aware of their relativistic and often biased nature. Ideological and cultural dilemmas such as those of Muslim vs. Christian, left-wing vs. right-wing, Greek vs. non-Greek, man vs. woman become more and more irrelevant in the majority of these novels, even though they make an effort to depict the historical and cultural reality of the past as faithfully as possible. In other words, these novels attempt a re-evaluation of Greece's recent historical past. This re-evaluation according to the personal and subjective perspective of the writer (who is often a woman) is in itself a way of claiming that history is exclusively a matter of perspective.

## The Contributions to this Volume

This is the first book in English (and the first book in any language other than Greek) to offer an overview of Greek fiction produced since 1974. With the exception of the chapters by Konstantinos Kosmas and Dimitris Païvanas, the contributions to this volume are revised versions of papers given at a conference held in Oxford in January 2002.

In Part 1, entitled 'An Overview of Tendencies and Perspectives', Dimitris Tziovas attempts to delineate three categories of fiction that appeared during the period under examination. In his view, these are (*a*) an outward movement of fictional characters who travel away from Greece, (*b*) the depoliticization of fiction and (*c*) the emphasis on mediated discourse, in other words the use of paratextual material of a variety of heterogenous discourses, in an attempt to highlight the relativistic nature of experience and truth.

Part 2, entitled 'Shifting Spaces, Drifting Identities', deals with the encounter with the national, ideological, geographical and national Other. In a brief discussion of a variety of contemporary Greek fiction texts, Vangelis Hatzivassiliou examines the encounter with the Other both within Greece (in the case of immigrants working in Greece) and outside Greece (when Greeks themselves travel). Along similar lines, Vangelis Calotychos investigates the treatment of Balkan immigrant workers in Greece by discussing fiction by Sotiris Dimitriou, Menis Koumandareas, Christos Voupouras/Yorgos Korras and Michel Fais. He attempts to show how the reception of these Balkan immigrants in essence reflects the ever-changing relation of Greece to its own Balkan past and its European present and future. Mary Mike investigates the construction of identity in the age of globalization. In the fictional texts she discusses, place is the factor that both connects and alienates. In their dialectical relationship, the lived place of the present and the remembered place of the past prove that both global and local, travelling and homecoming are two sides of the same coin and are equally fragmenting processes. Finally, Eleni Yannakakis attempts a categorization of contemporary Greek novels in which characters travel abroad. Through the discussion of some representative works, she concludes that, whatever the motives, travelling in these texts is chiefly of an ideological character.

Part 3, entitled 'The Global as Local', examines the issue of locality within a globalizing culture. Through the examination of Sotiris Dimitriou's fiction, Venetia Apostolidou argues that locality does not necessarily oppose the global; on the contrary, the former appears to constitute an aspect of the latter. She concludes that in fiction 'locality no longer functions as a reduction of social and historical processes on a larger scale, but retains its role as a powerful means of constructing identities, by offering a wide set of social and moral values'. By a different route, and as part of an examination of the fiction of Yorgis Yatromanolakis, Vangelis Athanassopoulos investigates how locality and history, divested of their particular character, can take on the dimensions of the global. Here fiction appears to expand locality and give it a global dimension as part of an effort at a universal interpretation of the world.

Part 4, entitled 'Fragmented Worlds', examines the issue of fragmentation that has ensued from the internationalization of culture. Focusing on techniques rather than themes, Maria Kakavoulia investigates the function of embedded non-fictional texts and discourses in fiction by Thanassis Valtinos and Michel Fais. This mode of narrative discourse, which has perhaps been overused recently, aims at emphasizing the subjective and non-totalizing nature of truth and reality. In the only chapter devoted exclusively to the short story, Anastasia

Natsina examines the work of six contemporary writers, tracing the evolutionary process from the threatening suspicion of the world's plurality in older writers to the acceptance and promotion of this plurality among the younger ones. This evolution implies a move from a sense of disorientation and fragmentation to an affirmative acceptance of the multiple ontological planes implied by the post-modern world of globalization. Finally, Dimitris Païvanas deals with one of the few political writers in Greece today. Thanassis Valtinos's treatment of post-war Greek history and politics in *Data from the Decade of the Sixties* is ironic and deconstructive, while his technique, consisting of the juxtaposition of non-literary, documentary discourses, aims at emphasizing the perspectivism of all ideology as well as of history.

Lastly, in Part 5, entitled 'New Treatments of Old Themes', Angela Kastrinaki investigates the phenomenon of contemporary fiction whose characters are artists. She concludes that apart from the increased number of such cases in recent years, the artist is viewed positively in contemporary fiction, in contrast to the rather derogatory representation of the artist in the past. On similar, though more theoretical, lines, Argiro Mantoglou investigates the existence of the woman author within the novel; adopting a feminist approach, she attempts to delineate how these characters break through the tradition of male-dominated practice and assert their female subjectivity by means of writing. Finally, Konstantinos Kosmas discusses the revival of the historical novel. Investigating the recent proliferation of historical novels, he attempts to investigate how history and national mythology are deconstructed in these texts so that the relativistic nature of historical truth, as presented by nationalistic discourses in the past, is highlighted. The novel under examination, Panos Theodoridis's *The Audio-Novel of Captain Agras* (1994), takes up an intertextual dialogue with an older literary text in connection with the life and death of a Greek participant in the Macedonian Struggle (1904–8).

We hope that the present volume will offer the opportunity to non-Greek readers to get to know contemporary Greek fiction and, most importantly, encourage more research in the area.

## Notes to the Introduction

1. 'Ena simeioma tis Loris Keza'. It is significant that, though this note is in Greek, some words are written in Latin characters (CNN, MTV, CD), and in some cases an English word is used instead of the most obvious Greek equivalent. By

- contrast, the word *diadiktyo* (internet) is in Greek, despite the fact that the English version is regularly used in Greece; the names of the non-Greek writers mentioned are also given in Greek characters.

2. Though the local Orthodox Christian populations had to fight against the Ottomans for about ten years in order to gain their independence, their cause found support from a number of European governments because of Europe's own ideological search for identity. By contrast, the colonialist policy of Europe was strongly opposed to the autonomy of other populations who lived within the borders of the Ottoman Empire at the time.

3. See Constantine Tsoukalas, 'Greek national identity in an integrated Europe and a changing world order', in Harry Psomiades and Stavros Thomadakis (eds.), *Greece, the New Europe and the Changing Order*, 57–78.

4. Ibid. 66.

5. Greece's first king, Otto (1832–62), was the son of King Ludwig I of Bavaria.

6. This defeat was accompanied by an exchange of minorities between Greece and Turkey in which about 1,500,000 Greek refugees entered Greece, amounting to more than half of the already existing population. For the economic, political, social and cultural impact of the population exchange see Renée Hirschon (ed.), *Crossing the Aegean*.

7. This becomes clear in the few cases of novels of this generation in which the whole story takes place in European cities, or else cosmopolitan and Europeanized characters are transplanted into a Greek cultural environment. Both cases create the impression of a heterogeneous mixture of cultures.

8. This Hellenocentric tendency took the form of debates on issues of Greekness, but also led to a type of literature that exalted Greek ideals; some of these works were written by pro-European writers such as Theotokas himself. Related to this is a thematic turn to the Greek historical past in literary texts such as Stratis Myrivilis's *O Vasilis o Arvanitis* (1943), Yiorgos Theotokas's *To daimonio* (1938) or Angelos Terzakis's *I Pringipessa Ysabeau* (first version in instalments 1938; second revised version in book form 1945). For more information on this issue see Mario Vitti, *I Genia tou Trianta: ideologia kai morfi*, 196–212; Roderick Beaton, *An Introduction to Modern Greek Literature*, 169–80.

9. These include academics such as Constantine Tsoukalas, Nikos Mouzelis, Kostas Zouraris and the late Kostis Moskof, the composer Mikis Theodorakis, the late actress and Minister of Culture Melina Mercouri and the late Premier Constantine Karamanlis (who was also President).

10. There have been occasions, however, for instance during and after international events such as the wars in the former Yugoslavia and against Iraq, when anti-Western feelings have run high in opposition to the official American and European policies in these matters. This, however, does not reflect a hostility towards the peoples or cultures of Europe and America.

11. Yorgos Chouliaras, 'Greek culture in the New Europe', in Psomiades and Thomadakis, *Greece, the New Europe and the Changing Order*, 89–90.

12. See e.g. Amanda Michalopoulou's novel *Oses fores antexeis* (1998).

13. Dimosthenis Kourtovik, 'Ena dilimma choris noima'.

14. Arif Dirlik, 'The Global in the Local'.

15. Ibid.

16. In Chouliaras's view, 'As everywhere else in the developed—by global standards—regions of Europe, popular culture in Greece, too, has become equivalent to mass culture' (Chouliaras, 'Greek Culture', 92.)

17. As Chouliaras observes: 'If by "Greek culture" we understand a localized way of life, which is unambiguously distinguishable on the basis of material and behavioural traits, then this culture entered its swan-song phase some time ago. A new Europe can only mean an intensified commonality of consumption patterns' (ibid. 91).

18. According to the relevant literature, globalization is not entirely new: at least on the economic level, a similar phenomenon had existed at the beginning of the twentieth century (Mansoob Murshed, *Globalization, Marginalization and Development*).

19. For definitions of globalization see Roland Robertson, *Globalization: Social Theory and Global Culture*; Mike Featherstone et al. (eds.), *Global Modernities*; Featherstone, *Undoing Culture*; Manuel Castells, *End of Millennium*; Deepak Nayyar (ed.), *Governing Globalization: Issues and Institutions*.

20. In strictly economic terms globalization refers to the expansion of economic transactions and the organization of economic activities across the political boundaries of nation states. In other words, it can be defined as a process associated with increasing economic openness, growing economic interdependence and deepening economic integration between countries in the world economy (Nayyar, *Governing Globalization*).

21. The nation is gradually being replaced by a network of financially independent areas, without a fixed centre, strongly bonded with each other, which are under trans-national supervision and management. This has led to inter-country formations or regional free trade zones such as EU, NAFTA (free trade agreement between USA, Canada and Mexico) and NEPAD (New Partnership for Africa's Development).

22. According to Ulf Hannerz, these features lack local authenticity and are deprived of their local ideological connotations, since they have already been modified in the place of origin—he calls this procedure 'creolization of the centre'—both as the result of the contact between centre and periphery and with the aim of endowing them with a closer cultural relevance to the centre (Ulf Hannerz, *Transnational Connections*); for a definition of creolization see n. 24.

23. According to Manuel Castells, 'the global economy will expand in the twenty-first century, using substantial increases in the power of telecommunications and information processing. It will penetrate all countries, all territories, all cultures, all communication flows, and all financial networks, relentlessly scanning the planet for new opportunities of profit making' (Castells, *End of Millennium*, 374).

24. 'The notion of creolization [...] refers to a process where meanings and meaningful forms from different historical sources, originally separated from one another in space, come to mingle extensively' (Ulf Hannerz, 'Stockholm: doubly creolizing', 96). Creolization implies fragmentation, mixture and lack of authenticity; these are considered to be the features of the globalized culture of post-modernity that are gradually replacing the traditional culture of a single language, single nation-state, single set of customs and a common history (Hannerz, *Transnational Connections*).

25. The development of the local within the global in the age of globalization has acquired several different terms, such as 'global regionalism' (Dirlik, 'The Global in the Local'), 'glocalization' (Wayne Gabardi, *Negotiating Postmodernism*), or the Japanese term 'Globloc' (Rob Wilson, 'Goodbye paradise').

26. For more on modernity vs. postmodernity, see Mike Featherstone, *Postmodernism*; Andreas Huyssen, *After the Great Divide*.

27. Nikos Mouzelis, 'The concept of modernization'.

28. Dimitris Tziovas, *The Other Self*, 15.

29. Elisavet Kotzia categorizes these as the 'first post-war generation'. Such writers are Stratis Tsirkas, Dimitris Hatzis, Andreas Frangias, Spyros Plaskovitis, Nikos Bakolas, Alexandros Kotzias and Nikos Kasdaglis (Elisavet Kotzia, 'To ergo ton metapolemikon pezografon').

30. According to Elisavet Kotzia, who categorizes them as the 'second post-war generation', these writers include Yorgos Ioannou, Thanassis Valtinos, Menis Koumandareas, Christoforos Milionis and Petros Abatzoglou (ibid. 33). Some of these may have appeared in the 1950s but produced their most important work in the 1960s.

31. Categorized by Elisavet Kotzia as the 'first post-dictatorship generation', they include Aris Alexandrou, Alki Zei, Dimitris Nollas, Yorgis Yatromanolakis and Maro Douka (ibid. 34). The reason for including Aris Alexandrou, who had made his appearance as a poet long before this, is that his only novel—a seminal work in Greek literature—was published as late as 1975.

32. Aris Alexandrou, *To kivotio* (1975).

33. This altered perception of politics in literature is explained by Beaton, who argues that 'Bearing witness to history [related to the Civil War], during that time [1949–1981], was more than a literary trend: until 1981, official history was limited to a single version of what had happened in Greece during the 1940s. Only in literature could alternative versions of a contested past be represented. In public discussions, held in the early 1970s against a background of political oppression, first-rate writers [...] declared their principled refusal to 'invent' (Roderick Beaton, 'Land without novels?').

34. Tziovas, *The Other Self*, 25–6.

35. See Dimosthenis Kourtovik, 'I elliniki pezografia 1974–88', in id., *Imedapi exoria*, 48; Vangelis Hatzivassiliou, 'I elliniki logotechnia meta to '74'.

36. It is indicative that the narrator-character in Marilena Politopoulou's novel *Oikos enochis* (2002) claims that she never votes, while she advises her daughter to support Unesco. An international ideology seems here to have replaced a local one.

37. Elisavet Kotzia, 'Elliniki pezografia 1930–1999'.

38. This increasing phenomenon exhibits an effort to create a fiction that goes beyond the generic restrictions that traditional or even modernist approaches imposed on literature in terms of both themes and technique; this is attempted through the intermingling in the same text of various non-literary discourses from non-literary disciplines, such as mathematics, science, anthropology, gastronomy, history, linguistics and documentary. Such texts are Apostolos Doxiadis's *O theios Petros kai i eikasia tou Goldbach* (1992; rev. edn. 2000), Amanda Michalopoulou's *Yantes* (1996), Yannis Panou's *Apo to stoma tis palias Remington*

(1981) and *I istoria ton metamorfoseon* (1998), Michel Fais's *Aftoviografia enos vivliou* (1994) and Dimosthenis Kourtovik's *I nostalgia ton drakon* (2000).
39. See Vangelis Hatzivassiliou, 'From modernism to post-modern?'; id., 'Nuevos caminos de la narrativa griega'.
40. The view has been expressed that more and more Greek writers aspire to translations of their books in other European languages, and they use an easy and straightforward language so that their texts can be translated more easily and appeal to a readership that is unfamiliar with the culturally bound peculiarities and connotations of sophisticated Greek.
41. See Dimitris Tziovas, 'Residual orality'; id., *The Other Self*, 23–5.
42. For a thorough comparison between inter-war and recent cosmopolitanism see Elisavet Kotzia, 'Elliniki pezografia kai kosmopolitismos 1930–2000'.
43. Greek women today read more than in the past for several reasons: more women are educated today than before, they are financially independent and they usually have more leisure time than men.
44. The issue of high and low literature could be raised here, but this is beyond the scope of this introduction. It should be noted, however, that in Greece serious fiction and 'chick lit' are published by the same publishers, are promoted similarly, and indeed are not differentiated from each other in any way.
45. Tziovas, *The Other Self*, 49–50.
46. Some representative novels of this type are Niki Anastasea's *Afti i argi mera prochorouse* (1998), Eliana Chourmouziadou's *I idiaitera* (1998), Yorgos Symbardis's *O achristos Dimitris* (1998), Ersi Sotiropoulou's *Zig-zag stis nerantzies* (1999) and Michalis Michailidis's *I skyla kai to koutavi* (2002).
47. Zyranna Zateli, *Kai me to fos tou lykou epanerchontai* (1993) and Ioanna Karystiani, *Mikra Anglia* (1997).
48. Such representative novels of escape and encounter with the Other are Tasos Rousos's *O kairos tis Lize* (1993), Soti Triantafyllou's *Savvato vrady stin akri tis polis* (1995), Neni Efthymiadi's *I poli ton glaron* (1997), Dimitris Nollas's *Foteini Magiki* (2000), Faidon Tamvakakis's *Oi navagoi tis Pasifais* (1997), Argiro Mantoglou's *Virginia Woolf Café* (1999), Amanda Michalopoulou's *Oses fores antexeis* and Apostolos Doxiadis's *O theios Petros kai i eikasia tou Goldbach*.
49. The first tendency kind of novel includes Nikos Themelis's *I anazitisi* (1998), *I anatropi* (2000) and *I analampi* (2002), Theodoros Grigoriadis's *Ta nera tis chersonisou* (1998), Zateli's *Kai me to fos tou lykou*, Aris Fakinos's *To oneiro tou protomastora Nikita* (1998) and Soti Triantafyllou's *To ergostasio ton molyvion* (2000).
50. Such novels include Rhea Galanaki's *O vios tou Ismail Ferik Pasa* (1989), *Tha ypografo Loui* (1993), *Eleni, i o Kanenas* (1998) and *O aionas ton lavyrinthon* (2002), Maro Douka's *Enas skoufos apo porfyra* (1995) and Panos Theodoridis's *To ichomythistorima tou Kapetan Agra* (1994).

# PART 1

❖

# An Overview of
# Tendencies and Perspectives

CHAPTER 1

❖

# Centrifugal Topographies, Cultural Allegories and Metafictional Strategies in Greek Fiction since 1974

*Dimitris Tziovas*

Analysing developments in Greek fiction since 1974 is not an easy task, considering the explosion of fiction that has occurred in recent decades. Without aspiring to reach definite conclusions about trends or canons, the aim of this chapter is to highlight and analyse three major developments that have occurred in Greek fiction since 1974. The examination of these developments might justify the treatment of 1974 as a turning-point not only in Greek history and politics, but in literature too. Before embarking on a detailed analysis, let me first briefly outline these developments.

The first, which could be called spatial, involves a transition, in the topographical focus of Greek prose-writers, from a centripetal to a centrifugal pattern. Since the late nineteenth century the reference point of most of these writers has been Athens, even though very few of them were born there and the majority moved there gradually both physically and thematically. Around 1974 this centripetal trend towards Athens, which went together with the urbanization of Greece, was completed, and writers started looking beyond their metropolitan centre and set their plots outside Greece.

The second development has to do with the shift from politics to culture. Until recently most Greek novels could be described as national, social or political allegories, but now there is a growing trend for cultural allegories, exploring questions of identity, origin, gender, communication or border crossing rather than political or historical conflicts. This focus on cultural rather than political or social issues reflects the world-wide colonization of the political by the cultural.

The third major development pertains to narrative method and involves the shift of emphasis from experience to mediation. Modern Greek fiction has become increasingly aware of the crisis of representation, and authors, instead of laying claim to the raw and authentic representation of their experience or consciousness, tend to highlight the idea that experience is relativized, fragmented and mediated through secondary (written or oral) devices such as letters, historical documents, newspaper extracts or personal accounts. Contemporary novelists tend to subscribe to the view that the past is known to us through its textual traces; for this reason there is an increasing emphasis on textualization and documentation. Hence, the author assumes more the role of a subjective or mediating agent and less that of an objective or experiencing subject. The paradox is that although we witness a growing reliance on textual traces and documents, the authority of this textual or archival evidence is nevertheless contested or relativized. This is one of the main metafictional strategies, which involves building up an illusion and subsequently demonstrating that it is provisional or even dispelling it altogether.

It could be argued that these three broad developments, briefly defined as topographical, cultural and metafictional, have shaped the orientation of Greek fiction since 1974 and opened its horizons to wider, global issues and concerns. I shall be analysing each of them in turn by pointing out possible connections and ramifications.

As has been said earlier, from the late nineteenth century until around 1974 Greek fiction followed a centripetal pattern as writers gradually moved to Athens from the diaspora, or Asia Minor after 1922, or the Greek periphery. Writers did not simply move physically to the metropolis; often this transition also left a mark on their writing. The conclusion of this centripetal trend towards Athens soon after 1974 was related to the completion of the urbanization process of Greek society. The completion of this centripetal process could be seen in the work of Stratis Tsirkas, a leading representative of the Greek diaspora, who set his trilogy *Drifting Cities* (1960–5) in Jerusalem, Alexandria and Cairo, then moved to Athens, 'the most open city in the world' as it is described by the protagonist of *The Lost Spring* (1976), who returns home after eighteen years of enforced exile.[1] Similarly Dimitris Hatzis's repatriation is indicative of the social and political aspects of this process; his *The Double Book* (1976) portrays the difficulty of homecoming not so much to the metropolitan centre, but to the country itself. It could be argued, therefore, that around the mid-1970s the metropolitan centripetal trend in

Greek fiction reaches its climax, and, in turn, its narrative space is shrinking. What are the consequences of this topographical limitation for fictional writing itself and how has it been dealt with?

One of the main presuppositions of the novel is the dialogue, the antithesis and often the conflict between two or more worlds with their beliefs, ideologies, class differences and life-styles. These incompatible world-views may be represented by families, classes, societies or more often individuals as their symbolic embodiments or illustrative examples. In view of the fact that in the last two centuries Greek society has been marked by class fluidity and unstable social roles, it could not easily establish or foster social groups with clear and recognizable characteristics. Hence the worlds that are in interaction, dialogue or conflict in Greek fiction are usually topographically defined and separated by the incommensurability of the diasporic ideal and the local Greek reality, the ideological tension between Greek culture of the periphery and the metropolitan centre, or the social antithesis between urban development and provincial poverty or backwardness.

Considering that most of the leading Greek writers before the Second World War were not born in Athens, it could be said that they view the metropolis from outside, either as Greeks of the diaspora, as refugees or as internal migrants. From the 1830s to 1880, Athens represents an ideal that is often frustrated by reality, as can be seen in the novels of Grigorios Palaiologos (1794–1844) or in the anonymous *A Soldier's Life in Greece* (1870–1), in which the main character's ideal image of Athens is dissipated upon his arrival. Greek fiction of the mid-nineteenth century is informed by the clash between the ideal and the real, between an image of Athens inflated by its classical glory and its disappointing present.[2]

With the growing urbanization and industrialization during and after the late nineteenth century, the clash between the real and the ideal is supplanted by the antithesis between urban and rural (or in the twentieth century between the urban bourgeoisie and the lower social strata of the poor metropolitan districts). Writers and their characters flock to Athens and experience the harsh economic and social reality of the capital. In texts such as *Les Misérables of Athens* (1894/5) by Ioannis Kondylakis, the Athenian stories by Alexandros Papadiamantis (1851–1911), *The Vow* (1899/1921)[3] by Alexandros Moraitidis and the novels of Grigorios Xenopoulos (1867–1951), the difficult transition and adjustment to the urban environment is depicted. This theme, in various versions, would continue to feature in Greek fiction, as for example in *Young Man with Good References*... (1935) by Loukis Akritas, in the writings of Pantelis Prevelakis (1909–86), and even in those of contemporary novelists such as Christoforos Milionis (*Western District* (1980)), Evgenia Fakinou (*Astradeni* (1982)), Sotiris Dimitriou and others.[4] Following the transition from the countryside to the city, Greek fiction records the transformation of Greek society without, however, escaping nostalgic references to the birthplace or emotional memories of the lost paradise of childhood or adolescence. Thus the antithesis between the two worlds is often emotionally charged and acquires an elegiac tone, particularly in the narratives of writers originating from Constantinople or Asia Minor.[5]

In these texts the world of lost homelands is contrasted to the reality of the Greek state. The new and dynamic image of Athens with Syngrou Avenue, high-rise buildings and cars presented in *Argo* (1933–6) by Yorgos Theotokas could be compared to the Taksim Gardens in Constantinople described, through the eyes of a child, in his autobiographical novel *Leonis* (1940). A couple of decades later, Kosmas Politis, feeling an outcast in his own country as he states in his epigraph of his novel *At Hatzifrangou* (1963), returns to the Smyrna of his childhood, and thus the city assumes the role of protagonist in his novel. The explicit or implicit juxtaposition of two worlds, the difficult adjustment to the new urban reality, the nostalgic revisiting either of the birthplace in the Greek provinces or of Constantinople and western Asia Minor constitute one of the major preoccupations of the modern Greek novel, while the theme of uprootedness and alienation shape its poetics.

Once the cycle of urbanization had been completed, settlement in the capital had been achieved and nostalgia for the birthplace gradually waned, Greek fiction lost one of its major sources of inspiration and as a result had to find alternatives in order to reinvent the dialogue between the two worlds. Increasingly since the 1980s a centrifugal trend has developed in Greek fiction, a number of novels being partly set outside Greece while their characters are in constant motion, travelling and searching in various parts of Europe. The centripetal metropolitan trend might explain why before the 1980s 'one had to look hard to find stories focused exclusively on Greeks who had left Greece for work abroad. For some reason, neither the country nor its authors were ready to rework that timely subject.'[6] It seems to me that this view reinforces the argument that the focus at that time was on migration to the metropolis rather than abroad.

When the representation of internal migration had been exhausted, the attention turned to emigration outside the country. The old topographical and social oppositions gave way either to the expansion of narrative space or to a retrospective inflation of narrative time by turning to history. As a result the historical novel has flourished during the last twenty years, offering an alternative to the narrowing of narrative space by shifting the dialogue or conflict of different world-views into the past.

There are two writers who do not fit the centripetal metropolitan pattern that I have just outlined and were able to establish a dialogue between cosmopolitanism and locality. Georgios Vizyenos (1849–96) and Nikos Kazantzakis (1883–1957) managed to avoid being absorbed by the Athenian centre and developed a fruitful interface between their birthplace and Europe. On the other hand, the inter-war writers of Salonica were unable to achieve such a balance as they emphasized cosmopolitanism and virtually ignored the fact that Salonica was the most multicultural Greek city of the time. Only later did N. G. Pentzikis (1904–93) try to redress the balance, but during the inter-war period the eyes of most of the writers of Salonica were focused on European modernism. By circumventing the metropolis, Vizyenos and Kazantzakis succeeded in fusing Thrace and Crete respectively with European culture in their work, and this perhaps explains their high reputation today.

In their work these two writers portray characters of different ethnicity or religion; in particular, Vizyenos shows a great deal of sympathy towards Muslims. What may have contributed to this is the fact that both of them originated from areas with a substantial Muslim population, while their sojourn outside Greece for a number of years offered them a multicultural experience and the opportunity to make contact with people of different origin and culture. Both writers promoted a hybrid conception of culture based on their diasporic experience. Vizyenos is not a Thracian writer, nor Kazantzakis a Cretan one, to the extent that Alexandros Papadiamantis is identified with Skiathos or Yorgos Ioannou with Salonica. This perhaps explains why Kazantzakis's style irritates a number of Greek critics, since his language is neither regional nor standardized urban, but a peculiar mixture of both. Vizyenos and Kazantzakis are not writers of locality, exile or cosmopolitanism, but of heterotopia, engaging in a dialogue with places where they were born and lived, and developing a critical intercultural perspective out of their experience of both Europe and their native place. In their work at least two different worlds interact, pointing to a dialogue between East and West. Their example, however, was not followed by younger writers.

Nevertheless, contemporary Greek fiction reflects a new geographical consciousness of a decentred world of migration and mobility. One could argue that this development is part of a wider transition from territorially defined cultures (in terms of nations, regions, or localities) towards a conception of cultures as collective structures of meaning, carried and disseminated by transnational networks, which tend to overlap and mingle. A territorial culture tends to be centripetal, local and context-bound, whereas a culture as a structure of meaning is centrifugal, decontextualized, cosmopolitan and willing to engage with the Other. However, there is an interdependence in operation, as there cannot be a cosmopolitan cultural diversity without local specificity. In other words, there can be no cosmopolitans without locals.[7]

As soon as the Greek novel ceased to be the representation of the territorial reconfiguration of the nation and the rapid urbanization of Greek society, it aspired to represent its European orientation, even though this orientation might be at times uncertain or contradictory. Thus it demonstrated a cosmopolitan extroversion, focusing on universal rather than local or national issues. The earlier attachment and reference to place gave way to the aspiration of young Greek novelists to write European rather than Greek novels. By abandoning its role as a 'national allegory', the Greek novel highlighted the twofold function of the novelistic genre: the artistic and the entertaining. This development, however, caused some consternation, since few critics and writers were prepared to see the novel as a commercial and entertaining activity. The recent commercial success and dynamic presence of popular fiction caused an identity crisis in a highbrow Greek novel that faced the dilemma whether to retreat into formalist narcissism or seek a new social role compatible with the changes in Greek society. This reorientation of Greek fiction is related to the second major shift I outlined at the beginning.

In recent decades we have experienced 'the colonization of the social by the cultural', while a general 'culturization' of the political language has taken place.[8] Culture has become the new pervasive social 'dominant', like religion in the Middle Ages, philosophy in early nineteenth-century Germany or the natural sciences in Victorian Britain.[9] As Terry Eagleton argues, 'culture is a pre-modern and postmodern rather than modern idea; if it flourishes in the era of modernity, it is largely as a trace of the past or an anticipation of the future'.[10] What links pre-modern and postmodern orders is that in both, for quite different reasons, culture and social life are allied. This becomes clear in the transformation of aesthetics over the years. A term that initially signified perceptual experience later became specialized and applied to the arts, but today has come full circle and rejoined its mundane origin more as style and pleasure than as artefact. Aesthetics, like culture, now pertains both to the arts and to everyday life, and its two senses have been conflated in fashion, advertising, media and the like.[11]

The cultural turn in contemporary Greek fiction involves a preoccupation with material culture and lifestyles, as is testified by the number of novels dealing with food[12] and an aesthetic dimension that is manifested through an increased emphasis on the process of writing and the proliferation of artists and writers as fictional characters in the novels of the last twenty years or so. Culture, then, in recent Greek fiction is both material and aesthetic, being associated with pleasure and artefact, eating and writing. It is, however, more than that.

As Fredric Jameson has argued, culture is always 'an idea of the Other'.[13] Hence the increasing emphasis on otherness brings forth the idea of culture in the sense of accepting the difference, the relativity and ultimately the plurality of life-worlds. Culture, according to Eagleton, 'now means the affirmation of a specific identity (national, sexual, ethnic, regional) rather than the transcendence of it.'[14] Having been transformed into a terrain of conflict, it no longer constitutes a realm of sublimity and consensus. Culture as spirituality is eroded by culture as commodity, to give birth to culture as identity. In short, a transition has occurred from culture as art to culture as identity politics. It is not the solution any more, but part of the problem. It is no accident, according to Immanuel Wallerstein, that there has been so much discussion in the last few decades about the problematic of 'culture':

It follows upon the decomposition of the nineteenth-century double faith in the economic and political arenas as loci of social progress and therefore of individual salvation. Some return to God, and others look to 'culture' or 'identity' or some other realistic illusion to help them regain their bearing.[15]

This cultural shift has highlighted the tension between the universal and the particular, the global and the local. On the one hand, there is the promotion of diversity of cultures (in academia, for example, through the promotion of different canons) and on the other hand there are those who advocate the universality of Western civilization. The tendency towards one world or one nation contradicts the tendency towards distinctive nation-states or distinctive ethnic groups.[16] Stuart Hall argues that the weakening of the idea of the nation-state produces simultaneously two antithetical responses. It goes local with the emphasis on regional or ethnic elements and it goes above the nation-state towards supranational or even global formations. Hence global and local are the two faces of the same movement.[17]

Though one can argue that globalization and fragmentation are part of the same process, culture is by definition particularistic. The predominance of culture as a concept today entails an increasing recognition of cultural, ethnic and regional plurality and a perception of the world based on difference and otherness. The worldwide colonization of the social and political by the cultural has had an impact on Greek fiction, in that Greek society itself is now more preoccupied with cultural than political or social issues. We also witness a cultural reading of the past that has resulted in the proliferation of historical novels preoccupied with questions of identity or the reassessment of the past rather than with historical truth and authenticity.

Greek fiction of the twentieth century was preoccupied to a large extent with historical and political events. Texts such as *Number 31328* (1924/1931) by Ilias Venezis, *Argo* (1933–6) by Yorgos Theotokas, *The Broad River* (1946) by Yannis Beratis, *Pyramid 67* (1950) by Renos Apostolodis, *Drifting Cities* (1960–5) by Stratis Tsirkas or, more recently, *Mission Box* (1974) by Aris Alexandrou can be described as historical or political allegories. This description is not intended to detract either from the experimental aspirations or the aesthetic value of these texts, but simply to indicate the engagement of these narratives with the historical and political situation of the time. Perhaps this illustrates Fredric Jameson's distinction between first-world and third-world literatures and his argument that third-world texts could be read as 'national allegories' whereby personal stories tend to be read in primarily political or social terms:

Third-world texts, even those which are seemingly private and invested with a properly libidinal dynamic—necessarily project a political dimension in the form of national allegory: the story of the private individual destiny is always an allegory of the embattled situation of the public third-world culture and society. Need I add that it is precisely this very different ratio of the political to the personal which makes such texts alien to us at first approach, and consequently, resistant to our conventional western habits of reading?[18]

The case of Alexandrou's *Mission Box* makes clear that historical or political allegories survived in Greek fiction right up to 1974; later, however, events are filtered through a highly personal perspective, as is the case with *Fool's Gold* (1979) by Maro Douka and *Achilles' Fiancée* (1987) by Alki Zei. Though the ambition of Greek writers for epic reconstructions of Greek history and political life might not have diminished, particularly among older writers, as the cases of *Crossroads* (1987) by Nikos Bakolas and, more recently, *Twice Greek* (2001) by Menis Koumandareas suggest, in the last two decades, as Greece has enjoyed the longest period of democracy and peace in its history, the idea that the personal is the political has been gaining ground, and in turn historical or political allegories have given way to cultural ones. This cultural dimension in the form of identity politics could be found even in novels such as *The Life of Ismail Ferik Pasha* (1989) by Rhea Galanaki, *The Silver-Grass is Blooming* (1992) by Vasilis Gouroyannis, or *May Your Name be Blessed* (1993) by Sotiris Dimitriou, with firm historical background and explicit references to historical events or political tragedies. These writers do not revisit the past to restore its authenticity or to vindicate a point of view; their narratives take the form of ethnographic explorations rather than historical reconstructions into a hitherto hidden past (Ottoman and Balkan). They explore the significance of divided worlds and broken families, the impact on personal identity of cultural hybridity and political suppression, and the importance of crossing ethnic, linguistic and cultural boundaries.

Similarly, Maro Douka's Byzantine novel *Come Forth, King* (1995) can be seen as a cultural allegory, in that it undermines the notion of historical 'objectivity', highlighting the contemporary resonances of the story. The fictional narrator of the novel, a little-known officer and faithful follower of Emperor Alexios Komnenos, has retired to Pontus after his master's death and tells the story of Alexios's reign to the Emperor's grandson. He emphasizes the subjective character of his narrative and claims that he is not omniscient, nor does he intend to write history. In the novel, Alexios appears to be caught between East and West, Muslim Turks and Catholic Europeans. His position could be seen as a metaphor for the present position of Greece, as the author herself has implied. Douka states in a note at the end of the novel that she is not writing a historical novel, but she is interested in a kind of dialogue between past and present. She highlights the parallels between the end of the twentieth century and the twelfth century, thus pointing to the allegorical nature of her text:

As I buried myself in the time of Alexios Komnenos, I realized that we, at the end of the second millennium after Christ, aren't that different from those who ushered in the twelfth century, thoughtlessly undermining their own present, completely alone between East and West. The Byzantines, who called themselves Romans, spoke Greek and struggled for their correct Christian faith, as I experienced them and came to love them, left an indelible imprint on us: without them, our identity today would have been different. So, having decided to write a book about the life and work of Alexios Komnenos, I was to write a book about our own time, by way of this present that keeps us and defines us.[19]

After the end of the Cold War, the fizzling out of political passions and the growing presence of migrants in the country, we have witnessed, as I have said, a cultural turn in the Greek novel. Increasingly, contemporary Greek fiction aspires to represent the cultural dilemmas and debates within Greek society, its increased westernization and most importantly the transition from monoculturalism to multiculturalism with the influx of immigrants and the emphasis on minorities. A number of contemporary Greek novels can be seen as cultural allegories which involve the fictionalization of otherness, identity and cultural communication.

The plot of these narratives often employs the pattern of a quest, and as a consequence geography and travel play an important role in its construction. The quest plot may take different forms or serve various purposes. For example, in *As Many Times as You Can Stand It* (1998) by Amanda Michalopoulou, the quest has a primarily erotic motive as the Greek heroine has a fling with Ivo, a Czech travel agent whom she meets in an Athenian bar and spends a few passionate days with. When Ivo goes back to his country, his wife and children, she embarks on a search for him which takes her to Prague, Munich, Geneva and Madeira. Though the plot seems initially to rely on a rather traditional and romantic form of quest, Michalopoulou ultimately ironizes it, as the focus of the quest gradually shifts to European identity and the reader becomes uncertain as to the real object of her search.

In *The Nostalgia of the Dragons* (2000) by Dimosthenis Kourtovik the quest all over Europe for Ibycus, a prehistoric mummy discovered on a Greek island and subsequently stolen from a museum, serves the generic identity of the text as philosophical thriller. The quest pattern is not simply used to galvanize the curiosity of the readers as to whether the sixty-year-old Professor Drakas and the beautiful young policewoman Andromachi Koutroumba accompanying him will eventually manage to recover Ibycus after searching for him in Genoa, Münster, Copenhagen, Berlin, Wrocław and finally the Balkans. It also conveys the constant probing into some important existential questions about origins. In this way the quest pattern helps to bring together philosophical inquiry with detective mystery. Ibycus becomes a metaphor for the primordial self-destructive tendency of the human race from prehistory to the present day, and this could warrant a description of the novel as a kind of cultural allegory.

The novels by Michalopoulou and Kourtovik involve a movement from Greece to the rest of Europe, as their main characters set out not only to find a beloved person or a missing object, but also to explore the make-up of Europe and its cultural legacy. Alexis Panselinos's novel *Zaida, or The Camel in the Snow* (1996),[20] on the other hand, deals with the visit of a Viennese musician to Greek lands. During the winter of 1791 the musician fakes his death and funeral and with a false identity moves to Italy, where he meets two young Italian fugitives. Fearing that in Italy he might be recognized by one of his enemies, he decides after seven years to leave Italy with the two Italians and, after a number of adventures, arrives in Corfu in February 1799 while the island's French garrison is under siege by the Russians and the Turks. There he meets Andreas Roilos, an exiled poet and revolutionary from Lefkada. Owing to the difficult situation in the island, the three Europeans, together with Roilos and his servant, move to the mainland opposite. After being captured by brigands in the mountains of Epirus, they escape and end up as visitors to the court of Ali Pasha. There in order to help a Greek lady to escape from Ali's dungeons, the Viennese musician and the Greek poet complete an unfinished opera 'Zaida' and stage it in front of Ali. The plan succeeds and all the characters flee Ali's court.

Here the object of quest is not clear, and hence the aim of this long and complex narrative remains obscure. This is perhaps due to its allegorical character, since there is an implicit association between the Viennese musician and Mozart,[21] who died in 1791, and the poet with the Greek poet Dionysios Solomos (1798–1857). What, however, is the point of this encounter between Mozart and Solomos in the mountains of Epirus or the court of Ali Pasha? This bizarre and imaginary encounter in a place none of them had ever visited serves as a cultural allegory, suggesting a dialogue between East and West. Panselinos sets his novel in a crucial historical period when Greece is about to emerge as an independent nation-state at the crossroads of classicism, nationalism and romanticism.

'Zaida' itself can be read as a cultural metaphor, as the musician admits that he was trying to graft elements from local music on to the sounds he already carried inside him. He also makes an attempt to understand the ethos of Eastern art and argues that this requires attendance at church services and participation in local fairs and other festivities. 'Zaida', with music by Mazarini/Mozart and libretto by Roilos/Solomos, represents a cultural osmosis of East and West, an opera with no national features, but open to local adjustments. 'The instruments whose voices he knew well echoed differently, to such an extent that it was as if they were telling him that sound has languages too and may vary as much as the different tongues of the human race' (564). It is clear that, with his historical novel, Panselinos is projecting into the past contemporary concerns about Greek cultural identity and the role of Europe in its formation. He finds in the past an image of the present or future.[22]

The same could be said about Theodoros Grigoriadis's novel *The Waters of the Peninsula* (1998), which gives an account of the journey of three men during the summer of 1906. The first is a young Englishman of aristocratic origins who sets off from Salonica following in the steps of earlier English missionaries who recorded sacred shrines in Thrace. He is accompanied by his Greek interpreter from Anchialos in Eastern Rumelia (in present-day Bulgaria) who has studied in Constantinople. At Philippi they are joined by an Ottoman student who has just escaped from the Imaret, the Muslim theological school in Kavala. Together the three head towards Philippopolis (Plovdiv in Bulgaria), from where they travel east towards Adrianople (Edirne) and finally Constantinople.

This is an adventure novel, taking place in turbulent times and volatile areas, but it is also a cultural allegory, since it explores the encounter and fusion between different cultures represented by the three main characters. The allegorical aspect of the narrative is underlined by the transformation of the Muslim into Orpheus and the development of a deep and erotic friendship with the Greek. Though the novel represents different religions and opposite viewpoints

(British Orientalism, Greek patriotism and Muslim mysticism), it also projects cultural hybridity and human understanding among people of different ethnic or religious backgrounds. Without ignoring war and violence, the novel highlights the deep bonds among the peoples in the Balkan peninsula at the beginning of the twentieth century, which could be seen as a metaphor for the present situation in the region.[23]

The quest pattern and the emphasis on travel in these novels urge associations with the Hellenistic novel, in which the 'central theme of the lonely traveller searching for his beloved [...] is an expression of the individual's sense of isolation in the world'.[24] Hellenistic society was different from the simple tribal community reflected in the Homeric epic, which was characterized by cultural homogeneity and uniform patterns of thought and action. In the Hellenistic period the small, closed world of the epic is broken down and fixed norms are questioned. In this respect it has been suggested that Hellenistic society 'has fundamental traits in common with modern Western society after the French Revolution. In place of stable traditions and fixed values there enters a vast multitude of conflicting desires and centrifugal tendencies.'[25] It could be argued that periods of fluidity and turmoil such as the Hellenistic period produce novels that fit their climate and reflect its transitory character. Periods of insecurity and wider social change are mirrored in literary forms and are often expressed through dynamic patterns such as travel or quest. Individual uncertainty and cultural amalgamation are translated into the restlessness of characters who constantly move from place to place, either in search of an elusive stability or by accepting nomadism as their centrifugal condition of life. Cosmopolitanism in the novel is usually associated with periods involving mass migration or social mobility such as the periods after the world wars and our own age.

Being a major feature of a number of contemporary novels, the quest pattern is associated with two other features that are exemplified in Panselinos's and Grigoriadis's novels. The first of these is the encounter, dialogue or contrast between two worlds or cultures that are often represented or epitomized by individual characters, and the second is the setting of this encounter in the past, which facilitates parallels with contemporary developments and thus increases the allegorical character of the narrative. In other words, narratives look backwards in order to move forwards.

It has been claimed that the nineteenth and a large part of the twentieth century were obsessed with history and time. As Michel

Foucault has pointed out, 'Space was treated as the dead, the fixed, the undialectical, the immobile. Time, on the contrary was richness, fecundity, life, dialectic.'[26] Over the last few decades there has been an increasing reassertion of space in critical thought, the development of spatial hermeneutic and an emphasis on human geography. A different way of seeing the relation of time and space, history and geography, sequence and simultaneity has emerged which does not lead to the displacement or subordination of history but to its spatialization. The idea of history as linear progress, being the ideal of modernity, gives way to the compression of time into perpetual present. The dissolution of time into space brings about a transition from history to geography and from modernity to postmodernity. This also involves a shift from modernist notions of expatriation and exile to postmodern notions of migrancy and nomadism. The nomad 'represents a subject position that offers an idealized model of movement based on perpetual displacement.'[27] This increasing centrality of space and geography in critical thought had a wider impact in the re-evaluation of spatial dimension in narrative.

In a number of novels the encounter between two worlds is the main theme, as we have already seen in Panselinos's novel. The contrast of these worlds echoes the paradoxical postmodern notion of culture as torn between cosmopolitanism and locality, globalization and fragmentation, universalism and particularism. While earlier Greek narratives record the often painful transition from the countryside to the metropolis, contemporary novels thematize the difficult adjustment and the identity problems of Greeks outside Greece.

Novelists, like historians, often embark on a rereading of the past from a contemporary perspective by focusing on the role of the Greek diaspora and discovering prefigurations of contemporary concerns about multiculturalism, migration and identity in the activities of Greeks within the context of the Ottoman Empire and beyond. Novelists such as Nikos Themelis fictionalize the migratory trends among Greeks before the twentieth century and highlight how trade made the ethnic, linguistic and commercial boundaries in south-east Europe extremely porous.

As they move from mountainous Zagori and Siatista to cosmopolitan Odessa, the lives of Thomas and Eleni, the two main characters of Nikos Themelis's novel *The Overthrow* (2000), illustrate how commerce at the end of the nineteenth century contributed to cultural interaction, the circulation of ideas and the fluidity of identities. Though the novel focuses on how historical, economic and political changes turn characters' lives upside-down, the multi-ethnic and multi-cultural character of certain cities, such as Salonica, is emphasized.

In his autobiographical narrative *Like a Novel* (1995), Yannis Kiourtsakis often compares Greece with western Europe through the eyes of his brother Haris, who studied in Belgium in the early 1950s and corresponded frequently with his parents and his brother.[28] Though his narrative is highly autobiographical—the author explores the formation of his selfhood by looking back at his relationship with his parents and his brother—the underlying theme of the book is the contrast between Greece and Europe:

> Yes, this is a Greek story, and as you're writing it you seem to be writing about contemporary Greece itself, which forever journeys towards Europe and forever returns from Europe, which forever seeks itself in Europe. (350)

An interplay between self and other, home and abroad, exploration and *nostos*, Greece and Europe, takes place in this text, pointing to the idea that the aim of this narrative extends beyond autobiography to cultural allegory.

If Kiourtsakis's text focuses on Europe, other novels deal with the experience of Greeks in the USA. One of these novels is *Underground Heaven* (1998) by Soti Triantafyllou, which gives an account of the life of Billy Morrow, son of Harry (Haralambos) and Helen (Eleni) Moropoulou who emigrated to the USA in the early 1960s from a village in Arcadia. Billy is unable to go to college because his parents do not have the money; hates everything Greek (church, language, social gatherings) and is attracted to cars, music and girls while he dreams of California. His parents are not at all well-off and after thirty-six years in America they do not feel either Americans or Greeks; his father, however, keeps sending money to his sisters in the village, though he has visited them only three times since he emigrated.

This novel contrasts real and imaginary Arcadias: the Arcadia from which Billy's father escaped to seek a better future, and his son's imaginary Arcadia represented by California. Somewhere in the middle lies the boring and suffocating life of an American Midwest town where the family lives. By representing different worlds, generations and lifestyles, Triantafyllou highlights the identity crisis of Greek immigrants. In her narrative she blends utopian dreams, social frustration and the desire for adventure, avoiding either the elegiac nostalgia for the homeland or the optimism of a success story of a Greek who made it abroad. Though the themes of identity and heterotopia give way to adventurous travel towards the end of the novel, she successfully encapsulates in her narrative the social impasse and the cultural dilemmas of migrants. Centred around a Greek-American family, her novel could be linked to Karystiani's novel *A Suit in the Earth* (2000),[29] which has as its main character a leading Cretan scientist who lives and works in the USA for many years, haunted by a long-standing vendetta back home.

In Karystiani's novel two different worlds are juxtaposed: the traditional world of the mountainous Sfakia and its culture of vendetta, and the technological world of a health research laboratory in the USA. These two worlds seem to be miles apart; both, however, are inhabited by loneliness, silence and muted feelings. After twenty-eight years away from Crete, Kyriakos Rousias thinks that different ways of life produce different attitudes and thoughts. He appears to have escaped the violence and poverty of his native place by moving to the USA when he was fifteen, but it still weighs heavily upon him. As the narrator suggests, his destiny is still Crete:

There are some places that, when their people leave for elsewhere, they take with them. They take the landscape, the town, the river from here and put them down somewhere far away. There are other places that don't sit tight, but eventually go of their own accord and find the fugitive.

In either case, Rousias and Crete were bound to find each other again. (70–1)

Even though, on his brief return to Crete in 1998, he does not take revenge for the killing of his father back in 1972 and thus breaks the vicious circle of the vendetta, he realizes that he cannot escape the past:

He usually admired those who had the capacity to rid themselves of the weights of the past and look forward, to rid themselves of the weight called Greece and quickly become assimilated elsewhere. He himself had tried but failed. It was a failure that didn't upset him in the least; on the contrary, he felt grateful and listened to his heart beating gently and lazily, as was appropriate in the middle of a perfect August day. (302)

For Kyriakos Rousias time seems to have stopped in the early seventies. Though he represents the forefront of scientific research, he still listens to the Greek songs of that period. In a sense he represents a paradoxical combination of scientific progress and cultural nostalgia or even backwardness. In this way, Karystiani avoids a stereotypical contrast between the two worlds and is able through streaks of humour to blend the primitivism of the Cretan landscape with the globalization of technology. Without idealizing the Cretan landscape, she shows how its mystical attraction and natural beauty are dotted by cars, guns, mobile phones and modern sounds. Karystiani skilfully fictionalizes Rousias's oscillation between destiny and liberation from the past, tradition and modernity by presenting this ambiguity not as a choice but as an internal struggle.

Kyriakos Rousias in Karystiani's novel is haunted by his birthplace in the same way as Ismail in Galanaki's novel *The Life of Ismail Ferik Pasha* (1989). In this novel the two worlds, that of Crete, where Ismail was born as a Christian with the name Emmanuel Kambanis Papadakis, and that of Egypt, where he was taken captive and became Minister of War, are clearly demarcated as the world of myth and the world of history. The novel consists of two parts and an afterword. The first part, bearing the title 'The years in Egypt: The Myth', is narrated, as is the afterword, in the third person, whereas the second part, 'Days of Homecoming: The History', is narrated by Ferik himself in the first person. Myth and history represent the two lives of Ismail Ferik Pasha, associated with Crete and Egypt respectively. Although Ismail finally returns to Crete where he dies, and the two worlds are sharply contrasted, even in terms of narrative mode, Galanaki is able to maintain the ambiguity about Ismail's identity and homecoming. Thanks to this ambiguity, *The Life of Ismail Ferik Pasha* is able to transcend the constraints of its historical context and assume the role of an allegory, addressing contemporary concerns about ethnic and cultural identity.

Cultural allegories and what Linda Hutcheon calls historiographic metafiction[30] both highlight the contemporary resonances of the narration of past events or of a historical period. This could explain the linguistic or other anachronisms in novels on historical themes such as those by Rhea Galanaki. A number of critics argued that Galanaki's representation of the nineteenth century in her novels is not convincing, and it might have been better to set her stories in her own time.[31] They particularly object to the way her characters think and speak, which they do not consider compatible with their historical period. I think this criticism arises from the fact that they judge Galanaki's novels according to realistic criteria and treat them as historical novels rather than as historiographic metafiction with an allegorical dimension. Galanaki's novels are as much about the present as they are about the past. Writers such as Galanaki and Panselinos use the past to voice contemporary cultural concerns, often in a metaphorical manner or even in a poetic language, and this explains why they shun verisimilitude.

Some of the novels I have mentioned try to combine the self-referentiality and inwardness of modernism by flaunting the writing process with a renewed interest in plot which often employs travel, mystery and love in order to excite the curiosity of the readers. Plot, being the dynamic element here, is associated with cosmopolitan nomadism and search for identity, while the emphasis on the writing process represents a pause for reflection and self-analysis. The frequency of travel in these narratives is often identified with the exploration of the other, whereas narrative self-consciousness is associated with the exploration of the self. A play between extroversion and introversion, otherness and sameness takes place in these narratives. This becomes clear in Alexis Stamatis's novel *Bar Flober* (2000).[32]

In this novel, Yannis Loukas is editing the autobiography of his father, a leading writer. Sorting out his father's personal archive, he finds the manuscript of an unpublished novel by somebody called Loukas Matthaiou. He embarks on a search for this mysterious and unknown man whose manuscript fascinates him and contains encoded directions. As a result, his search takes him to Barcelona, Florence, where he meets Matthaiou's daughter Katerina, and Berlin, where he finds his wife. Eventually Loukas tracks him down in a village in Arcadia where Matthaiou lives in isolation with a young woman whom he found some years ago, when she was sixteen and living rough in the area. Eventually Loukas realizes that Matthaiou is his real father.

By means of the exploration and search for the unknown writer, who is the stark antithesis of his father, Yannis Loukas explores himself as a human being and writer. The exploration of otherness through his adventures in Barcelona, Florence and Berlin leads to his understanding of himself and the realization of sameness (i.e. that Matthaiou is his real father and Katerina is his half-sister). This explains his attraction to Matthaiou and his fascination with his manuscript. Ultimately otherness seems to be transformed into sameness. The travel plot acts as a conduit for self-discovery; its outwardness at the end serves the inwardness of self-analysis as cosmopolitanism gives way to the emphasis on isolation, locality and return to roots.

Though the novel appears to be about cosmopolitanism, inasmuch as Matthaiou has spent some time in America and is acquainted with the representatives of the Beat movement, it nevertheless expresses a desire for self-exploration and the discovery of origins. The quest for the missing author, having the features of a detective novel, becomes the search for a return to a real and imaginary Arcadia. The cosmopolitan peregrinations of Loukas and Matthaiou in America and Europe lead to the desire for something simple, primordial and true. The novel, however, does not simply signify a return to beginnings; it also suggests the renegotiation of the past and the reinvention of literary tradition, considering that Loukas's 'father' Markos represents the dominant realist tradition, whereas Matthaiou represents the suppressed attempts in Greece at experimental and playful writing. Stamatis's novel is as much about travel and discovery as about artistic creation and the writing process. This brings me to the third major development since 1974.

Stamatis's novel suggests that the past (in this case Matthaiou's life) becomes known through its textualized traces. Yannis Loukas is able to reconstruct his life and movements by decoding Matthaiou's text. The increasing textualization of the past is often assisted in a number of Greek novels by paratextuality, that is to say the incorporation of written documents or footnotes in the narrative.[33] These secondary devices help the narrative to highlight the contrast between verisimilitude and fictionalization, validity and fabrication. A case in point is Panselinos's novel *Zaida, or The Camel in the Snow*.

This novel is based on a batch of letters that the author, in the introductory chapter, claims were given to him in 1980 by an Austrian musicologist and friend. These letters appear to have been written between 1792 and 1800 in Italy and Greece by a German musician, who does not reveal his identity, and are addressed to Sophie, his sister-in-law. Convinced that the writer of these anonymous letters is Mozart, the author translates and edits the letters, using them as the basis of his novel.

The letters as a narrative device have at least three functions in Panselinos's novel. First, they help to switch from first-person narrative (letters) to the third person of the narrator who fills in the gaps left by the letters. Secondly, the letters offer the opportunity for all sorts of details regarding the history, geography and literature of the period, and, thirdly, they occasionally register the linguistic variety of each region. The letters are central to Panselinos's aim to write historiographic metafiction by giving the impression that he meticulously reconstructs the historical and cultural atmosphere of a period, while at the same time he undermines this intended verisimilitude with the allegorical aim of his novel and the fictitious encounter between Mozart and Solomos. The letters as false documents convey both the desire for an accurate reconstruction of history and the idea of its fabrication and fictional embellishment. In this way an objective, scholarly and archival sense of history is blended with its imaginative reconstruction. It could be said of Panselinos's novel what has been said of postmodern fiction in general, that 'there is a contradictory turning to the archive and yet a contesting of its authority'.[34]

What Panselinos's novel shares with Amanda Michalopoulou's *As Many Times as You Can Stand It* is the emphasis on editing either letters or a novel, which is normally considered to be the job of a scholar rather than of a fictional writer. This narrative strategy is different from that of the author-as-editor who presents forgotten or newly discovered manuscripts in order to support the authenticity or realism of his story, often used in earlier Greek fiction. Here the aim is not so much the authentic representation of either historical events or individual consciousness through diary notes or other recording devices as the introduction to an ironic and playful game with the readers' expectations concerning distinctions between past and present, fact and fiction.

In Panselinos's novel the author assumes the role of the editor right from the beginning, while in Michalopoulou's novel there is an afterword by the editor, Otto Spilman, who reveals that he is not a film director, as readers have been led to believe, but a poet and professional editor who has been invited to edit the only novel by the little-known writer Grete Samsa, which is posthumously published under the title *As Many Times as You Can Stand It*. This parodic device represents the culmination of other devices involving Grete Samsa, who has been considered by critics to be a kind of reincarnation of Kafka (the main character of his story 'Metamorphosis' is called Gregor Samsa, while Grete is his sister).[35] Kafka is very much present in Michalopoulou's novels as the narrator interpolates quotations from his diaries, printed in italics, into her own narrative. Thus the novel becomes a textual universe, allowing humour, irony and parody to surface.

Michalopoulou's novel is among a number of Greek novels inhabited by other voices or constructed by other narratives.

Experience is mediated through writing or reading, as letters, diaries and extracts from newspapers, reports or other novels are embedded in the narratives and narrators are often engaged in reading or processing other texts. A number of novels rely on paratextual documentation.[36] The purpose of these paratextual strategies is 'to remind us of the narrativity (and fictionality) of the primary text and to assert its factuality and historicity'[37] by pointing to a parodic interplay between the documentary and the fictive, textual inscription and fictional subversion, historical credibility and narrative illusion. This interplay and the use of written material as a source of reconstructing one's life leads to the blurring of the distinction between life and fiction, as is claimed in Yannis Kiourtsakis's *Like a Novel*:

Now you see it in the distance: this teenager was already attempting to write the book you're struggling to write today (he already saw life as a novel). And when you're writing this book, essentially all you're doing is writing the texts that he left unfinished—besides, it's with these that your book is being written.[38]

Centred around the Zimmerman test, which proves whether somebody has an artistic talent or not, Nikos Panayotopoulos's novel *The Gene of Doubt* (1999) can be seen as another text using metafictional strategies. It begins with a prologue by Dr Friedrich Clause, to whom the writer James Wright (his name alludes to the act of writing, as is suggested in a footnote) entrusted his manuscript 'A portrait of the artist as a dying man' just before his death in a London hospital in April 2063, and ends with an afterword signed by Panayotopoulos himself. Apart from the framing and the device of posthumously publishing somebody else's manuscript, the novel deals primarily with the process of the production and evaluation of literature. It subtly explores the role of the writer, of talent and criticism within the network of relationships defining art. *The Gene of Doubt* constitutes a defence of the writer and his freedom, but at the same time it suggests that art could be a trick:

Clause's contribution to the opening of a new era for Art could only be called a hoax, just as had happened with the Zimmerman test during the first period after its presentation at the Ottawa conference, demonstrating that, even if time isn't the *unique and ultimate judge of Art*, it is certainly the greatest hoaxer.[39]

At the end it is doubt, uncertainty and scepticism that invigorate and support art and not the pseudo-scientific test for ascertaining the existence or non-existence of the creative talent. *The Gene of Doubt* is a novel within a novel since it incorporates into the narrative James Wright's 'A portrait of the artist as a dying man' which is a parody of Joyce's title *A Portrait of the Artist as a Young Man*, while one of his novels, according to a reviewer, relies heavily on Albert Camus's *The Plague*.

In Evgenia Fakinou's most recent novel, *Who killed Moby Dick?* (2001), there is an emphasis on the process of writing, as a well-known writer, Takis Apostolou, has been invited from Athens to write a book on commission about a seaside town near Lamia that is trying to boost its image and attract more tourists. The mayor who commissioned the book has high hopes for its success, but the town itself has no ancient monuments or long history to provide the material for the book. The writer, with the help of the local 'historian' Asimakis, tries to collect exciting stories from the people of the town and is finally offered a summary of Herman Melville's *Moby Dick* (1851) lifted from illustrated books for children. Though his book would not bear his name, the writer realizes that the inclusion of an abridged version of *Moby Dick* could damage his reputation as a writer, and after receiving a warning, he decides to rewrite the story:

He turned back to the beginning of the text and reread it carefully. It was absolutely fine. The adventure of a certain Antonis on a whaler that was simply hunting whales in a general way. It definitely had no connection with the original text. It was bland and uninteresting, but it was harmless. No clever bastard would be able to make the connection and say, 'But what's he talking about? This is the story of Moby Dick.'[40]

Fakinou's novel is about (re)inventing history, collecting documents and the writing process to satisfy media attention. The writer is presented here as a compiler of oral narratives and a collector of documentary material who is unable to invent an exciting story about the past of the town, but relies on recycling well-known stories from either *Moby Dick* or *Gulliver's Travels*. As a fictional writer is involved in writing a historical book about a small town, writing, like history, is presented as a process of fake reconstruction. Through the inhabitants' claiming that someone from their town was part of the crew in the story of *Moby Dick*, there is a tendency in the novel for the boundaries between fiction and reality, history and invention to be erased.

Thus we witness the increasing textualization of Greek novels and the growing role of writers and writing in the plots. Novels present themselves as multilayered and multivocal; historical details are extracted from texts and events are partially reconstructed by means of written material or oral accounts. These novels demonstrate a crisis of representation and narrative reliability. Narrative information is mediated through texts or other devices; as a result novels become opaque and the illusion of realist transparency is irrevocably lost. The use of this secondary material as mediating agent represents both the crisis of representation and the solution to this crisis. What these novels suggest is that if the past is known through its textualized traces, then, like all texts, it is open to interpretation and reconstruction. As the dialogue with earlier writers in Greek fiction is not fully developed, the intertextual dialogue of contemporary Greek fiction is not directed so much to earlier Greek narrative texts or genres as to other textual sources.

On the basis of the increasing use of documentary material in contemporary Greek novels, one can talk about a kind of 'documentary metafiction', which is similar to Linda Hutcheon's term 'historiographic metafiction' in the sense that both use realist conventions that simultaneously seek to subvert. In 'documentary metafiction', as in its historiographic counterpart, the novels present themselves both as documentary and artifice. The reader has to acknowledge the referential and non-referential nature of literature at the same time. 'While he or she recognizes that the historically verifiable events, people, and places exist(ed), he or she must also recognize them, in Hayden White's terms, as discourse.'[41] The use of textual documents suggests that history and the past are not self-structured bodies of pure, non-linguistic facts. Instead both are realized in language.

It should be said here that the emergence of documentary or historiographic metafiction has to do with the increasing awareness that the discourses of history and fiction converge or overlap. Hayden White has been instrumental in pointing out that 'there are many histories that could pass for novels, and many novels that could pass for histories, considered in purely formal (or, I should say, formalist) terms. Viewed simply as verbal artefacts, histories and novels are indistinguishable from one another.'[42] By questioning the opposition of history to fiction, which dates back to the period of the French Revolution, one points to the indeterminacy of historical knowledge and to the documentary construction of fiction.

Documentary metafiction, like its historiographic equivalent, involves the tension between subjectivity and objectivity, discourse and narrative, or in Hayden White's terms narration and narrativity, that is to say, in his words, 'between a discourse that openly adopts a perspective that looks out on the world and reports it and a discourse that feigns to make the world speak itself and speak itself as a story'.[43] Narration adopts a more subjective viewpoint and draws attention to the narrative voice, while narrativity is 'a form for the representation of events construed to be real rather than imaginary'.[44] If we view, as Hayden White does, 'narration and narrativity as the instruments with which the conflicting claims of the imaginary and the real are mediated, arbitrated, or resolved in a discourse',[45] we realize that in documentary metafiction there is a creative tension between subjectivity and objectivity, historical representation and its subversion.

What differentiates the self-consciousness of contemporary novels from the self-referentiality of modernism, however, is the emphasis on plot. Recent novels aspire to present themselves both as textual artefacts and as good stories—in other words, as narratives that might attract and puzzle the reader at the same time. This difficult, and often paradoxical, combination cannot easily be found in either European modernist texts or even Greek ones such as those by Melpo Axioti or N. G. Pentzikis. In their novels, narrative fragmentation, free association or stream of consciousness techniques are more important than constructing a plot that makes the novel readable and enjoyable. On the contrary, a number of contemporary Greek novels attempt to strike a balance between difficulty and readability, narrative experimentation and intriguing plot. The valorization of the plot, which is assisted by the mystery of the quest pattern, may well be due to market demands and the writers' desire to reach a wider audience and to see their books become best-sellers. In this way, highbrow Greek fiction tries to retain the notion of high and difficult art without ignoring the attractions of consumerism. This can also be seen as an attempt to erode the boundary between 'high' and 'low' culture. Contemporary Greek fiction, then, like postmodernism, spans the demotic and the esoteric, the commercial and the aesthetic.

## Notes to Chapter 1

1. See also Mitsos Alexandropoulos's novel *Mikro organo gia ton epanapatrismo* (1980).
2. See Dimitris Tziovas, *The Other Self: Selfhood and Society in Modern Greek Fiction*, 33–4.

3. In these double references the first date belongs to the publication in serial form, the second to the first publication as a volume.
4. Rhea Galanaki, in her essay 'Topos, mia speira atermoni (i peri entopiotitas, ethnikou, Anatolis, Dysis)', discusses the dialogue between Crete and Athens, periphery and metropolis, East and West in her work.
5. For an account of Greek fiction about Asia Minor and Constantinople see two publications by Peter Mackridge: 'The two-fold nostalgia', and 'The myth of Asia Minor in Greek fiction'.
6. Artemis Leontis, 'In the eyes of strangers', 11.
7. See Ulf Hannerz, 'Cosmopolitans and locals in world culture'.
8. In *The Idea of Culture*, Terry Eagleton points out that 'what gradually took place was a shift from this politicized culture to cultural politics' (127). See also Nina Yuval-Davis, *Gender and Nation*, 39.
9. Eagleton, *The Idea of Culture*, 126.
10. Ibid. 29. For the pre-modern and the postmodern order, culture is associated with difference, locality and identity. For the Enlightenment, however, difference was largely a reactionary doctrine that denied equality among people and prevented them from entering world citizenship.
11. Ibid. 30.
12. Amanda Michalopoulou, *Yantes* (1996), Andreas Staikos, *Epikindynes mageirikes* (1997), Eleni Yannakaki, *Peri orexeos kai allon deinon* (2001), Yannis Efstathiadis, *Me gemato stoma* (2002).
13. Fredric Jameson, 'On "Cultural Studies"', 34.
14. Eagleton, *The Idea of Culture*, 38.
15. Immanuel Wallerstein, 'The national and the universal: can there be such a thing as world culture?', in King (ed.), *Culture, Globalization and the World-System*, 104.
16. In these contradictions, according to Immanuel Wallerstein, states have played opposite roles. 'In one case, they have used their force to create cultural diversity, and in the other case to create cultural uniformity. This has made the states the most powerful cultural force in the modern world and the most schizophrenic' (ibid. 99).
17. Stuart Hall, 'The local and the global: globalization and ethnicity', in King, *Culture, Globalization and the World-System*, 27.
18. Fredric Jameson, 'Third-world literature', 69.
19. Maro Douka, *Enas skoufos apo porfyra* (1995), 507–8.
20. Alexis Panselinos, *Zaida, i i kamila sta chionia* (1996).
21. This implicit association, which has been made explicit by critics, is reinforced by the fact that Panselinos translated Mörike's 'Mozart auf der Reise nach Prag' into Greek in 1996.
22. In an interview with Olga Sella, Panselinos argues that some contemporary Greek historical novels, including his, are not driven by romantic nostalgia, but are allegories that can comment on the present better through the mask of the historical past ('Ta vivlia einai viomata', *Anti*, 636 (6 June 1997), 56–8).
23. See Dimitris Tziovas (ed.), *Greece and the Balkans: Identities, Perceptions and Cultural Encounters since the Enlightenment*.
24. Tomas Hägg, *The Novel in Antiquity*, 89.
25. Ibid. 89.
26. Michel Foucault, 'Questions on geography', in id., *Power/Knowledge*, 70.

27. Caren Kaplan, *Questions of Travel*, 66.
28. Yannis Kiourtsakis, *San mythistorima* (1995), 287, 353.
29. Ioanna Karystiani, *Koustoumi sto choma* (2000).
30. Linda Hutcheon, *A Poetics of Postmodernism*, 105–23.
31. See Elisavet Kotzia's review of Galanaki's novel *Eleni, i o Kanenas*; Vangelis Hatzivassiliou, 'Sti skia tis istorias'; Dimosthenis Kourtovik, 'I nostalgia gia ton Kanena'. See also the exchange between Aris Marangopoulos, *Avgi*, 18 Oct. 1998 and Elisavet Kotzia, *Kathimerini*, 25 Oct. 1998.
32. The name of the bar in the title plays on 'Florence', 'Berlin' and 'Flaubert'.
33. For paratextuality see Gérard Genette, *Seuils*, esp. 7–12.
34. Linda Hutcheon, *The Politics of Postmodernism*, 81.
35. Spyros Tsaknias, 'O Kafka kai oi alloi'.
36. Examples include Thanassis Valtinos, *Stoicheia gia ti dekateia tou '60* (1989), Michel Fais, *Aftoviografia enos vivliou* (1994), Aris Marangopoulos, *Oi oraies imeres tou Veniamin Sanidopoulou* (1998), Thomas Skassis, *Elliniko stavrolexo* (2000), Kostas Akrivos, *Kitrino rosiko keri* (2001), Pavlina Pampoudi, *Chartini zoi* (2003) and Tasos Chatzitatsis, *San spasmena ftera* (2003).
37. Hutcheon, *The Politics of Postmodernism*, 85.
38. Kiourtsakis, *San Mythistorima*, 536.
39. Nikos Panayotopoulos, *To gonidio tis amfivolias* (1999), 222.
40. Evgenia Fakinou, *Poios skotose ton Moby Dick?* (2001), 311–12.
41. Alison Lee, *Realism and Power*, 36.
42. Hayden White, 'The fictions of factual representation', in id., *Tropics of Discourse*, 121–2.
43. Id., 'The value of narrativity in the representation of reality', in id., *The Content of the Form*, 2.
44. Ibid. 4.
45. Ibid.

# PART 2

❖

# Shifting Spaces,
# Drifting Identities

❖

# CHAPTER 2

# The Greeks in the Balkans, the Balkans in Greece: Greek Fiction's First Steps towards Acknowledging the Other Next Door

*Vangelis Hatzivassiliou*

The Balkan turn of modern Greek fiction is an offspring of the last decade of the twentieth century. I use the word 'turn' with some hesitation, as I believe that we are not yet dealing with an entirely systematic and established phenomenon.

There are essentially two ways in which contemporary Greek writers open out towards the Balkans (I have opted to restrict my spectrum to those who made their appearance in literature after the political change of 1974). One way is static and inward and implies a sort of observation post—in this context, the Balkan foreigner represents a hero who, having just begun to move to the tune of Greek society (and while he tries to attune himself to it) is converted to the object of an initial recording and exploration. The other way is outward and entails moving the field of observation beyond Greece. The observation post exists in this case too, but in an inverse relationship with reality, as the observer is now the foreigner himself—a foreigner faced with an obviously transitional society in which he tries to catch and understand social changes as they occur.

The writers who adopt the former way are inevitably led to the consequences for everyday life of the structural changes (on the economic as well as on the social level) that have occurred in Greece in the last twenty-five years. From being a society of emigrants, which experienced a continuous drain of its members to the USA (early twentieth century), to Germany, Belgium and Australia (in the period following the Second World War) or to France (with the brain-drain of the mid-60s), Greece after 1990 (by which time the changes had become fully operative) was converted into a host country of Balkan migration that arose and swelled in the wake of the collapse of Soviet socialism.

The settlement of Balkan migrants in Greece and the multiple situations it provoked (from expulsions and xenophobia to various mutual contacts) make up the living material of several contemporary prose writers who observe foreigners in the large urban centres and record the focal points of their meeting with the natives and attempt to trace the lines of their convergence with the host country as well as their divergences from certain more or less significant parameters of its material culture and its mentalities.

This point clearly summarizes, to my mind, the basic features of the former type of approach to the Balkan foreigner (including by extension the economic migrant from countries of the former Soviet bloc), namely observing and describing the Other in terms of one's own nativeness, which is safe in its guaranteed order.

Let us now have done with our preliminary remarks by passing on to the latter way. The writers adopting this course (or at least their heroes) have to travel and move in order to locate and identify the Other in his own environment—in the conditions (as far as this is possible) of his own nativeness. So we see the protagonists of the narrative crossing borders in order either to look for traces of their recent or remote collective history or to discover entirely new experiences, which they endeavour to place within a new perspective, namely one that is, by definition, free of the narrow national framework.

The most interesting feature, of course, is the combination and interlinking of the two ways in relation to the overall horizon of contemporary Greek fiction, and the illustration (albeit at a very initial and preliminary stage) of their basic trends.

Speaking of an overall horizon, let us not forget, before we go any further into the discussion of our subject, that the contacts between contemporary Greek prose writers (from the older ones to those who are just making their first appearance) and the outside world are not limited to the Balkans: on the contrary, they extend to Western Europe and the USA (sometimes even reaching beyond the European and the American continents) and assume many forms, frequently very different among themselves (I am referring chiefly to novels of the last decade): distant, frozen Strasbourg;[1] oppressive Austria in the time of Mozart;[2] Poland, Egypt, Belgium and the Bay of Biscay;[3] the names of French intellectuals (Victor Hugo, Edgar Quinet);[4] suffocating Belgium of the 1950s;[5] ultra-modern medical research centres in the USA;[6] a Germany of casinos and Greek migrant workers;[7] early twentieth-century gangsters in New York;[8] the age-old tribes of the Pacific islands;[9] the circulation of revolutionary ideas in the Europe and Russia of 1917;[10] the spread of the commercial spirit during the nineteenth century in Asia Minor, Trieste and Odessa;[11] and frenetic races with powerful motorcycles in today's Italy, France and Spain.[12]

So not only does the leaven already exist, but it actually swells every now and then—sometimes indeed with the strangest and most un-expected methods, in a perspective of the unceasing interlinking of Self with Other, or, to put it another way, of the foreign with the domestic and the local with the international. In this way, the leaven for the Balkans is gradually produced. At this point, I shall proceed to the image of the Balkan foreigner who lives and works in Greece while forming a wide range of relations and ties with the natives.

Let me begin by noting that we shall never be able to see and understand these ties correctly and in depth unless we take account of some literary works that are not strictly of the present but refer to moments in the historical past and to some instances of osmosis that have defined Greek identity through various paths. Always in the context of the Balkan foreigner's presence in Greece, I am thinking, for example, of the story of Olga in *Three Concentric Tales* (1986) by Rhea Galanaki, where a girl of Muslim background (Islam standing here beyond the Balkan picture as the nationally experienced East) pays dearly for her emancipation in Crete at the dawn of the twentieth century, or of the novel *I Grow Old Successfully* (2000) by Yorgos Skambardonis, where we find bitter memories of the Bulgarian occupation of Thrace (with the blessing of the Nazis) during the Second World War. I am also thinking—to linger for a while longer in the area of the historical past—of Vasilis Gouroyannis's novel *The Silver-Grass is Blooming* (1992) in which the leading roles are played by Chams, i.e. Albanian-speaking Muslim inhabitants of Epirus, many of whom collaborated with the Germans and the Italians during the Occupation, arousing the hatred of their Christian compatriots. The historical Balkan Other, then, is represented both as an oppressed social entity, which only glimpses its freedom from afar without the slightest real hope of achieving it, and, at the other pole, as an oppressive political and military power exercising undisguised violence against the local Greek Christian population.

But what of the Balkan foreigner in the immediate present? In Michel Fais's collection *From the Same Glass and Other Stories* (1999), two of the stories provide a picture in relief: 'Halima, Desdemona, Boubou' and 'Upper and lower limbs'. The former is dominated by the collective inter-Balkan perspective with direct reference once again to the historical element: two cats, together with a woman who is transformed into a cat, relive the history of the Balkans in the century just ended, sketching its blood-soaked landmarks in fragmentary outlines. In the second story, the purely individual drama is firmly established: a woman of Greek origin from Russia finds again, in the foreign country, the man she had deeply loved, now an invalid.

Interracial coexistence in love (this time in marriage) is also the subject of the novel *Kilroy was Here* (1992) by Dionysis Haritopoulos, in which the hero tirelessly proclaims his admiration for an immigrant woman from the then still united Yugoslavia, who is married to a Greek from Preveza.

But the strongest coexistence between Greeks and Balkans, this time expressed on the social level, is found in the novel *Broken Greek* (2000) by Thanasis Cheimonas, in which the narrative brings together two heterogeneous and essentially opposed worlds: on one hand the well-to-do middle class of the salubrious Athenian suburbs of Psychiko, Filothei and Ekali, and on the other, shown in anything but a Manichaean way, a parade of miserably deprived Eastern Europeans, chiefly of Balkan origin, in all forms and varieties, struggling to survive in a wealthy, foreign and often hostile country.

Thus, when depicting the immediate present, Greek writers strip the Other of his demonic stereotypes and approach him for what he is or rather what he struggles every day to be: a citizen and a complete individual entity in a still alien and inhospitable society.

Now it is time we took a look at the Balkans outside Greece. In the collection of short stories by Vasilis Tsiamboussis, *Sweet Bonora* (2000), trans-border assignations and cohabitations are the main theme. The heroes move across the Balkans, but also across a wider European landscape: from Greece to Bulgaria and from Bulgaria to Greece, from Spain to Skopje (the capital of FYROM) and from Skopje to Spain and Greece, or from Greece to Germany and from Germany to Greece. In this case one might speak of heterogeneous identities and racial and cultural mixtures or even (if a vocabulary of older coinage were needed) of mixed outcasts and marginalized strata sinking into a void under the pressure of their inescapable routine and their ruthless social fate.

From the fictional *Nostalgia of the Dragons* (2000) by Dimosthenis Kourtovik and the endless wanderings of its heroes between Italy, Denmark, Germany, Poland and Bosnia, suffice it to pick the scene in Bosnia, where the protagonists, instead of clarifying an already highly complicated situation, founder in an even greater ignorance under the influence of the religious raving and armed insanity of the local political-military bands.

With the novel *The Waters of the Peninsula* (1998) by Theodoros Grigoriadis we return once more to the historical past: an English journalist, a translator from Thrace who works at the British Embassy in Constantinople, and a Muslim student who has dropped out of the religious seminary at Kavala get mixed up with Greeks, Turks and Bulgarians during the sweltering summer of 1906 and become involved in the national and racial passions shaking the Balkans in that period. The dominant element in Grigoriadis's work is nature, a nature that, while never detaching itself definitively from history, hastens to embrace the three men, removes them from their collective cares and introduces them into an endless play with the mysterious and the divine, to which they finally become entirely converted. The historical past to which we are taken back by Grigoriadis does not alter the angle from which contemporary Greek fiction sees the Balkan foreigner outside Greece. Just as in the case of those dealing with the immediate present, the effort here is directed at understanding the Other through the vital needs of his community. Now the truth is the truth of otherness, or, to be more precise, the multiple (and of course mutually conflicting) discourses of inter-linked othernesses.

I do not wish to close this sampling tour (it is no more than that and it is certainly no more than indicative) without briefly touching upon a composite case, in which the inward and the outward approach to the Balkan foreigner converge in ideal balance. In the novella *God Tells Them* (2002) by Sotiris Dimitriou, the Self as Other and the Other as Self become inextricably, inevitably and fatally interlinked. Some Greek building workers meet with Albanian, Vlach, Romany and Northern Epirote colleagues on a desolate hillside in Epirus, where an émigré is building his house. There they exchange stories, which despite their variety nevertheless serve to highlight the common fate of these people:

the protagonists of these stories are condemned to a life of relentless torment, suffering and ill-treatment.

The chief characteristic of Dimitriou's book is the painful yet ultimately futile wanderings of his anonymous everyday heroes in two areas that are at the same time familiar and alien (Greece and Albania), where their yearning to be able to live and create is gradually transformed into an utter failure to secure even the most basic necessities of life. Some escape from under the noses of the Sigurimi (the Albanian security police) to face the snares of the Greek border, others are thrown into Albanian dungeons, only to see the light of day thirty years later, while others are forced to abandon their comrades to their fate during their escape, only to have this on their conscience for the rest of their lives.

The stories constantly related by Dimitriou's heroes are not linear: they begin from the middle or the end, they are interrupted by interventions from other characters, become confused with one another or provide the basis for other narratives, which keep their flame alive throughout the plot. As for the characters of these stories, it would be a mistake to try to find their individual characteristics. All those who appear on Dimitriou's narrative scene constitute an indispensable part of a collectively stymied destiny, organic elements of a double identity that is every so often dissolved, only to pick up its pieces quickly and start over again, thus continuing *ad infinitum*. On this trajectory, the protagonists do not exchange stories so much as their burning breath, in a text that represents, in an ideal manner, oral speech and the purely physical preconditions under which it functions and manifests itself. The people who gather together on the desolate hillside in Epirus in order for each one of them to lay his stone as a contribution to the building of the émigré's house are united by overwhelming experiences. The weight of these experiences, together with the similar geographical background of all the speakers, activates their age-old traditional linguistic idiom, giving it an exceptionally high degree of internal force and warmth. Besides, Dimitriou has sought to purify his words of all ornamentation, converting the orality of his text into a dramatically distilled expression that is highly active even when it is silent.

*Translated by Eleni Dalabira and Peter Mackridge*

## Notes to Chapter 2

1. Maro Douka, *Ourania michaniki* (1999).
2. Alexis Panselinos, *Zaida, i i kamila sta chonia* (1996).
3. Dimitris Nollas, *O tymvos konta sti thalassa* (1992).
4. Rhea Galanaki, *Tha ypografo Loui* (1993).
5. Yannis Kiourtsakis, *San mythistorima* (1995), *Emeis kai oi alloi* (2000).
6. Ioanna Karystiani, *Koustoumi sto choma* (2000).
7. Antonis Sourounis, *Meronychta Frankfourtis* (1982), *Mison aiona anthropos* (1992), *Gas o gangster* (2000).
8. Apostolos Doxiadis, *Ta tria anthropakia* (1997).
9. Faidon Tamvakakis, *Oi navagoi tis Pasifais* (1997).
10. Soti Triantafyllou, *To ergostasio ton molyvion* (2000).
11. Nikos Themelis, *I anazitisi* (1998) and *I anatropi* (2000).
12. Nicole Roussou, *Stoichimata me tous theous* (2000).

CHAPTER 3

❖

# The Alpha Males and Worker Bees of the Balkan Honeycomb: Economic Migrants in Contemporary Greek Fiction

*Vangelis Calotychos*

[...] because they remembered that they too were Greeks,
they too once upon a time were citizens of Magna Graecia;
and how low they'd fallen now, what they'd become,
living and speaking like barbarians,
cut off so disastrously from the Greek way of life.
                    C. P. CAVAFY, 'Poseidonians'[1]

Despite his hatred for the 'filthy gypsy Skopjans who want to take our Macedonia', the red-blooded Greek narrator of Michel Fais's short story 'Buzz, Buzz, Buzz'[2] befriends a Skopjan, the beekeeper Milko Popofski. 'Now he, he was a human being!'[3] This was no small feat at a time, in the 1990s, when the Greek government was locked in a rancorous diplomatic dispute with the fledgling government of its neighbouring northern state that sought to name itself 'Macedonia' and so, in Greek eyes, usurp the former's classical heritage. Ordinary Greeks were swept up in nationalist fervour and proceeded to name this state 'Skopje' after its capital, and the country's inhabitants Skopjans. In this climate, the friendship struck up by Fais's narrator with one such 'Skopjan' is refreshing, even if it unfolds in the afterlife. The narrator speaks from beyond the grave and the luckless Milko passes away in a hospital ward in Ioannina *en route* to thank the narrator's uncle for saving his son's life at the hands of racist thugs on the terraces of a Greek football ground. Aside from Milko's resolve, a Skopjan *filotimo* [sense of honour], he leaves behind an embalmed hawk that he had carried with him all the way from Skopje as a token of appreciation for the narrator's uncle. Upon his death, a swarm of bees nesting in this hawk's stomach disperse in the hospital wards and cause sheer chaos, buzz–buzz–buzzing about, swarming around and bothering one and all. Try as they might, doctors, nurses and patients are unable to shoo them out. Swatting, chasing and expelling them does not work and soon the bees are everywhere. The migrant bees, tucked away like in the belly of a modern Trojan horse, have got in and are here to stay.

Fais's figure is an enduring monument to the imminent threat of contamination and disorder that economic migrants from the Balkans and Eastern Europe were thought to bring with them into Greece. After 1989 these refugees swarmed across shifting borders to all corners of the European Union. By the early 1990s, the western press was warning about the challenges posed by 'barbarians at the gates'. And Greece, a country that for decades had supplied emigrant labour to Europe, and before that to the United States, found itself in the unaccustomed position of playing host to just such immigrants. Greeks were psychologically, socially and logistically unprepared for this influx. After all, the liberalism and Europeanism that Greek élites had pursued since the 1930s had predicated itself largely on the suppression of the often associated perils of Balkanism, communism and Slavism. The Cold War and Greece's ideological separation from the peoples of the Balkan peninsula only reinforced this distance from Balkan specificities.

Happily, the Macedonian dispute, though still unresolved, has been defused and the small state has survived, having seen little of the violence that ravaged the former Yugoslavia. More recently, it has enjoyed Greek diplomatic support and financial assistance. Indeed, more generally, yet only after some initial defensiveness, Greeks have gradually demon-strated greater understanding in negotiating their place in the Balkans. The process has not been painless. At a state level, Greeks did so while submitting themselves to austerity measures designed to help them achieve modernization and closer integration with the European Union even as territorial and ethnic wars rumbled ominously at their borders. Circumstances have changed to the point that Greeks are seeking to enhance their European profile by foregrounding their relation to other Balkan societies and even championing the region's interests to their

European partners. On a social level, individual Greeks have had to free themselves of their own prejudices in their dealings with these immigrants. Unfortunately, the migrants were swept up into the vortex of broader fears about the effects of globalization, neo-liberalism and Europeanization, and even became symbols of disaffection with these phenomena. All in all, reorientation has been much slower on this level as persistent forms of racism and exploitation remain ingrained in everyday practice as well as in some of the functionings of the state apparatus towards these people.

This chapter focuses on interpersonal relations between Greek characters and economic migrants both in Greece and across its borders in order to comment on the anxieties that underlie a reconfiguration of identity conditioned by the treatment of a multiculturalist difference in Greek society and through the Greek novel. Greek writers have struggled with the notion of a common humanity shared with these people. For, typically, as nation-states enter a crisis of legitimation, some of the accepted traditions of natural affinity or belonging have been thrown into question. In this context, an examination of the embodied experiences of affinity in matters of speech, cleanliness, bodily movement, health and language in the contemporary novel will inform the likelihood of a reappraisal (or a restriction) of the scope of affinity between Greeks and others. The identity of the citizen in Greece, as elsewhere, can no longer be built on the self-identification of the Alpha-male type of Fais's benevolent yet red-blooded Hellenic male, the product of an overwhelmingly homogeneous society. The bees buzzing around us pose new challenges for that identity and the processes for defining it. I have space here to consider briefly works by Menis Koumandareas, Christos Voupouras/Yorgos Korras and Sotiris Dimitriou. The perspectives identified in this analysis are as much a symptom of, as a comment on, the power differential at the core of Greeks' relations to these migrants. While this article limits itself to a discussion of encounters between men, and different types of men, it is worth acknowledging that a more wide-ranging analysis of novels, short stories and films that discuss immigration must face the experience of women too.[4] The trafficking of women throughout the Balkans, including Greece, has reached staggering proportions and demands the urgent attention of all sectors of Greek society.

In the 1990s, with geographic precision, Balkan difference located itself in the heart of Greece. Omonia, the square situated right in the centre of Athens, has become the symbol of the decade's otherness.

This actuality carries with it a set of ironies. Preparations for the 2004 Athens Olympics move forward apace with the renovation of the square and the coincidental expulsion from its environs of heroin addicts and migrant workers, who have made the square their hangout. New shopping centres and renovated neoclassical hotels in Omonia by day provide the backdrop for rampant prostitution, some of it by young immigrant men, by night.[5]

While Greek modernity seeks its symbolization in the staging of a successful Olympic Games contingent on the development of the city's infrastructure, this is built in part on the backs of migrant, often undocumented, workers. In the space of a decade, projects such as these have contributed to rates of growth that run at twice the EU average, which have catapulted Greece from European whipping boy during the wars of the Yugoslav succession to a respected place at the Euro-table in 2004. But the ironies and anxieties are never far from view and persistently irrupt. The very party held to celebrate the New Year 2002 and Greece's full entry into the European Monetary Union (EMU), in the more bourgeois square in the heart of Athens, Constitution Square, was marred by a fist-fight between Kurdish and Albanian refugees.

Omonia Square has become a symbol of a ubiquitous demographic and spatial change that is taking place across the capital and beyond. For example, the once eminently bourgeois nearby neighbourhood of Kato Patissia is now rundown. Rents have plummeted and the apartments are inhabited—some Greeks say 'overrun'—by Eastern European and African immigrants. It is in just such a neighbourhood, in a ramshackle local barber's shop, that Menis Koumandareas sets his collection of stories *Their Smell Makes Me Want To Cry* (1996).[6] In this bastion of male solidarity, the barber, named Euripides, banters with a motley crew of customers. In the fourth of nine tales titled 'The Romanian Kid' ('To Roumanopoulo'),[7] a gay artist, named simply Phaedon—it is common for Greek artists to go by one name—shares with Euripides his view of how geopolitics and globalization, dislocation and migration have transformed daily life in Athens by referring specifically to Omonia: 'Omonia has become a meeting place for many peoples. [...] From the Balkans, Eastern Europe, the Middle East. As if Greece were becoming *Magna Graecia* again! The one we read about in books, with its colonies back again' (106). Phaedon sees a multicultural wonderland, but one that cannot shake off his own brand of cultural hegemony:

Get out of your house on Sunday morning and take a look at the proud Africans with their colourful clothes, look at the tiny Filipinos, the Albanians, always by themselves, the Poles with their families. That's why I'm telling you, we have become a centre for all peoples, in this crossroads of the world. And we give them a second country, we teach them our language. Think about it, what better way to make Greek a universal language? (106)

Here, as in the other stories, the folksy Euripides listens and nudges the conversation along. A 'man's man' with a curiosity for the perverse, he channels the excesses of his customers' tales through his own well-worn, mainstream ideology. He has the sympathetic eye of one who has long confronted others in a barber-shop mirror—trimming away from their observations, lightening their soul, cropping their heads into a uniform short-back-and-sides. Yet Euripides does not see himself in the mirror of others' stories. The reader, by contrast, inhabits the space between Euripides and his customers, s/he reflects on Euripides' perspective, as well as his or her own, on these peoples of a different creed, colour, language and sexual inclination, on the 'Roumanopoulo', and on what it means to be categorized as such. Euripides, a practising heterosexual, does not share Phaedon's opinion of such multiculturalism: 'I looked at him, nodding my head. I was not a racist but I could not share his enthusiasm. And I couldn't care less if he thought me a housewife or a senior citizen' (106–7). Clearly, to do so would emasculate him. Where Phaedon exults in the freedom of foreigners coming and going as they please, Euripides attributes the reason for 'why we witness some murder or other every day' to this *laissez-faire* immigration policy (106).

Certainly, Phaedon's account of his infatuation with a Romanian lad, the son of a famous pianist, who has turned to male prostitution to survive on the streets of Athens, does not breed much optimism. It does, however, offer a window on the ambiguities of really knowing and loving 'a stranger' or a 'foreigner', of differentiating between using him and respecting him in the bedroom or in the workplace. It is an exercise dependent wholly on his foreignness, his status as 'the Romanian kid'. For all projects of romanticization and exoticization, artistic or otherwise, are more safely undertaken from a distance, or when an initial objectification disallows the coming together of two people as equals. This is not unlike whoring, which is just how this tryst begins: Phaedon, the artist, pays for the company of the gorgeous son of the concert pianist. In his turn, Leonard the 'Roumanopoulo' agrees as long as Phaedon respects the fact that Leonard has a girlfriend in Canada and that his kisses are reserved for her. It is predictable, then, when the two do not sleep together on their first night. For by exchanging money but not consummating the transaction sexually, Phaedon wishes to delude himself that he is no longer party to a transaction. Both seek by their actions to preserve or elicit a common humanity or remain, in their minds, who they know they no longer are. The social and cultural inequality between them escapes in some of Phaedon's more unguarded moments: Phaedon strives to close this gap with a gesture that can not conceal an approximation-cum-appropriation reflective of a long-standing Greek cultural hegemony over its Balkan neighbours:

Yes, the Romanian lad. Sounds a bit like *Romaniot* or *Romios*. It is related to Romans, Byzantium, Rumelia, the word *Romios*.[8] It encapsulates the union of so many cultures and leads in all kinds of directions: the Balkans, of which Romania is the northern extension. Once, in fact, many Greeks lived there [...] a part of diaspora Hellenism had its centre in Bucharest, Jassy and Constanza. (94)

Even by story's end at a chance meeting, when they are no longer together, Phaedon's self-pity requires the crutch of the claim to a common humanity. Leonard has pilfered money from Phaedon's friend, to whom Phaedon entrusted him, and then disappeared. With the ill-gotten proceeds, Leonard contends that he went to Canada to see the love of his life. The trip, however, signals the end of his idealized relationship and he returns to Athens to join his friends working in a gay bar called 'Queen'. Leonard's disappointment and his decision to seek refuge in a coterie of gay co-workers appeals to Phaedon and makes him see in this something of his own plight: 'Poor Leonard. Poor all of us. Weren't we all victims? Sides of the same coin, the one that we handed out to them and that they would take, unhesitatingly. The same used banknote that was passed from hand to hand and that no longer bore any significance as long as it passed by some bed somewhere' (108).

Phaedon's belief that he and Leonard share a common plight brings to the fore issues of (homo)sexual difference in Greek society. Greek aesthete and Balkan immigrant, homosexuals both, are victims of a wider economy of exploitation examined in the book. These aesthetic and sexual allegiances break down ethnic differences and recompose prevailing norms by creating new alliances, in new spaces in the face of a masculinist, nationalist self-definition. Even Phaedon the artist and Euripides may be 'sides of the same coin'. The former dabbles in art because it is useless in the Kantian sense and the latter, a pragmatist, would not dabble in anything that did not make him money. Yet neither is immune from the kind of self-examination undertaken as a result of their interaction with Balkan Others. Phaedon's concern for Leonard is moved by his desire to convince himself that their relationship transcends the transactual terms of their original meeting, that it is always something more than this. Euripides, too, opens the tale with reflections on his own transactions with foreigners, not in bed, of course, but in his barber's shop. He has hired 'a Turkish lad—I'm not prejudiced—honest but slow.' He replaces him with a Pole:

He was so polite I couldn't bear it. Why did I get rid of him, you ask? He would get there half an hour before me and stand shivering outside on the stoop of the shop. I'd get off, he'd stay on. I'd cut hair, he would clean up, dust off; like he had ants in his pants or something. I got rid of him with two months wages. Anyone would think I had money to spare. (82)

Euripides would seem to have fired these workers because they are either too lazy or too diligent, not because they are foreigners. He claims to see beyond ethnicity and the stereotype. What role differences play in Euripides's evaluation of them is not fully clear. Nevertheless, the tale ends with a reaffirmation of the basic economy as Euripides knowingly introduces Phaedon to a new customer, Hassan.

Greek novelists and film-makers in the 1990s have set this economy of performative interaction of Greece and the Balkans in tales that cross borders. There are numerous examples: Theo Angelopoulos's *The Suspended Step of the Stork* and *Ulysses' Gaze*, Sakis Totlis's novel *The Combination: Edessa-Zurich* (1991) (better known in the form of Stelios Goritsas's film *Balkanisateur*) and Nikos Themelis's *The Overthrow* (2000) take difference on tour into the Balkan hinterland. Others have re-examined the place of difference at the heart of national identity: Rhea Galanaki's *The Life of Ismail Ferik Pasha* (1989), Vasilis Gouroyannis's *The Silver-Grass is Blooming* (1992), Theodoros Grigoriadis's *The Waters of the Peninsula* (1998) and Diamantis Axiotis's *The Least of His Life* (1999). A work that places both a Greek's contact with an immigrant and a crossing of borders at the centre of its consideration of identity is Christos Voupouras's and Yorgos Korras's *Mirupafshim* (2000), which originally appeared as an award-winning feature film in 1997.[9] What begins with a young Greek leftist's well-meaning attempt at befriending a group of Albanian migrants on a city bus, turns into a relationship doomed to failure. A set of socio-economic inequalities and cultural differences examined closely in the narrative throws precarious intimacies into a tailspin. The resulting anxieties engendered allow traditional values of faith, family and nation to reassert themselves defensively and fill that space of uncertainty. In other words, a close encounter with the Others elicits the very resistances that reinforce our most 'essential' barriers to them.

This is a very peculiar film and novel. For though it sets out precisely as a kind of liberal experiment in multicultural living, it takes an extremely unexpected turn that is as narratologically refreshing as it is politically disturbing. For, eventually, Christos, our protagonist, accompanies his Albanian friends back over the border to Albania. Once there, he experiences otherness himself amidst the constraints of the Other's own social and cultural mores as well as by their designs upon him—primarily, they want him to sponsor visas for their whole family to be allowed into Greece. All this unfolds as he drifts about Albania with them contemplating the embattled status of the Albanian Orthodox Church and the ethnic Greek minority. Personal and public realms become intertwined in the figure of Aphrodite, the ethnic Greek wife of one of the Albanians, whom Christos cautiously probes for insights into Albanian culture. She becomes progressively a figure of gendered and ethnic imprisonment in this intensely patriarchal family and state structure. Concurrently, Christos's frustration at his increasingly unworkable relationship with his Albanian friends projects itself onto his reading of the Albanian public sphere. Indicatively, it is as they tour Muslim mosques and Orthodox churches that their most heated disputes take place. Eventually, Christos does not obtain the visas for the Albanians, and he returns to Greece.

Once back in Greece, Christos undergoes something of a transformation. He dutifully pays a visit to his ageing parents and, quite uncharacteristically, holds his mother's hand; he expresses great love for his daughter and vows to be a better father, and he reminisces fondly on Church services of his youth to intone that 'life is memory'. In short, the wayward leftist is brought back into the fold of family, patriarchy and religion. This catches both his reader and his daughter unawares:

'Daddy, I don't understand anything you're saying...'
'Let me explain to you. Have you seen on television when they brand the buffaloes?'

'Of course, I have, yes.'
'Well, that's how we got our identity. It's branded on us.'[10]

With this patriotic turn, it becomes unclear whether *Mirupafshim* is a knowing critique of the Greek Left's courting of ultra-nationalist and religious movements in the 1990s (especially during the Macedonian crisis) or if it is a strident affirmation that cultural essentialisms *are* there, after all, and run more than skin-deep. That we are indeed irrevocably different. Be the cause essentialism or unrelenting social construction, *Mirupafshim* cautions us that cultural differences will complicate and perhaps even inflame even the most well-meaning of contacts between Albanians and Greeks.

The crossing of borders and contact with the economic migrant is captured in the bilingual title of this last work, *Mirupafsim tha pei: kali antamosi* [*Mirupafshim Means Till We Meet Again*]. The excavation of hybrid languages and previously hushed micro-histories is prevalent in a host of works of contemporary fiction, like Michel Fais's *Autobiography of a Book* (1994) or Markos Meskos's *Muharrem* (1999). The three tales that comprise Sotiris Dimitriou's *May Your Name Be Blessed* (1993) are delivered in a thick Epirot idiom.[11] The third tale, which is best known because it formed the basis of Sotiris Goritsas's acclaimed film *From the Snow*, tells of the trials and tribulations of a group of migrants who have smuggled their way into Greece from the snow-covered mountains of Albania. In the original book, the two preceding tales offer a short family history of these long-suffering migrants that stretches back sixty years. The first tale, set during the Occupation and the early Greek Civil War in Thesprotia, depicts the women of the village embarking on a journey to provide food for their starving families. The men are absent; either working abroad in Australia or America, or else fighting in the Civil War. The carefully noted names of the protagonists (Yori-Kaisarina, Vangeli-Stolaina) contain the names of their husbands, to whom they would seem to be inextricably tied. However, the irony lies in the fact that all the men are absent and the women shoulder all the traditionally male responsibilities. They travel in a landscape before national borders, in a local cartography that resonates with names foreign-sounding to a metropolitan Athenian ear.[12] The women's sufferings are not wrought upon them because of their ethnicity. Indeed, they are treated with kindness time and time again—Cham women (Albanian-speaking Muslims living in Greek Epirus) give them food, as do Christians and

Albanian Muslims as well as Gypsies, who cheerily inform the narrator that they will come to her village one day and expect a reciprocal gesture. It is only the communist partisans who spoil this picture: they rape the women and, on three occasions, steal their corn. The communists regard the women as fascists with a binary logic that, by the second tale, prevails and imposes itself on the landscape in the form of a border drawn between areas controlled by the army and the communists. 'Greece' and 'Albania' institute a new ideological and geographical but also linguistic regime: 'We'll have no "cousin this" and "cousin that" no more,' [the *kapetanios*] snarled at her. 'What do you mean cousin? It's comrade or nothing now' (36). The border separates one of the women, Sophia, from her family. Though her village is only three miles away, she can no longer reach it. Political and ideological barriers have interfered and disrupted the functioning of a pre-nationalist ecosystem. In Dimitriou's landscape, men are in prison or abroad, women are separated from their mothers, their sisters, often their children, even within national borders.

By the third tale, Sophia has reared children and grandchildren in Albania, who are 'ethnic Greeks' living in repressive conditions, which eventually force them to learn a new language of 'minority' identity and 'discrimination' (56). With the 'bridle gone, the fear'd gone' (60), Shpëtim, Sophia's grandson, 'pisses off home' (62) over the border to Greece, where, once away from the border regions, he is mostly treated as just another filthy Albanian. In an ending that stresses more the instinctual will for survival and perseverance and offers no clear resolution, Dimitriou also offers a glimmer of hope or, at least, respite: Shpëtim meets a Greek at a bus stop much in the way Christos meets his Albanian companions in the opening scene of *Mirupafshim*:

I spoke to a young lad. 'Listen,' I say to him, 'can you tell me how to get there?'

'Here,' he says to me, 'I'll take you to the bus stop. It's on my way. Are you from Albania?'

'Yes', I answer.

We fetched at the bus stop.

'Got a ticket?'

'No', I say to him.

'I've got one if you want.'

'You've done me favour enough already.'

'Some favour!' he says to me. He gives me the ticket.

'What your name?' I say to him.

'Dimitris.'
'May your name be blessed, Dimitris.'
He smiled. He waved.
I climbed onto the bus, I was feeling somehow better. That lad'd poured
balsam on my soul. (83–4)

At one level, this scene instils a dose of common humanity into all the
brutishness. On another, it encapsulates Dimitriou's yearning for a
different economy of personhood and coexistence in keeping with the
local topography of the first tale. Here and in his interviews, Dimitriou
favours a realm free from the ideologies that come with nationalism,
modernity and urbanism.[13] Like the nostalgias often evoked by
postcolonial writers and critics, he claims an authenticity untouched
by and in spite of history, a resilient pre-nationalist consciousness that
is often intensely folkloristic, communitarian and ingrained. There is,
of course, a peril with this vision that it might lapse into the one
represented in *Mirupafshim*, an ardent localism branded on our skins.
Of course, Dimitriou's is not a nationalist vision. But, when, in the first
tale, Dimitriou's stoic women characters affirm that they can depend
on 'our own people' (6) from villages all around—and by this they do
not mean Greeks—the question remains what makes someone our
own? The problems of integration encountered by thousands of 'our
own' ethnic Greek Albanians and Pontians from the former Soviet
Union who have returned to settle in Greece have painfully taught
us the ambiguities of employing such an identification casually. For
the concept is built on possession and inclusion, dispossession and
exclusion. Such notions, like the idea of a common humanity, are
difficult to maintain *in* history. The Greek novel has been charged with
exploring the senses in which Balkan migrants will and will not become
'our own people'.

## Notes to Chapter 3

1. C. P. Cavafy, *Collected Poems*, 193.
2. This is the first tale ('Vzzzt, vzzzt, vzzzt') from Michael Fais, *Ap' to idio potiri kai
   alles istories* (1999).
3. Fais, ibid. 18.
4. For an admirable beginning in this endeavour, see Georgia Farinou-Malamatari,
   'The representation of the Balkans'.
5. The acclaimed film by Constantine Yannaris *Stin akri tis polis* (*On the Edge of the
   City*) considers just this subject in the lives of teenage Russian Pontian 'returnees'
   of Greek descent.
6. Menis Koumandareas, *I myrodia tous me kanei na klaio* (1996).

7. Translated extracts are cited by pages in the original Greek text. However, the translation itself is taken from Patricia Felisa Barbeito's and my translation, 'The Romanian Kid'. Our full translation of the entire collection of short stories (Menis Koumandareas, *Their Smell Makes me Want to Cry*) will appear in the Birmingham Modern Greek Translations series, published by the Centre for Byzantine, Ottoman and Modern Greek Studies, Birmingham University, in 2004.

8. A Romaniot is a Greek-speaking Jew. *Romios* was the traditional word for a Greek Orthodox, from the fact that the Byzantines called themselves Romans. Rumelia was an area of the Balkans where many Greeks lived; Eastern Rumelia briefly became autonomous in 1878 until it was annexed by Bulgaria in 1885.

9. Christos Voupouras and Yorgos Korras, *Mirupafsim tha pei: kali antamosi* (2000).

10. Ibid. 253.

11. Sotiris Dimitriou, *N' akouo kala t' onoma sou* (1993). Translations are taken from Sotiris Dimitriou, *May Your Name Be Blessed*, translated by Leo Marshall.

12. Very innovatively, Marshall conveys this by adopting lexical and syntactic forms of expression that are rural and somewhat outdated but which have no specific regional characteristic. 'The unfamiliar terrain' produced 'belongs to a different and unfamiliar world', as he explains in his translator's preface (p. xxiv).

13. See e.g. his remarks in an interview in the periodical *Anti*, 21 Dec. 2001, 46–7 or in the newspaper *Kathimerini*, 20 Apr. 2003 ('Itan pio eleftheroi apo mas, gematoi ormi kai zoi').

❖

# The Dislocated Self in a Global Situation

*Mary Mike*

In Greek novels written within the last twenty-five years, a certain turn can be observed towards a mode of thinking and writing that deals consciously and persistently with descriptions of personal intro-spections and of intimate quests, both inwards and outwards; with the representation of an opening to the other, of contact and interaction between native and foreign characters. This intense preoccupation with the coordinates of the self, the mapping of its limits, has resulted in a shifting of the concept of Greekness that leads, among other things, to a new problematic, a new conceptual scheme.

These mutable boundaries both increase the nature of imagined belonging and kinship between the national and international literary production and expand a cultural/spatial field. This eclectic com-munity is mainly located in the inconsistencies and internal conflicts of the subject, in the realization of the fact that there cannot be such a thing as a 'single' person, in the projected and explored multiplicity that puts in question the concept of a concrete, cohesive and autonomous self. Multiple focalizations of the same event at different moments and from diverse points of view, the endless play of spatial and temporal perspectives, constant displacements between the national and the international, the real and the fake: all these indicate a preoccupation with the construction of an identity in progress, through, not outside, difference, which does not hesitate to bring out its multiplicity and diversity—on the contrary, it aspires to do so.

The concept of identity deployed here is not an essentialist one, but a strategic and positional one. That is to say, directly contrary to what appears to be its settled semantic career, this concept of identity does not signal that stable core of the self, unfolding from beginning to end without change throughout the vicissitudes of history. It accepts that identities are never unified and increasingly fragmented and fractured; never singular but multiply constructed across different, often intersecting and antagonistic, discourses, practices and positions. They are subject to a radical historicization, and are constantly in the process of change and transformation.[1]

Nevertheless, this common attitude towards the fragmented global individual seems to place local history in a different perspective. In this sense, local history does not quite constitute one of the ends of a temporal scale (from local history to global individual) but returns changed and affected, injected in the meanwhile with the altered gaze or perception of the wandering subject.

Besides, the locality of national culture is neither unified nor unitary in relation to itself, nor should it be seen simply as 'other' in relation to what is outside or beyond it. The boundary is Janus-faced and the problem of outside/inside must always itself be a process of hybridity. Hybridity interrupts the representation of the fullness of life and resists totalization. It incorporates new people in relation to the body politic, generates other sites of meaning and inevitably, in the political process, produces unnamed sites of political antagonism and unpredictable forces for political representation. What emerges as an effect of such incomplete signification is a turning of boundaries and limits into the in-between spaces through which the meanings of cultural and political authority are negotiated.[2]

Thus, in literary texts in which *nostos* (homecoming) is a central theme, multiple aspects of so-called locality (e.g. space, time, people, language, memory, the possibility of self-reflection in the eyes of others) are explored and elaborated. People too must be thought of in a double-time; they are not simply historical events or parts of a patriotic body politic, the historical 'objects' of a nationalist pedagogy. They are also a complex rhetorical strategy of social reference, they are subjects of a process of signification.[3]

Since it is through the internal orbit of the mind that the external landscape takes its place and unfolds, it is to be expected that the relation between the subject and the rediscovered place oscillates between two poles: that of total reconciliation and acceptance—something extremely rare, as the texts indicate—and that of complete alienation and misrecognition. The native locus might be a trap, a dangerous spider's web, a place of exile, an envied refuge, a consolatory fantasy that

weaves together scattered threads, a machine that grinds dreams and
expectations, or a blank page that has erased time and place, a repository
of one's memories, recalled events and accumulated cultural symbols.
The discourse on birthplace depends upon culturally constructed
images depicting and representing the past.

Without maintaining that the literary texts used here as exemplary
are representative of more totalizing tensions in modern Greek fiction
over the last twenty-five years, I have chosen to analyse *A Suit in the
Earth* (2000) by Ioanna Karystiani for the subject's effort to be
reconciled with place and *We the Others* (2000) by Yannis Kiourtsakis
for the dynamic of a writing of exile.

In *A Suit in the Earth* we read about the life of the emigrant scientist
Kyriakos Rousias. A painful cycle of blood, a Cretan vendetta, forces
Rousias to leave for America, where he studies and makes a brilliant
academic career for himself, to keep the past and the figure of the
murderer father at a distance, to decorate his home with posters of
the Greek Tourist Organization (thus creating an idyllic composition
of reality), and to postpone for many years the homecoming to the
island.

When at last he decides to return, the cycle of blood is breaking,
the reconciliation is successful, and time, space, language and memory
take on new dimensions that accompany him in America. It is as if for
the first time in his life he had acquired a father's grave, a childhood,
a cousin and other relatives.

Let us study the ways in which this reconciliation comes about.
When the physicist comes back after twenty-eight years to the Cretan
mountain plateau, he discovers the conspiracy of memory and oblivion, the painful process of the recollection of bloody events marked
by the dark zones of death, and also the terror that goes along with
absence.

The enforced exile and his detachment for so many years from the
vital space of the (m)other language lead him, while he is in America,
to planned meetings with Greek emigrant friends who listen to the
same songs and enjoy themselves in the same way, but also to endless
silences, to scientific castrations, to a disguised rejection of the past,
that is, to an illusion of the rejection of time and place. Can we say,
therefore, that the enunciation of cultural difference problematizes the
division of past and present, tradition and modernity, at the level of
cultural representation and its authoritative address? It is the problem
of how, in signifying the present, something comes to be repeated,

relocated and translated in the name of tradition, in the guise of pastness.[4]

Homecoming becomes a desire for reconciliation. If Rousias wants to rediscover space, he will have to retrace the threads of his life backwards until exactly that point where they were suddenly cut, thus initiating the cycle of blood:

> He sat down, it takes a great deal of work to find a forgotten place, he murmured, a great deal of work, a world half known and half unknown, places that reveal something and hush something else up, trivial things of the past and of the imagination that emerge one by one and, first of all, the hot stone that suddenly burned his backside (53).

> What am I doing here, Rousias wondered, as if all at once he had dried up; he closed his eyes and saw it—the physicists may deny its existence but they accept its necessity in everyday life—a soul, his soul, becoming solid like wet cement and cracking his chest. His tongue heavy like cement too. Not a word could come out (95).

Space demands to be rediscovered, and the possibility of claiming an origin for the Self (or Other) within a tradition of representation that conceives of identity as the satisfaction of a totalizing, plenitudinous object of vision is almost zero. By disrupting the stability of the ego, expressed in the equivalence between image and identity, the secret art of invisibility, of which the migrant scientist speaks, changes the very terms of recognition of the person.[5]

Each time the encounter with identity occurs at the point at which something exceeds the frame of the image, it eludes the eye, evacuates the self as identity and autonomy and—most important—leaves a resistant trace, a stain of the subject, a sign of resistance. We are no longer confronted with an ontological problem of existence, but with the discursive strategy of the moment of interrogation, a moment at which the demand for identification becomes, primarily, a response to other questions of signification and desire, culture and politics.

Given that the subject becomes a speaking subject only through its commerce with the system of linguistic differences, we should bear in mind the efforts that have to be made by exiled subjects to find the proper words for the symbolic representation of things and the social effect of the relation to the other.

The Bakhtinian idea that there are no 'neutral' words and forms—words and forms that can belong to 'no one'—seems to be borne out; language lies on the borderline between oneself and the other, has been completely taken over, shot through with intentions and accents. Each word tastes of the context or contexts in which it has lived its socially charged life; all words and forms are populated by intentions.[6] It is not easy, Bakhtin goes on, to detach and to appropriate a discourse that is half-alien. In many cases a discourse appears extremely resistant and cannot be easily appropriated. Consequently, if an act of enunciation can never exclusively attributed to speakers but is rather the product of an interplay between two or more inter-locutors, what is really terrifying in the fact that dialogue is impossible is precisely the lack of response.[7]

Thus, when the silenced Rousias returns home, he painfully remarks that 'others' words were running around, his mind was running to the past and, in the meantime, he was becoming aware of gaps, words whose meanings he had forgotten and things whose words he had forgotten' (76).

The locus resists, redraws, does not offer itself with the same ease and generosity. It does not surrender; that is why Rousias

did not know if he had been right to return. And he didn't want to think about it. He was walking around, looking at the surroundings as if they were new to him. Partly because of his long absence, partly because of deliberate oblivion, some images in his memory had faded and superimposed them-selves on each other like double exposures (65).

When Rousias's reconciliation with memory succeeds, a new literary locus is constructed, a new geography, which, in order to respond to the needs of the subject, must function as a double space, a super-imposed image, it has to be coined from the very beginning as one and the same place. Of course the way a place is deciphered differs according to its readers. In the case of the mutual acceptance of subject and place, the landscape ceases to be a threatening or picturesque space and becomes infused in the body, becomes an object of dreams, fades away when necessary and comes back again, as if in a live personal relationship:

He counted the forty-three years of his maturity, having reconciled his two places, which were light-years away from each other. However, stories obliged them from time to time to travel together, to converge, to fall on top of each other, to become one.

That happened from time to time. Then they separated again, one place in a thousand pieces, as many pieces as there were people's stories, as if it were people who put their stories down, their strictly personal wanderings, and draw maps accordingly (376).

In *We the Others*, the narrator-protagonist narrates his successive introspective phases to maturity within the span of twenty-five years (1960–85) in different places and in different horizons. Studies in Paris, adventures of a new love and discussions about Greece create an unbearable feeling of nostalgia and an idyllic image of the native place. However, this image is dissolved after he settles back in Greece. The frightful observation that a sense of exile is always present wherever the narrative subject may be and that he, the narrator, without knowing it, is reliving the adventures of his dead brother lead him to write a new text, in other words to form a new writing self.

In *We the Others* the way to maturity and adulthood is mapped out through the absence of a concrete point of reference, a stable and engaging horizon, through the painful oscillation between the imaginary reconstruction of another place and the almost permanent feeling of misery and intolerance that affects the subject, thus creating a new space for its utopia. At the same time, the birthplace is also affected by multiple changes that, in the meanwhile, have altered the gaze, the way of seeing, the ability to comprehend, to reflect on selfness and otherness:

how can you return to your homeland, when foreign places have bewitched you, when they have changed you so radically that every bridge connecting you with those left behind has been cut? But again, how can you travel, how can you truly open yourself to other places, when homesickness torments you so much that every other desire in your soul is paralysed? It would be vain, since you, who travelled to a foreign land, have become a foreigner yourself [...]

So, how could he really find himself again in his home, his home that he had so much missed while in Paris? We do not really miss just one place, we constantly miss the time that passes by, carrying away with it all the places where we live—how could we ever return to the same place, when every place in our lives never stops being transformed and lost in time? (125)

The Proustian phrase that the memory of a particular image is but a regret for a particular moment seems to be borne out. The lost home and the found home have no relationship to one another. Thus nostalgia, as a historical emotion, is a longing for that shrinking 'space of experience' that no longer fits the new horizon of expectations. Thus, every return of the protagonist to his actual birthplace or ancestral land gives him the same sensation of returning to where he has never been.

The object of nostalgia is further away than it appears. Nostalgia is never literal, but lateral, and it bears a secret hermeneutic affinity to irony; both share a double structure, an unexpected twin evocation of both affect and agency—or emotion and politics. Nostalgia, like irony, is not a property of the object itself but the result of an interaction between subjects and objects, between actual landscapes and the landscapes of the mind.[8] The past is remade in the image of the present or a desired future, collective designs are made to resemble personal aspirations and nostalgic reconstructions are based on mimicry.

The destructive changes in the urban landscape, the simultaneous deletion of both memory and time, the subversion of the established order, of persons as well as of things, the constant interchange between the same and the other, the rejection of the old hierarchies and the abolition of traditional values set off a process of constructing and adopting new roles on behalf of the subjects who, consciously or not, attest to the historicity of their (disrupted) construction and, consequently, their direct relation to the era in which they were raised, when they feel overruled by a torturing sense of exile:

Would he have written all the things he had written, would he have sensed so deeply the relativity of any 'I' or of any 'we' and the hidden otherness of every superficial identity, would he have talked as he had talked about the subversive philosophy of the carnival, if he hadn't lived in this era, which had turned all human beings, all peoples on this earth into others and constantly overturned things, abolishing every hierarchy, every value? How strange!— he could see it now: much as he hated his time, he was a child of this time himself. And his loneliness, this feeling of being cut off from every community, every collectivity, this taste of exile he always bore in his mouth wherever he went, this constant wandering with no homecoming, what was all this after all, if not the sense experienced by every contemporary human being, every man who lived anywhere on this earth in this era, as long as he had the courage to look deep inside himself? (372)

*We the Others* operates in a world where the level of communications, the widespread politics of insurgent nationalism, and the existence of large international cultural organizations have made the topics of nationalism and exile unavoidably aware of one another.[9] The division between exile and nationalism represents itself as one not only between individual and group, but between a mood of rejection and a mood of celebration. In literary terms, the division is suggested by the tension between monologue and dialogue, confession and proclamation.[10]

If we accept the belief of Franz Fanon that 'national consciousness, which is not nationalism, is the only thing that will give us an international dimension',[11] and that—as we have already said—the problem of outside/inside must always itself be a process of hybridity, it is at the heart of national consciousness that international consciousness lives and grows. A kind of exile. A simultaneous recognition of nationhood and an alienation of it.

The homecoming is doubly impossible, first because the subject cannot remain the same, and second because space itself resists and pauses, functioning as a protective shield. The speaking subject that is defined by and inscribed in language experiences an unavoidable decay and a deep rupture from the moment that it senses the violent change in the way it comprehends itself and the others.

The constant interchange in Kiourtsakis's novel between two places, two languages, self and the other, results in an intensification of the sense of exile and in an internal split between here and elsewhere and, even more, in the very core of every single one of the above-mentioned categories. The other, the elsewhere is never outside or beyond us; it emerges forcefully within cultural discourse, when we think we converse most intimately and indigenously with others.

I hope it has become evident by now that the literary course from local history to global individual is neither linear nor unimpeded. Although we have definitely left behind us the literary period of the exclusive preoccupation with local history, that does not mean that locality is the pole of the past and globalization the pole of the present and maybe the future; also, it does not mean that locality is disappearing or that it is simply restricted to a merely decorative role. On the contrary, what emerges from the texts is that the imagining of the global and the local is part of a wider ideological, discursive consciousness and that they are interrelated within societal discursive practices. So, how can one talk about binaries? Besides, the origins of national traditions turn out to be as much moments of disavowal, displacement, exclusion and cultural contestation as they are acts of affiliation and establishment.

The process of globalization, apart from diminishing differences and spaces, is also fragmenting the imagined unity within the same country and represents an enormous intensification of conflicts. Multiple narratives and new identities are emerging. Local ethnic and gender identities form an examplary site for postmodern politics.

The self, just as is has definitely moved away from the security and comfort of *ithografia* (the realistic fictional representation of traditional Greek life), has definitely moved away from conceptions about its cohesive representations. On the basis of attractions, rejections and conflicts, through dramatic sequences of discontinuous actions and spasmodic gestures, the identity of the literary subject brings about its fragmentation, its painful suspension between the desire to be reconciled with memory, space and time on the one hand, and the urge to explore new options of being on the other. Cultural difference must not be understood as the free play of polarities and pluralities in the homogeneous empty time of the national community. It results in the jarring of meanings and values generated in between the variety and diversity associated with cultural plenitude; it represents the process of cultural interpretation formed in the perplexity of living, in the disjunctive, liminal space of national society. The aim of cultural difference is to rearticulate the sum of knowledge from the perspective of the signifying singularity of the other that resists totalization.

But the way one conceptualizes places is peculiarly intense and is probably determined by heterogeneous factors. Since space and locality are utterly interdependent with temporality, they cannot remain an immobilized surface awaiting our arrival or our home-coming. Besides, for Jorge Luis Borges, Ulysses returns home only to look back at his journey as if creating an emotional topography of memory, while for Freud the only way of returning home is by analysing and recognizing early traumas, that is by privatizating and internalizing nostalgia, which is both a social disease and a creative emotion, a poison and a cure, as is the case in Karystiani's *A Suit in the Earth*. Because, contrary to national memory, which tends to make a single teleological, coherent plot out of shared everyday recol-lections in order to recover identity, shared everyday frameworks of collective or cultural memory offer us mere signposts for individual reminiscences that may suggest multiple narratives.[12]

## Notes to Chapter 4

1. Stuart Hall, 'Who needs identity?'
2. Homi K. Bhabha, 'Introduction', in id., *Nation and Narration*, 4.
3. Id., 'DissemiNation: time, narrative and the margins of the modern nation', ibid. 297
4. Bill Ashcroft, Gareth Griffiths and Helen Tiffin (eds.), *The Post-Colonial Studies Reader*.
5. Homi K. Bhabha, 'Interrogating identity: the post-colonial prerogative'.

6. Mikhail Bakhtin, *Problems of Dostoyevsky's Poetics*, 270–1; id., *The Dialogic Imagination*, 293–4.

7. V. N. Vološinov, *Freudianism: A Marxist Critique*, 118; id., *Marxism and the Philosophy of Language*, 153. See also Tzvetan Todorov, *Mikhail Bakhtin: The Dialogical Principle*, 49.

8. Svetlana Boym, *The Future of Nostalgia*, 353–4.

9. Timothy Brennan, 'The national longing for form', 62.

10. Ibid. 61. See also Melpo Axioti's last text, *Kadmo* (1972), a text of exile.

11. Franz Fanon, *The Wretched of the Earth*, 199.

12. Svetlana Boym, *The Future of Nostalgia*, 53.

CHAPTER 5

❖

# Geographical and Ideological Wanderings: Greek Fiction of the 1990s

*Eleni Yannakakis*

While I am aware that generalizations and schematizations are limiting and abstracting procedures, I shall start with the assumption that in contemporary Greek fiction the 1980s were a decade of introversion, of private life winning over public life, of personal histories overriding important historical events, all this taking place largely within Greece's geographical borders. By contrast, during the 1990s, novels ventured beyond Greece's borders: personal, family or existential problems faced by fictional characters were exported and thus brought into line with similar problems that people and fictional characters were facing abroad, since all these were seen to be universal in nature and could thus emerge anywhere in the world. The writers of this decade seem to have thought of Greece as a poor source of experience for their characters and a confining space that had to be expanded in order that novel-writing could gain in perspective and possibly increase its readership. The exodus of fictional characters from Greece has been massive and ever-increasing and is still continuing today. Of the nineteen novels that I refer to in this chapter, only three were published before 1995, while five appeared in 2000. In addition, even more novels are now populated by foreign (or at least not typically Greek) characters, that is by characters who bear foreign names or who, though Greek, have lived most of their lives abroad and return to Greece, where the main part of the plot takes place.

Place will be the chief parameter in my examination of these novels, since travelling implies a transposition in space. On the other hand, place is in itself an important factor in the construction and continuation of cultural, ethnic and national identities. Literature belonging to a particular culture or nation is usually located within the territorial borders of that nation. In this context, shifting places means shifting identities. The question is whether this systematic shift in the location of contemporary fiction also implies an ideological shift on the part of Greeks towards a more pro-European, global or simply less nationalistic identity. In other words, are these geographical wanderings in essence ideological ones?

Before proceeding to a detailed discussion of some representative individual novels, I shall attempt to trace some common features and tendencies. To start from their titles, nine out of the nineteen imply either a place or a journey; for instance *The City of Seagulls* or *Sentimental Journey*. As far as travel itself is concerned, in nine of the novels the destination is Europe, in two the destination is both Europe and America, in one it is Europe and the Middle East (Israel), in four it is America, in one it is Canada and in another one it is Africa; of the remaining two, the destinations are Europe and Asia respectively, but both are treated as utopian places. As for technique, the great majority of these novels adopt a fairly realistic narrative and the action develops in a straightforward temporal sequence. There are some exceptions of highly elliptical and allusive discourses, such as Argiro Mantoglou's *Virginia Woolf Café* (1999), Neni Efthymiadi's *The City of Seagulls* (1997), Angela Dimitrakaki's *Antarctica* (1997) and Dinos Siotis's *Ten Years Somewhere* (1995). Modernist techniques are also used in various combinations in a number of the texts under examination.

The nineteen novels can be broadly divided into three categories. After having sketched the chief outlines of these types, I will proceed to examine some representative samples from each category. The first type seems to be preoccupied with a kind of intellectual search that will lead to a fuller and deeper self-awareness and possibly give a meaning to life. Travel here is not an end but simply a means that will allow the characters to attain ultimate truth and personal happiness This search often acts as a metaphor for the attainment of art and for the very process of writing a novel. In *Lize's Time* (1993) by Tasos Rousos, a Greek professor of linguistics at a French university travels to a region of France, unexplored by scientists and anthropologists, in order to solve a mystery. In this way, he travels to utopia and backwards in time, to the early Middle Ages, where he meets a group of Goths who had invaded France many centuries ago. Similarly, in

*The Castaways of the Pasiphae* (1997) by Faidon Tamvakakis, a group of friends travel on a sailing boat from Greece to Asia. After their boat is wrecked, they find safety on an island that does not exist on maps and is inhabited by people who have stayed alive for many centuries. In *As Many Times as You Can Stand It* (1998) by Amanda Michalopoulou, a Greek woman travels to Europe in search of her half-Czech, half-Greek lover who proves to be, in part, a reincarnation of Kafka. In a similar search, the character in *Bar Flober* (2000) by Alexis Stamatis travels across Europe to find the unknown author of an unpublished novel whose manuscript he had discovered in his father's archive. Back in Greece, he finally meets the man, who proves to be his natural father. In *Virginia Woolf Café* (1999) by Argiro Mantoglou, the Greek character wanders the streets of London where she is temporarily based, following a request by Thomas Hardy to find the heroine of a half-finished story of his. In *The Hyena's Diet* (2000) by Vasiliki Kappa, the members of a club of bulimic people have to travel all the way to Kenya in order to discover the key to eating a lot and still remaining slim. Finally, in both *Uncle Peter and Goldbach's Conjecture* (1992 and 2000) by Apostolos Doxiadis and *The Nostalgia of the Dragons* (2000) by Dimosthenis Kourtovik, there is a search to solve intellectual puzzles. In Doxiadis's novel, the sought-for object is a mathematical problem that exists in reality and has so far remained unsolved. In Kourtovik's novel, the target is a mummy originating from a Greek island that will offer the key to the mystery of the origins of man. In both novels, the characters come very close to discovering the solution but finally fail to find it. However, apart from being an intellectual search, on another level, as we have said, all these novels are allegories for the attainment of art.

In the second type of novel, the characters literally escape to other places, either because Greece is too confining for them or because it creates their problems or simply cannot offer them any solutions. Here, travelling is an escape rather than a journey in search of a truth. In *Tomorrow Another Country* (1997) by Soti Triantafyllou, the family of the narrator (who tells her personal story as a *Bildungsroman*) end up in London to start a new life. In both Antzela Dimitrakaki's *Antarctica* (1997) and Thanasis Cheimonas's *Ramon* (1998), the young characters choose to leave Greece because their personal lives have reached a deadlock: in the former the character leaves Greece for Britain and then for America, while in the latter he leaves for Germany. In *The Zero and the One* (2000) by Fani Papageorgiou, the heroine travels to America to study, cannot adjust after her return to Greece and, facing family problems, retreats to the island of Patmos, where the father of her American husband-to-be owns a house. In Efthymiadi's *The City of Seagulls*, a middle-aged Greek flees to Canada after separating from his wife; there, he commits suicide after a long wait for a business meeting that never takes place. Finally, as we learn retrospectively, the character in Ioanna Karystiani's *A Suit in the Earth* (2000) is forced by his father to flee Crete for America so as not to be murdered in a vendetta in which his family is involved. When he returns, he is already sufficiently Americanized to be incapable of continuing the vendetta and taking revenge for his father's murder. In all these cases, travelling does not satisfy an internal need to explore the unknown but is a means of emotional and physical survival for those characters who choose to leave.

In the third group of novels, the characters have been living abroad for studies or work, and they give an account of their experiences. That is what the characters do in *Ten Years Somewhere* (1995) by Dinos Siotis, *Saturday Night at the Edge of the City* (1995) by Soti Triantafyllou and *The Magic Hole* (1999) by Dimitra Kolliakou. The characters have lived in America (in the first two novels) and in Britain (in the third). In *Sentimental Journey* (1998) by Filippos Drakontaeidis,[1] the character is sent to Paris to attend a conference on issues of European culture. In Michalopoulou's *Wishbone* (1996), the character spends some time in London, where she comes across the manuscript of a short story written by her student brother, from which she gets the idea she will develop in her own novel.

I shall now proceed to a more detailed look at a representative sample of novels. In Michalopoulou's *As Many Times as You Can Stand It*, which belongs to the first group, the female character starts an affair with the half-Czech half-Cretan travel agent Ivo, whom she meets in Athens. After he leaves Greece, she goes in search of him, first to Prague, then to Munich, Geneva and finally Madeira. This intellectual and existential journey leads to the realization that both Ivo and his half-sister, Grete Samsa (who is also half-Greek and a well-known novelist), are reincarnations of Kafka; it also leads to the completion of the novel-within-a-novel. The search for Ivo is gradually replaced by the search for an end to the writing of the novel itself.

This novel functions on different levels. First, it is about the relationship of Greek literature to the rest of European literature:

Greek literature is related through blood and emotion to the extensive and world-famous canon of western literature; the origins of this western culture are partly Greek, as is indicated symbolically by the fact that Kafka is reincarnated as a Greek. Secondly, this novel is about issues of identity, and more precisely about Greece's new status as a member of the European Community. Throughout this novel there is this sense that Greece belongs to Europe and to its civilization, and is part of a broader European identity; Greece seems to be present in one way or another in all manifestations of European life. Finally, this novel is about Greece's perception of being culturally a western country in contrast to the otherness of the newly westernized democracies of Eastern Europe: there is often a sense of superiority over the people of Eastern Europe, who frequently appear unfamiliar with aspects of western culture.

Above all, the ideology of the novel as far as identity is concerned is straightforwardly pro-European. Here the ideology of the global is expressed in its individual, local manifestations. It is summarized in the following phrases:

And now I came here, because there are many routes, *viele*, none being the last, you insisted on that. I don't know where my home is, I have no citizenship, at least the kind of citizenship that says stay here, grow like a bush and wait and see what will happen [...] Foreign languages soothe, and diminish despair. Just imagine if all people said 'life' and meant the same thing (371).

This, however, seems to be the ideology not only of Michalopoulou's novel but also of the majority of those I am examining.

Mantoglou's novel *Virginia Woolf Café* takes place in London from March to October 1996. The Greek character, Anna, answering the phone in one of London's red phone boxes on her way home one night, is asked by a man (who turns out to be the English writer Thomas Hardy) to locate and ultimately write about a heroine, named Ella, in a half-finished story of his. By way of her readings, Anna manages to travel back in time and listen to the problems faced by the heroine, a poet. In this sense, Anna appears to be finishing Hardy's story. At the same time, and under the guidance of Virginia Woolf, Anna writes her own novel (whose text is embedded in Mantoglou's novel in italics) about a contemporary woman called Emma (which in Greek means blood) who is facing relationship problems similar to those of Anna herself. In this highly experimental text, the writer sets up mirrors in all directions: Emma's text reflects that of *Virginia Woolf Café*, and both texts reflect those of Thomas Hardy and Virginia Woolf.

The action of the novel takes place in various areas of London, including a café in Bloomsbury named after Virginia Woolf, where Anna usually gets together with another Greek who is also 'in exile'. The novel is about the intellectual journey of a Greek researcher who, by way of her readings in English literature, manages to write her own novel. But the fact that this takes place in England and not in Greece, together with the almost non-existent references to features of Greece or Greek culture, is ideologically significant. Similar intellectual and intertextual endeavours have been the subject of novels in other periods of Greek literature such as the inter-war period. However, the novels of previous periods exhibited an awareness of their Greekness by setting part of the action in Greece or having Greece as the point of departure, or by making references to Greek culture or Greek literary and historical tradition, while Mantoglou's novel is devoid of such references and could easily have been written by a non-Greek.

To move on to the second group, Angela Dimitrakaki's *Antarctica*[2] tells the story of a 24-year old student named Vera, who has just returned to Athens after a long journey to America and Europe; she has been reunited with her Greek friends and is trying to readjust to the Greek way of life, which entails existential, personal, financial and family problems after the liberating experience of travelling abroad. At the end of the book, her flatmate, Stefi, starts her own journey to similar destinations (albeit not Antarctica) and for similar reasons. This is a novel about coming of age, or possibly trying to postpone the coming of age and the adjustments to the requirements imposed on adults by contemporary life in Greece: all the characters in the novel seem to find it difficult to come to terms with both the surrounding youth pop culture—which seems to be the only viable alternative left to them— and the traditional cultural values espoused by the Greek family.

Vera leaves Greece after her personal and family life and her life as a student at the university have reached deadlock. She leaves without the necessary financial means to support herself, so she has to rely on friends and casual acquaintances to support and accommodate her, or else to find casual jobs in the various places she moves to. Travelling itself has offered her stimulating experiences, and she constantly returns nostalgically to her travel memories after coming back to Athens (the 'present' of the novel), but it has not solved any of her problems. So, whereas the motives for travel we encountered in the first group are related to a systematic and conscious search for intellectual and/or personal happiness, in Dimitrakaki's novel travel is simply an attempt to escape from personal deadlocks and to postpone the moment when one has to conform and commit oneself to an established set of values determined by the surrounding culture. Back in Athens, Vera spends her time trying to find some means of maintaining herself without working, starts some new affairs, goes to parties, visits bars, takes drugs and alcohol, listens to music and attends concerts given by her friends who have formed a band.

What is of great interest for us here is the fact that this youth culture, as depicted in the way of life and thinking of these young people, is not in the least Greek; it could be the cultural setting of a story written in any western language by a writer of any western nationality and taking place anywhere in the world. It is an internationalized culture that cancels out all differences and tends towards a cultural and ideological uniformity. By contrast, traditional Greek values, expressed through Vera's family background, are presented as out-of-date and incapable of offering a sustainable alternative to this overwhelming and homogenizing international culture. The text is full of words, phrases and quotations in English, printed in Latin characters, which are intertextual references to songs and international literature or cinema (there is not a single reference to any Greek source of a similar type) or English words that have become part of an internationalized culture. Interestingly enough, Vera's flatmate, Stefi, keeps a diary in English.[3]

From icy Antarctica we move to cold Halifax in Canada in *The City of Seagulls* by Neni Efthymiadi, which also belongs to the same group of novels. The main character Konstantinos Konstas, a businessman, escapes from Greece to New York in order to attend a business meeting with a Greek-American businessman named Peter Pappas. As the venue of the meeting continually changes, he travels to Halifax and stays in a hotel for several days in the hope of meeting Pappas there. When the man fails to appear he commits suicide. In the meantime Konstas has encountered several people, either during his journey to Halifax or in the hotel, who to some degree become involved in his story and who face similar problems to his own: they are in search of somebody or something akin to Beckett's Godot who never arrives. The events and situations are narrated from the point of view of these characters as soon as they are introduced on to the scene, so we learn their own personal stories but also get different perspectives on the events surrounding Konstas's wait for Pappas, while the other characters also provide information about the protagonist's personality. By the end of the novel, we have found out that the journey to Halifax was in essence Konstas's excuse for postponing his suicide, which must have been planned while he was still in Athens. The reason for this suicide is not clear, though we assume that it is related to his separation from his wife, who had accused him of not making enough effort to prevent the arrest and deportation from Greece of a group of illegal immigrants who were friends of hers.

What is interesting in this text is that, though it is written by a Greek and is entirely in Greek, it takes place entirely outside Greece—in fact, it starts with the main character landing at New York—while the majority of the characters are American and not related to Greece in any way. The plot itself is irrelevant to Greece: the main character could have originated from anywhere, in the sense that there are no descriptions of a physical environment or references to particular loci that would necessarily recall Greece; even in the events that took place in Athens before the journey and are presented in flashbacks, most of the characters who are involved in the break-up of Konstas's marriage and thus indirectly contribute to his decision to commit suicide are not Greek but an international community of immigrants—with the exception of his Greek wife, Anna, and his Greek colleague Pavlos. On the other hand, the psychology and the family situation of the non-Greek characters gradually gathering in the hotel in Halifax are similar to that of the main character, depriving him even more of any distinct national or cultural features that might pinpoint his Greekness. Identity is not an issue either. On no occasion does the reader get the impression that Konstas feels in any way Greek—a feature that would differentiate him from the rest; he even accepts a change in his name when he starts arbitrarily being called 'Al' instead of Konstantinos for reasons of convenience by one of his American friends in the hotel. *The City of Seagulls* is another case of a Greek novel that is devoid of any local colour, with characters who have no sense of a Greek national or cultural identity and no collective aspirations, while the private nature of the characters' problems and experiences renders them replicas of characters in international fiction.

I shall conclude with two examples of the third type of the novel. In Drakontaeidis's novel *Sentimental Journey*, a Greek poet is sent to Paris as the Greek representative at a conference on European cultural identity. His mission is also to influence the organizing committee to choose the ancient Greek site of Delphi as the base for the European Academy of Poetry. Through a detailed account of what happens during the conference (individual speeches, descriptions of menus, informal discussions between the participants, the Paris scenery, the participants' amorous encounters between the sessions), the organizing of conferences is itself parodied, together with the very idea of achieving a common European culture. For, in the novel, the achievement of a unified culture seems to depend on and be jeopardized by the individual discourses, choices and behaviours of the various participants, who seem to be looking to their personal interests and ambitions rather than the goal of achieving a single European culture. As to the main character in the novel, the Greek participant, it is his complicated sex life during the conference that ruins Greece's chances of housing the European Academy of Poetry at Delphi.

Parody or not, it is interesting here that European cultural convergence and general issues of culture that are not typically or exclusively Greek have already infiltrated the subject-matter of a Greek literary text. According to this novel, Greece participates confidently in European cultural life. This is important to the novel's ideology, but the novel also seems to emphasize the nature of this unified European culture, in other words that it is a totality of differences. Cultural differences should be accepted positively as being aspects of the same phenomena that make up European culture, like the various functions of the different limbs of the same organism. The words of one of the conference participants are illuminating in this respect:

> Let me say that for me, the first priority is to understand the loci of memory, which are our points of contact. For example, the Rhine, my dear friends, is a different thing when somebody views it from Germany, another when one views it from France, or when one sees it from Holland or Switzerland. Of course, it is the Rhine, which is our contact, our memory. Similar points of memory, like the Rhine, are the Dnieper, the Mediterranean and the Alps. They are at the same time points of common dreams, which differ from place to place but are nevertheless inscribed in our heritage, in this memory that allows us to partake of the same hope. (214)

Kolliakou's novel *The Magic Hole* narrates the experiences of a

Greek girl, Marina, who goes to Britain for postgraduate studies, becomes readily assimilated into a non-Greek culture, and secures an academic job abroad and a non-Greek partner. The story takes place in Edinburgh, Athens, Groningen and parts of Israel. However, it is Athens and Edinburgh that compete with each other in importance in relation to Marina's feelings and sense of belonging. Athens represents the homeland that shelters the memories of her childhood and teens but also the place of the present of the story which she often visits either during vacations or to say a final farewell to her mother and aunt who die of cancer within a short space of time. On the other hand, Edinburgh is the place where the character comes of age, becomes emancipated and fulfils her dreams and goals in relation to her career.

The two places seem to be culturally far apart: though her mother looks for purity and quality in the label 'Made in England' or 'Made in Scotland' in the clothes she buys, she is appalled when her daughter splits up with her Greek boyfriend in order to start a relationship with a Jew whose mother is English and whose father an Israeli. In the following paragraph, the character comments on her feelings when her mother phones her on New Year's Day: "'Have you felt anything about New Year's Day over there in the company of the unbeliever?' she asked insolently. She said it in such a way as to suggest that if this unbeliever disappeared, all our problems would automatically be solved' (289). It seems that the main difficulty her mother faces is to accept that her daughter might marry somebody who is not only not an Orthodox Christian (even a Protestant wouldn't be good enough for her, according to her mother), but is a Jew. Moreover, though she is proud of her daughter's successes in academic life, she does not relish the idea of her daughter staying abroad after the completion of her studies in order to work.

However, Marina consciously chooses to live away from Greece; at a certain point in the novel, she states that she never missed Greece even when she first arrived in Edinburgh, while the fact that her ex-boyfriend, Yannis, missed Greece so much contributed significantly to their separation. She loves Greece, she likes spending time there, especially because her father and sister are still living in Greece, but she is quite happy to live and work permanently outside Greece. It is interesting that the narrator-character Marina often satirizes Greek culture and particularly the Greek stereotypical views about non-Greeks, non-Christians and even Christians who are not Orthodox, as well as Greek views about life abroad, as they are expressed by her mother. By contrast, she is entirely positive about ways of life outside Greece. Moreover, the Greek text is full of English words, though most of them are written in Greek characters—even words that could be easily translated into Greek, such as 'term' or 'porter'.[4] Moreover, a male voice that reminds her, as soon as she wakes up every morning, that her mother is dead speaks to her half in Greek and half in English.[5]

In conclusion, the plethora of novels whose plots are set outside Greece, together with the character of these wanderings, suggests that these are not superficial phenomena that are following a temporary trend. In other words, for these fictional characters and possibly for their creators, exploring the geography of the rest of the world appears to be more an ideological choice than the temporary adoption of the current trendy discourses on globalization. On the other hand, given the absence of a purely touristic mentality in these texts or a shallow cosmopolitanism designed to impress, it seems to me that Greece's ideological borders have expanded considerably in recent years. Europe in particular, apart from being the physical and relatively familiar neighbour, appears to act as a close relative of Greece, the ties between them dating back to Ancient Greece's primordial role in the rise of western civilization. Modern Greece feels that it is an equal, and wants to be treated as such by its European neighbours, because it constitutes not only a cultural and geographical part of Europe but also the legitimate heir of the ancestors they all share.

## Notes to Chapter 5

1. The title is an obvious intertextual reference to the book by Laurence Sterne, to whom Drakontaeidis's volume is dedicated.
2. The title seems to symbolize first the desire to go to a place far away—and thus immune—from contemporary culture; moreover, both the whiteness and the freezing temperature of the icy landscape of Antarctica signify, in my view, a kind of purification. However, Antarctica remains only an unfulfilled desire and an impossible escape, since Vera never visits it.
3. It is interesting that the cover of the book is a collage of two roads, one in Athens and one in Arizona, while one of the 'a's in the Greek title of the book is printed in Latin and is placed in a circle as if to attract attention to it.
4. The fact that none of the writers of the novels who intermingle Greek with English provides a glossary is an indication not so much of the writers' confidence in Greeks' knowledge of other languages as of the fact that English is now a systemic part of contemporary Greek culture.

5. This disembodied and unidentified voice often seems to be reading a letter to her with the title 'Reminder', this word not being translated but written simply with Greek characters.

# PART 3

❖

# The Global as Local

CHAPTER 6

❖

# From the Underworld to Other Worlds: Political Attitudes in Contemporary Greek Fiction

*Venetia Apostolidou*

The topic of the present volume forces us to reconsider the meaning of the notions locality and globalization as far as cultural and, in particular, literary production is concerned. Moreover, the discussion on the local and global dimensions of fiction cannot and must not ignore two more aspects that are strongly connected with the former, namely the national and the social. The title of our volume implies those two additional notions. We see this clearly if we ask two simple questions: Was local or national history really the dominating theme of former periods? Does the global individual really exist, irrespective of national frontiers and, if it does, does it exist irrespective of social definitions? Thus what we have to deal with is a new kind of interrelation between local, national, global and social elements in contemporary Greek fiction. This new interrelation means practically a new vision of the world and differentiated political attitudes. I feel the need to start with some thoughts on the new meanings of the above-mentioned notions, in order to lay the basis for comparing contemporary fiction to that of earlier periods.

While the discussion on the various facets of globalization seems endless, the notion is often misunderstood and deliberately misused. As Arjun Appadurai points out, globalization does not necessarily imply cultural homogenization; it is rather a deeply historical, irregular and even localizing process. As far as the materials of modernity are appropriated differently by different societies, there is still ample room for the production of localities. A variety of instruments of homogenization (advertising techniques, language hegemonies, clothing styles) are absorbed into local political and cultural economies, only to be repatriated as heterogeneous dialogues. Locality itself is a historical product, subject to the dynamics of the global, and the frequently repeated cliché that locality, as a property or distinctive feature of social life, is being threatened in modern societies should be re-examined.[1] Locality has always been a fragile social achievement, and we should not forget, in this respect, the tension between the local and the national during the nationalizing process that takes place within the nation state.[2] So, if something is in danger in our globalized world, this may be nationality rather than locality, and some people are already talking about a postnational imaginary. Yet a framework for relating the global, the national and the local has yet to emerge. The task of producing locality (as a structure of feeling, a property of social life and an ideology of situated community) is an increasingly crucial struggle in the modern world, a struggle affected by new factors, such as the disjuncture between territory, subjectivity and collective social movements, or the electronic media, which produce virtual communities in the place of spatial communities. Under the influence of those contradictory factors, we are witnessing, in our day, an increased engagement in the construction of locality by the many displaced and transient populations that constitute today's ethnoscapes.[3]

To move on to the realm of contemporary Greek fiction, we all acknowledge that a shift has taken place during the past twenty-five years, although the shift itself has so far been described superficially and misleadingly. When we say, for example, that the fiction of former periods was concerned with major political and social issues, while contemporary fiction focuses on personal problems, we reduce the change to a merely thematic level. On top of that, we forget that earlier fiction has gone, more or less, through a canonizing process, out of which a corpus of works has been chosen to represent so-called post-war Greek fiction, whereas, at the time, there was a plurality of themes, just as there is now. On the other hand, the fact that we experience today's fiction as an ongoing process and each one of us has a fragmented view, prevents us from making a fair and even-handed comparison, if we assume that this is possible and that our judgements are not subject to our ideological and aesthetic beliefs.

I shall now discuss the characteristics of contemporary Greek fiction, focusing on the differentiated, implicit meaning of the notions local, national, global and social, instead of the alleged change in themes or settings. Locality has always been, and still is, a persistent property of Modern Greek fiction, as it is, I think, of fiction in general. Even science fiction produces some kind of locality, no matter how odd, fantastic or alien this may be.[4] The difference lies in the use of locality by the authors. Although major Marxist authors of the post-war generation such as Dimitris Hatzis or Stratis Tsirkas set their stories in a local environment, such as 'our small town' or the Greek anti-fascist movement in the Middle East, they used locality as a means of depicting ideological, social and political processes on a national scale.[5] Hatzis's 'small town' can actually be identified with Greek society as a whole, whereas Tsirkas's 'drifting cities', despite their cosmopolitanism, depict ideological struggles within the Greek communist movement, as well as other characteristics of Greek politics such as the factor of foreign interference. It is widely acknowledged that these authors perceived their work as part of a general project governed by certain political ideas.

Locality in contemporary fiction, no matter whether the story is set on a Greek island, in Athens or in London, is much more particularized and lacks any intention of symbolizing larger processes of national interest. It creates small worlds that are literally small, in the sense of David Lodge's novel *Small World*, governed by a closed system of values, not valid outside their borders. Sometimes this small world can be identified as the underworld, but this identification is not of vital importance. The point is that, even if it is not situated on the social margins, it is treated as a marginalized, displaced world. Thus we can describe the shift so far as a transition from high to low, from large (national) scale to small (local) scale, from mainstream to underworld, from holism to particularism.[6]

It would be a mistake to interpret this shift as the abandonment of political and social concerns in favour of purely personal and ideologically indifferent issues. Problems of an everyday and individual nature may be discussed irrespective of national frontiers, but never irrespective of social and moral values, which, in turn, are always socially and culturally produced. Contemporary fiction may suggest a different social perspective that we need to comprehend rather than either condemning its ideological indifference or praising its liberation from the obsession with historical and political issues. Furthermore, we should ask to what extent this different social perspective is influenced by globalization, in other words, in what way this particular kind of locality and sociality is global.

I shall take as an example the work of Sotiris Dimitriou, which has already received its fair share of interest and praise. The fact that it is considered an exception within contemporary Greek fiction because of its social orientation might provoke the question how is it possible to study the major characteristics of a body of literature using an exception as an example.[7] All the contributors to the present volume are investigating a rather contradictory and unsettled literary production, which does not allow us to distinguish between canons and exceptions. I believe that Dimitriou's work displays, to an excessive degree, properties and characteristics that are traceable in many other contemporary works. Therefore, precisely because of its excessiveness, it can very well serve my purpose of examining the differentiated meaning of the local and the social.

Starting from his first collection of short stories, *Djallth im Christaki* (the first part of the title is an Albanian phrase meaning 'my little boy') (1987), critics noticed his excessive use of particularity and the absence of any generalizing aspiration.[8] The next two collections, *A Boy from Thessaloniki* (1989) and *The Vein in the Neck* (1998), as well as the recent *The Tardiness of Good* (2001), have confirmed the sense of locality in its most absolute version: the stories are set in small villages on the north-west borders of Greece or, when in Athens, on the most extreme social margins. His characters are socially alienated and psychologically disturbed, enclosed in their isolated world, from which it is impossible to escape. Some of them do not even speak the standard Greek language of the cities but a local dialect of the author's native Epirus. Dimitriou's fiction is governed by feelings of depression, deprivation, disorientation, displacement and exile. Although his two novels, *May your Name be Blessed* (1993) and *God Tells Them* (2002) deal with problems and situations that are apparently produced by historical events and processes, such as the collapse of the communist regime in Albania and the subsequent migration to Greece, they never desert locality as a structure of feeling, with the effective help of the local dialect. Nevertheless, the novels need to be examined separately, as the strong feeling of history that penetrates them, together with their synthetic ambitions, makes their sense of locality different from that in the collections of short stories.[9]

In what way does this strong sense of locality in Dimitriou's short stories imply a new function of sociality? Critics have expressed very different opinions about the social character of Dimitriou's stories. Dimosthenis Kourtovik has denied their social dimension altogether,

because of their vague definition of space and time. Dimitris Tziovas
believes that 'Dimitriou's stories negate the social and suggest a desire
to return to an elusive primordial state, a desire for the freedom of
nature and of carefree childhood'.[10] Elisavet Kotzia has wondered if
such deeply disturbed characters and situations allow the reader to
make any kind of generalization and move from the particular to the
universal, while Dimitris Kokoris has suggested that Dimitriou's work
is committed to the political struggle against social racism.[11]

The transition from the particular to the universal has always been
the most important presupposition for a socially orientated fiction. At
this point, I will seek the help of a leading author of an earlier
generation, Dimitris Hatzis. In an unpublished lecture on contemporary fiction given in 1980, Hatzis expressed a negative opinion
about the tendency he detected in contemporary fiction, namely the
focus on the underworld. He did not believe that characters who live
on the social margins can represent the core of society and thus offer
any kind of consolation or solution for the great mass of people, who
live a similarly empty and alienated life. He thought that dealing with
the underworld does not imply a revolutionary stance, since 'the
underworld is not the opposite of the mainstream but part of it'.[12] If
this is so, then have we the right to ask why it is impossible to reach
the whole through a part? This is actually what younger writers have
tried to do. Strangely enough, Sotiris Dimitriou, a writer who
followed the route that Hatzis rejected, is considered in many ways to
be his descendant. What we need to figure out is how, by dealing with
the underworld and producing a powerful sense of locality, he
provokes the reader's social awareness in spite of what older Marxist
writers believed.

The starting-point of Dimitriou's fiction is the loss of totality. The
author does not feel that he knows the rules that govern society and
life in general, he does not claim to possess the key to explaining social
procedures and structures. However, the awareness of his ignorance
does not cause him to abandon the effort to comprehend the human
being or society. In a recent interview published in the magazine *Anti*,
he said: 'I feel it's my duty to investigate unknown areas of the social
landscape. Literature is a search and a search always takes place in the
dark.'[13] Therefore, choosing to investigate the underworld is just
another way, or a shortcut, to get to the world, or to other worlds as
well. The extremes and exaggerations do not function as a means to
shock the reader for the sake of yet another powerful aesthetic

experience; rather, they point to the so-called mainstream so as to show up its false existence: to put it another way, the lightening of a dark area shades the former supposedly bright centre. As Dimitriou said, 'we all live, more or less, on the margins'.[14]

The protagonist of this fiction is the human individual, not viewed as a whole, but fragmented, the focus falling each time on different parts of body or soul. The human face takes priority, since it expresses desperation most eloquently. The author wants to draw new lines on the human face, in order to show its dignity, which persists in spite of unhappiness, poverty and utter dereliction.[15] A scene from the short story entitled 'Easter in April' from the collection *The Vein in the Neck* is characteristic. The scene takes place in the author's village on the Greek-Albanian border, where two Albanian illegal immigrants, hungry and miserable, have been arrested by the police and are brought to the village café, where the proprietor offers them *loukoumia* (Turkish delight): 'The Albanians ate the sweets greedily and the icing-sugar went all over their clothes. Although they were completely filthy, they brushed the sugar from their clothes with extreme care.'[16]

I do not share the view that this kind of fiction is not interested in moral values and does not bring the reader face to face with moral dilemmas.[17] On the contrary, it forces the reader to reconsider a series of moral issues that are fundamental to our society: incest, sexual deprivation, prostitution, racism and authoritarian violence. What it doesn't do is manipulate the reader according to a ready-made moral system, no matter how radical or alternative that might be. It is precisely the fact that it deals with a small, marginalized world that the reader cannot identify with, that forces him to a more cool-headed and therefore more effective reconsideration, as long as the reader is captivated by the narration and does not reject the work out of hand.

Dimitriou does not seem to wonder whether his fiction is local, national or global, or whether it is representative of Greek culture. Rather, he believes that, if fiction focuses on the human individual, his sufferings and passions, regardless of the national or social context, which is, in any case, inevitable, it will interest any reader whatsoever.[18] It is the insistence on the idea of locality that permits him to escape the vain dilemma between local and global. But this insistence on locality, in turn, is based on the absence of a well-founded sense of nationality. I am not sure if this is due to the fact that he was born and raised on the borders but, as he said in the above-mentioned interview in *Anti*, my mother in her village had no idea of belonging to a nation, she never saw a map and she couldn't imagine what Athens looks like [...] She felt free to think of her village as the centre of the world, similar to any other village anywhere [...] My grandmother didn't feel either inferior or superior to other grandmas all over the world, until she understood that she was enclosed in a nation and started making comparisons.[19]

What we see here is the tension between local and national rather than between local and global.

Literary critics have already discovered numerous intertextual relations between Dimitriou's fiction and previous Greek texts.[20] Although I have some reservations about many of those connections, it is impressive, for our discussion, that the kind of fiction Dimitriou writes cannot be considered as resulting from a gap between past and present; we should seriously look for continuities, at least as much as we look for shifts and changes in contemporary fiction.[21] If we care to align Dimitriou with global tendencies, I would note the affinity of his fictional world with the drama of Edward Bond, Sarah Kane or Sheila Stevenson, whose plays have recently been produced in Greece. One could also assume affinity with the contemporary Austrian author Josef Winkler, who sets his novels in a small Austrian village and writes about the awful moral pressures on the individual within a small community, the ruined lives, the suicides, the abuse of women, children and animals. As Jean-Yves Masson points out, his small world includes multiple voices from other similar worlds globally.[22]

The production of locality has always been a struggle that meant a lot to individuals and communities. For this reason art and literature have largely been committed to locality. Today the task of producing locality as a structure of feeling and a property of social life is still crucial but differently comprehended: locality is viewed as primarily relational and contextual rather than spatial—and definitely not national. New communities are being constructed in spite of or because of the erosion and dispersal of neighbourhoods as coherent social formations. In fiction, locality no longer functions as a reduction of social and historical processes on a larger scale, but retains its role as a powerful means of constructing identities, by offering a wide set of social and moral values. Consequently, literary criticism should move from the interpretation of the political dimension of fiction as commitment to a certain system of social values which aims at a universal consciousness and start appreciating particularity for what it is: a way of comprehending other particularities, a route to plurality which is nonetheless political.

## Notes to Chapter 6

1. Arjun Appadurai, *Modernity at Large*, 1–47.
2. Ernest Gellner, *Nations and Nationalism*.
3. Appadurai, *Modernity*, 178–99.
4. On the other hand, some critics stress the absence of any sense of locality in contemporary fiction; they talk of a 'literature of nowhere'. The characters of the novels have no homeland, they are always on the road, all places seem the same. See Marek Bienczyk, 'Metaxy alligorias kai alligorias', 32–41.
5. I am referring to Dimitris Hatzis, *To telos tis mikris mas polis* (1953/1963) and Stratis Tsirkas, *Akyvernites politeies* (1961–5).
6. Compare the shift in historiography from macrohistory to microhistory: Georg Iggers, *Historiography in the Twentieth Century*; Giovanni Levi, 'On microhistory'. The analogy between the shift in historiography and the shift in contemporary Greek fiction was first noticed by Yannis Dallas, 'Metapolemiki pezografia kai mikro-istoria'.
7. The literary critic Elisavet Kotzia has written that Dimitriou has been for many years the only socially orientated writer of his generation ('Mystikos, zontanos kosmos').
8. Dimitris Angelatos, 'I ek-plixi tis pezografias kai ton apokliseon'.
9. Dimitris Tziovas makes clear that 'unlike the stories, the novel does not focus on the particular case of some lonely individual, it deals with problems and situations that are more general and collective in character, acquiring thus a political and historical dimension' ('Introduction', in Sotiris Dimitriou, *May Your Name be Blessed*, trans. Leo Marshall, p. xiii).
10. Dimosthenis Kourtovik, 'I goiteia tou faux bijou', in id., *Imedapi exoria*, 276–80; Tziovas, 'Introduction', p. xii.
11. Kotzia, 'Mystikos, zontanos kosmos'; Dimitris Kokoris, 'Apo ti Valeria ston Spetim', 49.
12. Dimitris Hatzis, 'O syngrafeas brosta sti sychroni elliniki pragmatikotita'.
13. Sotiris Dimitriou, 'Anikoume ston koino paronomasti tou agnostou'.
14. Ibid. 46.
15. Id., 'Kinitra grafis', *Entefktirio* 33 (Winter 1995–6), 54–5.
16. Id., *I fleva tou laimou* (1998), 55.
17. Alexis Ziras, 'Synyfansi paradosiakou kai monternou', 204.
18. Sotiris Dimitriou, interview with Michel Fais.
19. Id., 'Anikoume', 47.
20. D. N. Maronitis has pointed to the relations with Dionysios Solomos's *I gynaika tis Zakythos*, Makriyannis's *Apomnimonevmata*, Stratis Doukas's *Istoria enos aichmalotou*, Marios Hakkas's short stories, and the eschatological writing of Yorgos Cheimonas, one of the older writers who praised Dimitriou's work (D. N. Maronitis, 'Paramethorios pezografia: to paradeigma tou Sotiri Dimitriou'). Michel Fais has added to this series Alexandros Papadiamantis, Konstantinos Theotokis, Thanassis Valtinos ('I grafi tis exorias', 52). Alexis Ziras has also pointed to Dimitris Hatzis (who is considered, in any case, the ancestor of many younger writers from Epirus), Yorgos Ioannou and Tolis Kazantzis ('Synyfansi', 199).
21. In order to forestall the objection that Dimitriou is an exception and does not represent the average tendencies of contemporary fiction, I note some authors

who can be related with Dimitriou, as long as, in each case, the connection is
made on a different basis: Michel Fais (especially his collection of short stories
*Ap' to idio potiri*), Yorgos Skampardonis (especially the novel *Gernao epitychos*),
Vasilis Tsiampousis, Kostas Sotiriou, not to forget the Epirus group, namely
Michalis Ganas and Tilemachos Kotsias.

22. Jean-Yves Masson, 'I idea tis pankosmias'.

❖

# 'The Ultimate Art of our Greek Corruption':[1] The Global as an Experimental Expansion of the Local in Yorgis Yatromanolakis's Fiction

*Vangelis Athanassopoulos*

## Cautious and Prudent Mixture

One of the most acknowledged characteristics of Greek literature in the first three-quarters of the twentieth century is its Greek-centred orientation. This tendency has been regarded as narcissistic, but the apparent narcissism was in fact an effort to disguise a much more dangerous syndrome, namely insecurity, whose symptoms were introversion and the turn to the East.[2] In the last quarter of the twentieth century, the syndrome of insecurity was radically diverted, though without any profound change regarding the place of Greek literature on the world map. The most characteristic manifestation of this diversion is cosmopolitanism. In addition to the specific objective circumstances that have determined the Modern Greek literary environment, the cosmopolitan choice of Greek novelists has been influenced by the phenomenon of globalization. In this ostensibly cheerful atmosphere of globalization, many Greek writers have been carried away by a superficial cosmopolitanism that is confined to the fictional settings (in an attempt to cover as much of Europe or the planet as possible), the foreign names chosen for the characters, and the themes, where the global is often falsely identified with the commonplace.

Greek writers tend to make this mistake because they are in a quite different position from writers who belong to one of the great

European literatures, yet they are unable to acknowledge this position. This difference is based on the fact that globalization, to a large extent, is a Eurocentric phenomenon, insofar as it is spreading from western Europe and the United States of America and resulting in the westernization of the cultures of neighbouring countries as well as the global community. It is obvious, therefore, that what sustains the realistic, personal and individual character in the work of a western European writer is evidence, or at least a condition, of mere standardization in the work of those Greek writers who are not embedded in the European literary tradition.

Yorgis Yatromanolakis is a special case in this atmosphere of superficial cosmopolitanism. At first sight, he appears to resist the tendency I have just described by insisting on the local. On closer examination, it becomes obvious that what he avoids are ostentatious references to the cosmopolitan, while he attempts a discreet promotion of the local to the global. For this reason, he does not choose foreign names for his characters, nor does he present them travelling abroad. Most of the time, their fate is determined by a specific area of Greece, and their activity has a national definition. Underlying these choices is the notion that in order to lend a global dimension to a character's action it is not necessary for him to have a foreign name, to cross a whole continent and to be deprived of any feature of locality. On the contrary, in order to be European or global, a hero has first of all to be local, to be, for example, Cretan. If this prerequisite is not fulfilled, then the European or global identity of the hero is spurious.

## The Representation and Creation of Landscape

In the five novels Yorgis Yatromanolakis has published so far, there is a narrative strategy that consists in an initially explicit specification of place, which is later expanded through the reversal of its pragmatic kernel and character. In all the novels, place and time are presented as purely existent, thus limiting their imaginary dimension. In the *Leimonario* the place is the island of Cythera, in *The Fiancée* it is Greece as a whole, in both *The History of a Vendetta* and *A Report of a Murder* it is Crete (in the former without being named, in the latter defined with reference to specific locations and by the charting of the hero's progress on the map), and, finally, in *In the Valley of Athens* it is Athens (in such a way as to make the novel resemble a guide to the city). In the non-fiction narrative of *Eroticon* (which, however, is tantamount to being a novel of the body), the place is the body itself, since the narration begins with the parts of the body and ends with its climax and death. Equally specific (and correspondingly realistic) is the definition of time in the five novels, the most characteristic examples being the fourteen days that constitute the heart of the action in *The History of a Vendetta*, the afternoon in *A Report of a Murder*, and the afternoon of 25 March 1996 in *In the Valley of Athens*.

Yet, after the realistic specification of place (which in some cases corresponds to a modern version of *ithografia*³), there begins its reversal, in a similarly realistic manner. This technique creates the impression that the depiction of the specific is not an end in itself, but rather provides the trigger and the material for its own reversal, which ultimately foregrounds the abstract. The place and the event acquire new dimensions: the story, space and time are endowed with universality, and, through the event, the *eikos* (the plausible) is foregrounded.

As a result, a double reality emerges on the level of fiction, a reality that is projected not as a metaphysical hypostasis but rather as a realistic perception of the world. A characteristic of Yatromanolakis's realism is the fact that this Other, this expanded place or altered time, is still described realistically. This type of description enhances a realistic notion according to which place, as a primary aspect of realism, is a palimpsest. Behind each place that is authentically existent lies another that is equally existent: what we see and what we think we see constitute two dimensions, forms, versions or levels of a single reality. In this way, constant references to familiar places do not refer to an external reality, but constitute a self-reference to a forest or a garden, in other words, not to a familiar place but to a notion.

The broadening of the local, which amounts to its reversal, is a medium for expanding the meaning of the story—with allegory as its furthest possible horizon—but at the same time, it goes beyond the local towards the global. A historically composed world is staged in order to be divested of its particular character through the reduction or abstraction of its locality and historicity. The real is not presented in a statically and one-dimensionally realistic way, but rather through a self-ignition and explosion that exposes it at the crowning moment of its existence. Thus in Yatromanolakis's novels the possibility of the abrogation or reversal of the real is the fundamental element of its hypostasis and the most apparent expression of its dynamism.

Yatromanolakis presents himself as a realist regarding indications of place and time, quoting irreducible facts (election results or the prices of agricultural products), yet at the same time he reverses this realism through a type of fiction that foregrounds the various or contradictory aspects of things, their division, thus revealing the dichotomy of the world itself. The initial means for broadening the local is fiction, as the fictional characters are involved in a double reality. The stages of their involvement, first in one aspect of reality and then in the other, are not contradictory because they manage to accomplish a transgression which in fictional terms is presented as a perception of a landscape that constantly opens out.

In *Leimonario* a specific island (Porfyri, i.e. Cythera) is presented as sunken, that is, non-existent. In *The Fiancée* a journey around Greece is made on her/its body instead of being charted on the map. In *The History of a Vendetta*, the villages of Crete are specific, but space expands (for instance in the chapter about the hiding of the fugitive) and becomes a place which is at the same time existent and non-existent, realistic and non-realistic. Even the objects that drastically cross this space are concrete, but in such a way that they reverse the pragmatic dimension, like the bullet that changes its course and kills Zervos.

In *A Report of a Murder* the narration is based upon the description of the events by the Crime Bureau of Crete and place is again specified, namely Crete, but it expands to embrace the sky, the universe and the signs of the zodiac: it becomes an axis that extends to the space where souls drift. An escalation in the process of this expansion of place is to be found in *In the Valley of Athens*, where, while the protagonist is taking photographs of the existing city, Athens appears denuded of its buildings, like a valley with rivers, a Valley of Souls; and when he descends into it, he finds himself in a landscape that opens out as he moves, giving him the impression that he is creating it.

## The Imaginary Expansion of Description

After fiction, description is the second means whereby the local is expanded, although on both levels of the real, its effect is equally or correspondingly realistic. Because of its constantly realistic perspective, and regardless of the pragmatic character of its object, description favours the examination of the nature of the narrative strategy whereby the local is broadened. Fiction and description are the means for adopting a strategy whose aim or scope is a universal interpretation of the world. In the context of this interpretation, and through the process of an extreme expansion of the local, the global is foregrounded not as an abstract notion or idea, but as a specific recognizable and familiar place.

Even in Yatromanolakis's first novel we notice a reduction of the realistic through an imaginary expansion of description. The pragmatic constituent of narrative or, on a second level, its realistic features, creates the impression that it serves as an occasion for the development of an imaginary that denudes, demystifies and undermines the pragmatic. This delicate relation of his prose to realism corresponds to the connection of his main characters with the social environment, which is determined, to a large extent, by a feeling of repulsion. In this way, the chief aim of the narration appears totally consistent, namely to distort and demolish a false reality, so that another, 'true' reality that lies behind it can emerge.

The true abandonment of the writer to realism is instantaneous, and takes place through brief descriptions that show a particular affection for the human functions, while narration is generally—and more intensely in his earlier fiction—the instrument of derangement. The protagonist is in a constant secret juxtaposition to an environment that wishes to adopt and raise him according to its own values, whereas he despises it as if it were a stepmother. Whatever exists as a fact and is described as such is at the same time presented through its illusionary reflection.

Yatromanolakis's relation to realism is also revealed by the descriptions that are presented as descriptions of photographs. This is especially evident in *A Report of a Murder* and *In the Valley of Athens*. Introducing a description not as primary but as secondary (i.e. not as a description of the real, but as a description of a photograph of the real) allows the writer to abandon himself to the innocent delight of representing the real without ceasing to undermine it, since he does not appear to believe in the possibility of a faithful, objective representation; yet what he describes is nothing but a previous description, and not the real itself. Additionally, descriptions of photographs (equivalent to the *ekphraseis* found in medieval Greek literature and the Hellenistic novel) do not serve any realistic necessity or any syndrome of the narration, because they are never a static descriptive element, but rather a part of the plot, as they crucially contribute to the construction of myth.

## The Determinism of Myth

In the myth of all Yatromanolakis's novels there is either a veiled or an explicitly stated determinism. This determinism not only constitutes the programme of the myth; it is also part of the myth. As a component of the myth, it facilitates the construction of the plot, so instead of being an element of the myth, it becomes a factor of the plot. The results of this multiple function of determinism are the abstract plots, which tend to turn into ritualistic ones,[4] but often become inflexible because the accidental is dramatically reduced and, where this cannot be avoided, the accidental is implausibly incorporated into the determinism of the myth. But this inflexibility is balanced by the fact that narration acquires a dynamic, because it gives life to a myth that follows a course imposed by the myth itself. As far as determinism is concerned, the self-imposed course does not identify with or correspond to logic or rationality, since the myth may be 'deranged': in this case the function of determinism is dramatically emphasized, because it guides and directs, in other words it provides a rationale for the irrational action.

The determinism of the myth has an additional function, not on the level of the plot, but on that of the characters. This is possible because determinism is personified as a character acting as a guide, who is present in all Yatromanolakis's novels, but has a leading role in *Leimonario*, in *A Report of a Murder* and in *In the Valley of Athens*. The person in whom determinism is incarnated is incorporeal; nevertheless, through the embodiment of determinism, the writer tries to lessen the abstract dimension of the plot by shifting it to an intellectual or even metaphysical level that is dangerously close to allegory.

The presence of a guide constitutes one of the motifs or narrative features which, directly or indirectly, serve the expansion of space and appear repeatedly in Yatromanolakis's fiction. Among them is the motif of the hero's progress that concludes in his being assimilated to the natural environment. Thus his progress is tantamount to the transition from a social reality to a natural one, combining the development of the action and the plot with the double dimension of space, as a place which is fake (the false and vulgar island of Porfyri, the false city of Heraclion in Crete, an Athens filled with buildings) and as a place which is authentic (the real island of Porfyri, the real city of Heraclion, Athens as an immense garden, like a verdant and evergreen valley). Anna's progress in *The Fiancée* corresponds to that of Yorgis, the embittered Orthodox Christian, in *A Report of a Murder*: the disappearance of the former in the mountains of Grammos in northern Greece is parallel to the assimilation of the latter into the nature of Mount Dikte in Crete. Yorgis's progress is also parallel to that of the murderer Dikaios in *The History of a Vendetta*.

The repetition of certain motifs, together with general similarities that can be detected in Yatromanolakis's novels, reveals the existence of a personal mythology. Defining this mythology is essential for the examination of the way the writer combines the immediate presence of the local with the suggestion of the global. This combination presents a particular narrative interest once we realize that the kernel of Yatromanolakis's mythology is Greece. Greece and its history is his obsession, an obsession that clearly stems from the realistic and bitter acknowledgement of his Mediterranean stigma, his anaemic existence in history. This acknowledgement is described in his novels: the transfusions, the waste of blood, the gaping wound of Greek need and the endemic Greek corruption. And this transgression of the national illusion is the best condition for a genuine development of a narrative from the local to the global.

## Conclusion

Globalization is a challenge for Greek fiction in a wider sense, because, for foreign readers, Greek fiction suffers from the stigma of the picturesque and folkloric: it is in the depiction of locality that foreign readers search for authenticity in Greek literature. It is common knowledge that local particularity may easily be transformed from a realistic object of the narrative into an anti-realistic condition. One way to sustain its role as a feature of fiction is to universalize it, namely to transform it into a universal particularity, in order to contribute to the literary formation of a global consciousness. A writer who belongs to a great literature does not face this problem because he is writing within a tradition that was historically a formative factor of global consciousness, and therefore his local particularity, to a large extent, corresponds to the global. This gives an advantage to the writer of a major literature over the writer of a minor one, because the latter has to cover the distance from the periphery to the centre before he can develop his narrative towards an evaluative horizon.

The question arises to what extent the aspiration of literary discourse to high quality is equivalent to a globalizing aspiration.

Under normal conditions, the answer should be positive, while a negative answer might mean that what appears and is established as global is something circumstantial, owing its central position not to its essential function but to cultural imperialism.

The process I described above is obvious in Yatromanolakis's fiction—especially in his two latest novels—and characterizes a writer of the periphery, that is to say a writer of a minor language and literature. What is most interesting are the ways in which the initial local particularity is first stated and then transgressed by being promoted to a global particularity. It could be argued that these ways constitute a crucial part of his poetics.

The local determination of a novel may have the narrow meaning of the national or regional particularity, but it can acquire the broader significance of a microcosm, in which universal relationships are reflected. Greek fiction has encompassed both these meanings in different phases. In the last two decades of the nineteenth century, Greek fiction relied on the first meaning, while in the corresponding period of the twentieth century it has been steadily aiming at the second. The relationship between these two meanings or phases and realism is equivalent because, as far as the representational intent is concerned, their object in both cases is as real as it is an ideological construction: the actuality and the fantasy of the village in naturalism have been replaced by the actuality and the fantasy of the global village in postmodernism.

Nonetheless, the universal dimension of the realistic, or the realistic representation of the universal, transgresses the acceptable limits of narrative realism, which have conventionally or historically been connected with the concrete or the particular, that is, with what has clearly defined borders. This transgression results in a situation where the universal perspective of the realistic with its extended meaning (first on the level of locality, and consequently on the level of significance) is supposed to have the potential of an allegory.

Yatromanolakis combines both meanings or phases of Greek narrative realism: he founds his narration on the first meaning of the realistic in order to experiment with its limits, testing its possibilities for expansion towards the second meaning. In this way, local particularity is not restricted to its national or regional character, but constantly seeks its universal dimension.

## Notes to Chapter 7

1. Yorgis Yatromanolakis, *Anofeles diigima* (1993), 259.
2. The 'East' in a Greek context refers historically and culturally to the Byzantine and Greek Orthodox tradition. The Greek turn to the East in the first three-quarters of the 20th century was opposed to the turn to the West and manifested itself in tendencies towards popular culture and Greekness.
3. *Ithografia* was the movement in Greek fiction in the late 19th and early 20th centuries that aimed at more or less realistic presentations of traditional life in specific Greek locations.
4. By 'abstract' I mean a plot that is stripped of events. Through the removal of the pragmatic dimension of specific circumstances, the plot appears to organize actions into an archetypal structure tending towards an output that possesses only the basic features of human activity, in which case the plot may be described as ritualistic.

# PART 4

❖

# Fragmented Worlds

CHAPTER 8

❖

# In and Out of the Text: Games across Genres in Modern Greek Fiction

*Maria Kakavoulia*

Since we are discussing, in this volume, a wide range of still unsettled
literary phenomena of prose writing, and since we are still unable to
canonize or evaluate the average tendencies of recent Greek fiction
production (1975–2000), I have preferred to narrow down the scope
of our discussion in the hope of avoiding schematic generalizations.
Therefore, this study focuses on a specific practice that links contemporary Greek fiction with its international counterparts: I mean the
way in which fictional texts incorporate and draw more freely than
ever upon various literary and non-literary sources, at the same time
questioning the representational value of literary narrative.

Since the restoration of democracy in Greece in 1974, Greek
fiction has experienced a flowering that is still going on. The number
of books of fiction published annually has tripled in the last fifteen
years. In this development the number of women writers is impressive. Techniques and attitudes towards form are more than ever
open to innovative experimentation, while the plots evolve around a
variety of topics such as human relations, political and social problems,
recent history, the distinction between public and private domains,
the tension between the conditions of urban and traditional life, and
the formation of cultural identity. We can discern various tendencies
in prose style in the post-dictatorship era. On the one hand, there is
a literary rhetoric that narrativizes historical or personal experience in
personal or dramatic modes of discourse, mainly in the manner of
historical novels, novels of magic realism or witness narratives. On the
other, we note an opening up of classical narrative structures, not in
the modernist sense of open-ended novels, but in practices whereby

heterogeneous discourse types are intertextually embedded within literary narratives.

As contemporary critics have remarked, oral narrative, printed media stories and other forms of narrative share common rhetorical and cognitive features across cultures.[1] Moreover, the media, the arts and the sciences seem more than ever to act as a source of inspiration for fiction on a global level. Journalism and fiction-writing have always been in close relation,[2] but nowadays the relationship has widened further: heterogeneous text types such as historical narratives, media narratives, interviews, letters, news reports and news articles, documentaries, small ads and other advertisements have been incorporated within the boundaries of the fictional text. Conversely, similar tendencies have been traced in the case of media narratives that seem to draw heavily upon literary poetics and fiction. The major concern of the present study, then, is to trace the tradition of a multifaceted type of narrative far beyond the generic boundaries in which implicitly or explicitly written and spoken inputs are introduced, demarcated or transformed within novels.

From a narratological point of view, one of the purposes of discourse embedding is to function as a way of distancing and disowning. It offers the possibility of reproducing forms of language that narrators or reporters dare not reproduce as their own discourse: colloquialisms, stylistically inappropriate wording, different text variations, official announcements, formal statements, etc.

Apart from the distancing effect mentioned above, the incorporation of various text and discourse types within the main corpus of narratives typically serves three purposes that apply to both media and literary narratives:[3]

(i) it makes the narrative more lively by 'convey[ing] a human and dramatic dimension to events';[4]
(ii) the narrator/reporter appropriates only those extracts that are convenient to prove his/her point or ideological framework;
(iii) it produces a rhetoric of factuality, i.e. it functions as reliable legitimization and powerful evidence; in both printed media and literary narratives the use of direct report or the quotation of historically reliable and valid sources corresponds to the ability of broadcasting to transmit the voice of the witness.

Deborah Tannen has already pointed out the invented nature of the illusion of the credibility of directly reported discourse in media texts,[5] and rightly so. Selection, quotation, sourcing and citing are just a few of the editing processes used to produce the final product in media texts. Thus, if the truthfulness and the documentary value of citation is already subject to doubt in media narratives, what happens when literary narratives employ similar strategies?

The incorporation, within a novel, of a variety of discourse or text types from different sources and contexts is not new in modern Greek literature. Prose writing that uses citational playfulness—a playfulness that destabilizes narrative linearity—can be traced back to nineteenth-century Greek fiction, in the novel *Pope Joan* (1866)[6] by Emmanouil Roidis (1836–1904), who used historical, literary and historio-graphical sources in a masterly way in order to produce the 'true' story of the only female pope in history.[7] The most interesting feature of Roidis's novel is the opening-up of fiction to its heterogeneous sources of inspiration. This opening—also traceable in recent fiction—establishes a tradition of what we may call multi-embedded narration. The complex intertextual substructure of Roidis's novel is apparent in a multi-embedded corpus of endnotes, footnotes and critical comments that ironically echo the structures of classical text-editing practices such as the *apparatus criticus*. At the end of the novel we find an appendix of footnotes that refer in detail to the textual sources used to produce the novel, such as Latin poetry, medieval literary texts, manuscripts and fragments of the Old Testament. The author uses a learned language that has the richness and eloquence of the classical languages, possesses subtlety of sentiment and a style that is at once ironic, caustic and delicate. The reader is invited to become part of this comic universe that balances between historical novel, ironic metafiction and 'medieval study'.[8]

A century later, we encounter a similar case of intertextual practices in the prose work *My Home* (1965) by the modernist author Melpo Axioti (1905–73).[9] Unlike Roidis, who uses notes and footnotes to indicate the real or fictive sources of his novel, Axioti uninhibitedly inserts a number of documents within the main flow of narrative. Typographically demarcated, these historical documents cast the lives of the people of the island in various periods of its history, under Ottoman rule and at times when its people sailed abroad to make fortunes. These documents—extracts from archive material, personal letters, historical or official documents, newspaper extracts, the log-books and journals of ships' captains, reports of sea-battles,[10] details of local community matters such as the deportation of a woman—stem from various dates.[11] References to the local history of the island of Mykonos range from the early seventeenth century to 1940. A mixture of personal memory, historical events and official documents bear each one their own language.[12]

With a mixture of homo- and heterodiegetic practices Axioti's narrator is at the same time a character, an addressee, a witness narrator and a reader. In general, the reader has to be actively involved in order to produce contextual links and to accommodate a narration that ranges from personal monologue to the historically specific linguistic usage of the inserted documents.

The two pre-1975 cases of prose works we have just considered (Roidis and Axioti) indicate the history and the background of this tendency of multi-embedded narration that has been flourishing more strongly in the last three decades. Whereas Axioti does not playfully undermine the credibility of the inserted documents, a more recent practitioner of the genre, Thanassis Valtinos (1932– ),[13] ponders precisely on this ambiguity. Unlike other works by Valtinos, his novel *Data from the Decade of the Sixties* (1989) is a multi-textured narrative consisting of a variety of text types within the course of its narrative.[14] The reader is actively engaged in restructuring, out of these fragmentary textual data, the Zeitgeist of the crucial decade of the Sixties that marked the emergence of a new era for post-war Greece.[15]

Whether fictive or genuine, the extracts from documents, chronicles, news items, oral narratives etc. in the text are reproduced as unprocessed raw material, justifying Valtinos's well-known love for oral and written testimony. He believes in the documentary power and value of anonymous personal narratives traced in heterogeneous discourse contexts such as public statements, personal dialogues, official government announcements, small personal ads, advertisements for various products, news items from newspapers, personal letters to the editor of a radio programme. These eloquently reveal the complex structures of contradictory ideological values and the equally concrete and elusive quality of reality that make up any current social, political and cultural history. A favourable text-type frequently used in *Data* is letter writing. We read letters to senior civil servants from people who want to emigrate in order to seek a better fortune, as well as letters from women to the editor of the radio programme 'Woman's Hour' ('I ora tis gynaikas'). These letters are cited in chronological order, so that we can draw conclusions concerning the development of a few of the story lines from the letters from the same writer.[16]

Valtinos's most recent prose work, *Diary 1836–2011* (2001),[17] continues along similar lines, but in a still more innovative and radical form. Far from constituting a typical confessional diary, entries occur randomly rather than in chronological order, and they include a wide range of text types: journal notes, letters, travel texts, tales and oral narratives, religious sayings, conversations, jokes, lexical and etymological puns, anonymous tales, lists of names and press reports. Valtinos's obsession with the documentary use of language is even more clearly manifested here. The use of the personal pronoun 'I' has a purely textual function, without any psychological depth or representative value. At the antipodes of narrative closure, the text offers unprocessed glimpses into Greece's recent history: civil war dramas (1946–9), the problems of the post-civil war state, the flow of emigration to countries in western Europe, especially Germany, during the Fifties and the Sixties, everyday rural life in the nineteenth century, the Asia Minor Disaster of 1922, etc. The almost two hundred years of the independent political state are here the main concern. The cognitive aspect of narrative, that is the construction of meaning, is here left to the act of reading.

Valtinos's, or maybe we should say perhaps Axioti's, 'school' of intertextual narration is taken up in a way by Michel Fais (1957– ) in his *Autobiography of a Book* (1995).[18] The background to *Autobiography* is Balkan Greece, and in particular the multi-ethnic town of Komotini in Thrace. The complex history of the relations among Jews, Pomaks (Slav-speaking Muslims) and Christians affects the political, social and cultural history of this provincial town through hybrid mixtures of cultures and languages. Through centrifugal narrative dynamics, the narration moves from the macro-level of life in Komotini to the micro-level of a family and the conflictual relations between its members.

The book consists of three parts. What is strikingly present from the very first page is that the narration is conducted through fragments and extracts from a variety of genres and text types: history and autobiography, historical narrative and oral narrative, personal experience in the form of diary notes, taped conversations, chronicles, news reports, confessions, personal narratives, etc. The time-span—as the press entries indicate—covers a period between 1927 and 1968. The first part of *Autobiography* consists of an archive-based narration, as Makis, one of the two protagonists, is trying to gather information to tell the story of his birthplace and to be relieved of the traumatic history of his own family. The narration is conducted as the presentation of archive material that is both real and fictional: tape-recorded oral narratives with specific indications of date and time,[19] extracts from the local Komotini press, fragments of court proceedings, interviews, advertisements, etc. The two main characters, Makis and his friend Efthymis, are close friends. Makis suffers from claustrophobia, and Efthymis suffers from a stutter. Makis is presented as author and narrator of an unfinished novel, while Efthymis plans to write Makis's biography.

The second part consists of four different drafts of a novel, while the narratives of Makis and Efthymis alternate with each other.

The third part includes a narrative in a woman's voice, that of Magda, who gives her own perspective on the characters of Efthymis and Makis. The excerpt that follows records an imaginary interview by Efthymis (here named as Edmond Bahar) with Yannis Achtalis, a native who is well acquainted with the complex history of multi-ethnic relations in that part of Thrace:

> *Photocopy No … : Transcribed (imaginary)*
> *Interview with Yannis Achtalis by Edmond Bahar:*[20]

'You told me over the phone, Mr. Bahar, that you are working on a book about Komotini. Could you explain to me, now that we are talking face to face, exactly what it is about?'

– I am collecting material, I am interested in anything: oral testimonies, diaries, letters, historical or folklore essays, even photographs or memorabilia concerning Komotini—roughly anything since the Asia Minor catastrophe. Certainly I am not a historian, and consequently I do not have any ambition to write a specialized study. Perhaps in the future this material will take the form of a picture-book.[21]

*Autobiography* explores the mediation between oral and written language, abuses a variety of narrative genres in the name of fictional reliability while undermining it with its own means, and points towards a notion of self as a trajectory of discourses that eventually tear apart any idea of self-contained subjectivity. The text engages interchangeably in issues of both personal and political history. Conversationalization of narration, transcription of recorded voices, lack of traditional 'concrete' characters, monologues, heterodiegetic narratives in the second person, oral, written and even photocopied documents—all these go to make up an uneasy complex narrative discourse that stresses narrative processing rather than narrative closure and totalization.

Narrative totalization—a story with beginning, middle, end—has been considered as one of the two chief strategies for constructing knowledge of the world, the other being, as Bruner has shown, paradigmatic or logico-classificatory thinking.[22] A fundamental resource for the development and refinement of human intelligence and cognition, narrative creates the very possibility of a relationship between self and society. Fais's *Autobiography* presents a problematic relational network precisely at this point. The traumatic relationship between self and society affects all levels of narration and is mirrored in the disorders of memory, the difficulties of speech articulation, and the distorted time and space perception from which the narrator suffers. We read a novel that takes shape within another novel. Only in the last thirty pages of the book can we recognize the panic of the two protagonists, their distorted and simulated worlds, their almost autistic psychologies.

*Autobiography* eventually argues, much more strongly than Valtinos's *Data*, against the myth of realism inherent in the use of documentaries or testimonies in the novel tradition. Fais succeeds in undermining their truth value from within, that is with their own means. To my mind, this strategy constitutes the major feature of Fais's work, namely irony, and in particular an ironic attitude both towards the genre of autobiography and—on a macro-level—towards novel writing itself, thus justifying the book's title. Fais's most recent work, *Aegypius monachus* (2001), similarly adopts a polyphonic stream-like continuum of narration that continues the writing style already adopted in the third part of *Autobiography*.[23]

Thanasis Valtinos and Michel Fais have successfully addressed the need for a renewal of the given patterns of story-telling without operating a dry formalism. As Valtinos says in an interview:[24] 'What is new is the mode. The exclusively personal view on things is what makes things look as though they are seen as for the first time. Otherwise, topics and themes have always been the same.' All the authors mentioned in the preceding pages of this study concentrate more or less playfully on the notion of transparent mediation, frequently revealing the non-literary sources or resources of fictional story-telling. They free narration from conventions and constraints, making the personal mediation of the social and the historical event into the central issue of their narratives. As Efthymis's interviewee in Fais's *Autobiography*, Mr. Achtalis, says:

When you narrate the event, the historical event, that is, it becomes a kind of personal experience—even though you haven't lived the event in question. Because language mediates. As a result, whoever claims that a particular fact 'speaks for itself' is either a liar or naïve. And I've been neither. At least, that's what I would like to believe. Let alone the fact that all along I've had a literally pathological obsession with historical accuracy. I considered facts as something sacred.[25]

A number of younger prose writers who have recently made their first appearance seem to be continuing prose fiction along the same lines, opening up yet further the boundaries of what is called prose fiction towards a dispersal of narration into its constituent parts. Such are the cases of Thomas Skassis's *Greek Crossword* (2001), Kostis Voulgaris's *Peloponnese Forever in Dream* (2001) or Kostas Akrivos's *Yellow Russian Candle* (2001).[26] These authors attempt—with greater or lesser success—to render the ambivalent reality of the historical past and present, having periods of national political history such as the civil war conflict as their fictional background yet again.

At the antipodes of this school of multi-embedded narration, a fresh mythology of reality arises from the work of the youngest generation of prose writers that appeared in the nineties and the most recent 2000–3 period. Turning the focus away from grand national and political narratives, away from obsessed autobiographism or ironic metahistory, they propose a topography of new sensibilities across a trans-national space. Free from political utopias, far beyond a narrative filtering of the personal micro-worlds through the magnifying lens of the exclusive use of first-person narration, they handle a series of topics around the themes of inter-personal relations, lifestyles and others, that only indirectly meet up with historical political reference.

## Conclusions

We have seen that, from the viewpoint of fiction, various non-literary text types of oral or written origin seem to have affected the literary devices of recent Greek fiction: radio voices, TV news reports, historical documents, letters, interviews, polyphonic structures, new hybrid types of narratives, etc. Dislocating and relocating a text type within a fictional framework can produce interesting results in the hands of talented writers. Conversely, from the point of view of media texts, research at a global level has already pointed out that print and electronic media have benefited greatly from fictional narrative practices. The case is not restricted of course to Greek prose writing only. And this gives the issue a trans-national value.

## Notes to Chapter 8

1. Jerome Bruner, 'The narrative construction of reality'.
2. See e.g. Joe Bray, 'Embedded quotations in eighteenth-century fiction'.
3. The comparison of literary and press language has yielded fruitful results. In particular, the analysis of speech presentation in the novel has already been successfully applied to the analysis of speech-embedding in news language by Mick Short, Wynne Martin and Elena Semino, 'Reading reports'.
4. Teun van Dijk, 'Discourse semantics and ideology', 243.
5. A number of theorists have questioned the truthfulness of direct speech quotation in media narratives. See e.g. Deborah Tannen, *Talking Voices*.
6. Emmanouil Roidis, *Papissa Ioanna* (Athens: I. Kassandrefs, 1866).
7. Set in the so-called Dark Ages, the novel tells the story of Joan, who, disguised as a man, rose to rule the church as pope in the 9th century.
8. Lawrence Durrell published a loose translation of *Papissa Ioanna* in 1954, thus earning Roidis a much wider audience in the 1950s and 1960s: Emmanouil Roidis, *Pope Joan: A Romantic Biography*, trans. Lawrence Durrell (London: Derek Verschoyle, 1954). The novel is not at all a sweeping historical drama, as is the case, for instance, with Donna Woolfolk Cross's popular *Pope Joan* (1996), which has recently become a bestseller in the USA.
9. Melpo Axioti, *To spiti mou* (1965). Leontis offers an interesting parallel reading of the political philosopher Agnes Heller's essay 'Where are we at home?' and Axioti's novel: Artemis Leontis, 'Primordial home, elusive home'.
10. Axioti, *To spiti mou*, 75.
11. Many of the archive documents reproduced in *To spiti mou* were first reproduced in the Mykonos local journals *Mykoniatika Chronika* and *Nea Mykonos* (especially in the volumes of the late 1950s and the 1960s).
12. Leonidas Zenakos writes in his review of Axioti's book: 'Axioti does not produce a picturesque representation of Mykonos in the manner of Kazantzakis. She renders the character and the expression of the island. People, events and situations emerge through different uses of language': Leonidas Zenakos, 'Melpo Axioti: "To Spiti mou"'.
13. Thanassis Valtinos is known internationally for his novels, short stories, plays and film scripts, and his collaborations with the film director Theo Angelopoulos. His work has been translated into French, German, Swedish, English and other languages. His own translations of classical Greek drama have been performed at annual theatre festivals throughout Greece.
14. Thanassis Valtinos, *Stoicheia gia ti dekaetia tou '60* (1989). The novel was awarded the Greek State Literature Prize in 1989 and short-listed for the European Aristeion Prize.
15. A less well-known prose work by Stefanos Tassopoulos entitled *Iliako orologio* (1988) presents an interesting mixture of multiple third-person narratives, news items from local newspapers of the 1950s, passages from encyclopedias, extracts from manuals of good manners from the 1950s and other material.
16. The first and last letters (9 Jan. 1960 and 22 Sept. 1969) are from the same writer.
17. Thanassis Valtinos, *Imerologio 1836–2011* (2001).
18. Michel Fais, *Aftoviografia enos vivliou* (1995). This novel, Fais's first, was translated into French in 1996.

19. Oral narratives had already played an important role in the formation of literary narration in Greek fiction of the 1930.
20. In other words, Efthymis of the third part.
21. Michel Fais, 'Autobiography of a Book' (excerpt), trans. Yiorgios Anagnostu, 186–7.
22. Jerome Bruner, *Actual Minds, Possible.*
23. Fais also experiments with the form of diary notes in the second work in this trilogy, a collection of short stories, *Ap' to idio potiri kai alles istories* (1999).
24. In the Greek newspaper *Ta Nea*, 14 Jan. 2000.
25. Fais, *Aftoviografia*, 203.
26. Thomas Skassis, *Elliniko stavrolexo* (2000); Kostis Voulgaris, *Sto oneiro panta i Peloponniso* (2001); Kostas Akrivos, *Kitrino rosiko keri* (2001).

❖

# The Individual within Multiple Worlds in Greek Short Stories since 1974

*Anastasia Natsina*

By leaving behind a restricted view of the world within national historical confines, Greek fiction since 1974 seems to have been engaging increasingly in the challenge posed by the coexistence and confrontation of different cultures to which the country has increasingly been opening up since the end of the dictatorship, culminating in the trend towards globalization. This widely shared assumption sets the socio-cultural subtext of my analysis.

An ever-increasing awareness of the role of language in the construction of reality, along with the unanswerable epistemological questions pertaining to a finite concept of world, has come to foreground the ontological dimensions of discursive plurality and emphasize the multiplicity of world-views as a multiplicity of worlds. In its many forms, this shift invariably involves considerable repercussions for the individual, as the uncontrollable proliferation of frames of reference disturbs the stability and meaningfulness of his/her selfhood; hence the individual's new position has been described in various ways, from utterly debilitating to blissfully liberating.

To turn to my specific topic, I would like to note the remarkable recurrence of the topic of multiple and often conflated universes in Greek short stories during recent decades.[1] For the purposes of this chapter I have chosen to discuss *The Preparation* (1991) by E. Ch. Gonatas, short stories from Dimitris Nollas's collections *Tender Skin* (1982) and *I Dream of my Friends* (1990), and the collections *Last Year's Fiancée* (1984) by Zyranna Zateli and *New Athenian Stories* (1989)

by Christos Vakalopoulos. In the succession from one author to
the next—which is also a succession from older to younger—I trace
a movement from a less rigorous to a more radical recognition of
multiple worlds and its concomitant repercussions on the individual
as these shift from a feeling of extreme ontological danger in
Gonatas through loss of orientation and often playful bewilderment in
Nollas to a sense of power and bliss in Zateli and Vakalopoulos
respectively.

In *The Preparation* by E. Ch. Gonatas (b. 1924) we follow the
repeatedly failed attempts of a retired doctor, Agelaos Avvakis, and his
assistant and disciple Prokopis to weigh the former's head by using an
old pair of scales with beams. The neutral description of the characters
in their mildly pedantic course of action and interpersonal behaviour
lends a sense of duty to their unusual project. Their undertaking takes
place in a shabby room, full of Agelaos's scribbled notes and calcu-
lations, which, along with the consideration of obscure parameters
such as the weight of his glasses or the vibration of his voice, sets the
framework for a scientific practice verging on recklessness. Further,
the application of the method of trial and error, which foresees the
seed of future success in a present failure that repeatedly gives different
and inconclusive results,[2] and the reliance on the mirror in deter-
mining the weighing (the mirror reflects the scales, which are difficult
for Agelaos to see otherwise, laying his head on the scale-pan as he
does), clearly point to a conception of world as unified and con-
forming to laws, layered in consistent interlocked chains of signifiers
and signifieds.

The two men's project takes this conception to the extreme by
bringing the major advocates of objective reality, reason and positive
method, to bear upon their human agent, in order to offer a con-
clusive measurement of a living individual. As any first-year medical
student would be quick to note, it is only by approximation that one
could weigh the head of a living human. The activity of Agelaos's
brain at the time of the measurement impedes any definite result, very
much in the manner described by Heisenberg's uncertainty principle.
The impossible task of self-referentiality, the ultimate project of
grasping totality, results in an irresolvable tension and an unbridgeable
division that presents itself in various forms in the text, not least
regarding individuals.

Reaching an impasse in their research once more, Prokopis offers,
rather as an interlude, to tell a story that seems to him relevant to

Agelaos's own task. It is of a man on a staircase in the darkness, who, when provided with the light he is desperately crying for, shuts his eyes and starts ascending and descending the stairs in a constant oscillating, pendulum-like movement. The voluntary blindness that leads the man of the embedded story to what seems like a repeated failure in his irrational task resembles Agelaos's activity. It is a similar blindness that leads Agelaos to try to accomplish a task that by definition defies accomplishment, to achieve a unitary totality fraught with irreconcilable tensions. Thus he seems to be reaching the extremes of a tradition opened up by a leading figure in the study of both gravity and the pendulum, Galileo, whose urge 'to measure what can be measured and make measurable what cannot be measured' summarizes the epistemological task of the modern era.

Moving from the interiors of this story to its immediate exterior, the same tension is portrayed in the next and final scene of the text. The two men interrupt their work and are drawn to the balcony by the voices of two women in the yard who go about their daily housework. The encounter is fraught with phallogocentric con-notations (the yard is earth, the women are ironing large bed sheets, and they complain that the two men 'up there' are enjoying the 'garden'—referring to the leaves of the tree), but as a pear falls down from the tree the women have no difficulty in weighing it empirically in their hands, thus bringing the two men of theory to despair. The fruit of the two men's failed mental efforts becomes in the discourse of the women an apple-pear, fraught with theological and scientific connotations (Eve's apple and the discovery of the law of gravity respectively) of closed systems, perfect within themselves which, projected onto the fruit of failure, show the aspiration of these discourses to permanence and all-comprehensiveness to be peels of various levels of fictitiousness.

This peculiar fruit, the apple-pear, as a 'one-word *mise-en-abyme*'[3] also brings to light the complementary relation of the two men, revealing Prokopis as Agelaos's double. Prokopis's active participation in Agelaos's self-weighing, his offer of the 'precious' mirror and of the embedded story to the same (mirroring) effect, his fear that if Agelaos fails in his task he himself will have to take his place, point to him as an apt portrayal of the innermost division of the subject when faced with the impossibility of oneness and closedness. Abiding by the venerable tradition of doubles in world literature, Prokopis teases Agelaos into (self-)destruction, concluding the story as he does by characterizing Agelaos as courageous, which is either a direct hint at beheading (so as to finally weigh correctly) or at least encouragement into a lost cause.[4] In any case, the consequences for the individual confronted with the inadequacy of his instruments to treat the gaps in a unitary concept of world are dire, even if, from another angle (one of the very many indeed offered in this story), imperfection and failure are highly valued. Treating the logical paradox of self-referentiality, the text shows the insufficiency of the logical system to describe reality, which turns out to be a mutable, self-contradictory non-unified 'system'. As they are led to confirm its failure in Gonatas's miniature masterpiece, Agelaos and Prokopis mark the turn from an epistemological concern to an ontological one.

In doing so they appear to mark the beginning of a number of short stories by Dimitris Nollas (b. 1940). In these the multiplicity of worlds is revealed as an inherent feature of the innumerable narratives that envelop human lives, as the metafictional strategies of the texts foreground the role of language in the construction of incommensurate universes of discourse. The individuals, often journalists or authors and generally aptly serving as first-person narrators, are shown to suffer from a loss of control over their own narrative worlds, experiencing an uncertainty that they might be inhabiting somebody else's story, or, worse still, their own which is made foreign by the mere act of its enunciation.

'Copyright', the closing piece of the collection *Tender Skin,* is based on the parodic frustration of the detective plot—the modern-istic/epistemological mode *par excellence* according to McHale[5]—as the police and two journalists fail to provide an explanation for the curious death of Th. Andoniadis (who holds a passport in the telling name of Georg Bleibtreu—George Remain-Faithful), which was caused by two bullets of differing calibre. Privileging storytelling over speculations pre-empted by the missing data ('in this story it is as though everything were missing', they say), one of the two journalists recalls a similarly enigmatic story where he was confronted with the disappearance of a woman he was flirting with in a bar; according to the barman, the woman had not appeared in the bar for a week and the supposed door to the lavatory through which she had disappeared was merely decorative. The man describes himself as enveloped in the story told by the barman, totally uncertain of the true course of the events, and concludes his narrative—and the whole story—by noting that the inability to control the fact is something that could kill somebody, thus providing a radically undermining interpretation of the last scene of 'what really happened' in detective stories, while suggesting the fatal consequences of conflated universes of discourse. This point recurs in Nollas's following collection, *I Dream of my Friends*, with varying degrees of playfulness. In 'I Knew You'd Be Waiting for Me' the hero–narrator returns to his fatal bar after long abstinence in order to meet his prospective publisher. In the flurry of subsequent drinks and toasts he is informed that long absence from the bar is a punishable offence and the offender is made to believe 'that one owns things he does not or has done things that did not happen'. When the man leaves the bar at the end he has completely forgotten about his plans, whereas his fellow-drinker, Mr Pagidis (Mr Trapman), who is described as the hero's double, his 'amphitryon', stays behind to wait for a meeting. The reader cannot help wondering whether the whole story about the pitiable hero's supposed meeting was not actually a punishment of the kind described earlier. But then the rule of punishment itself would be part of the same fallacious world and hence be ineffective, which thrusts the reader along with the protagonist into a *mise-en-abyme* structure similar to the paradox of the Cretan liar, interminably conflating subsequent levels of factuality and fictionality and understandably resulting in the disorientation and division of the hero.

Similarly, in 'The Writer's Passion' the self-conscious hero–narrator tells the story of his deception by a bookmaker who stole the money he was supposed to bet on the horse that eventually won the race. A few months later the bookmaker makes a sudden appearance, only to let the hero know that he has now turned to writing; whereupon he briefly relates the story he just sold, which is none other than that of the hero's deception. The man thus suddenly finds himself in the position of the authored/fictional character rather than that of the author, which he had occupied thus far, but only to move soon another level downwards when he declares that the story he has just heard is the one he finished writing the previous night. He is thus caught in a 'strange loop' that has shifted the narrative level twice,[6] conflating the different fictional levels and paradoxically bringing him to the original level without nevertheless restoring him to a position of power; rather, deceived for the second time, he unwittingly consents to his abuse and pays for the drinks.

The moral consequences of authoring a story are examined in Nollas's brilliantly executed 'Stories Are Always Foreign', which brings this matter to bear upon the confession of crimes and exposes its deeply alienating repercussions for the individual without recourse to metafiction. Two men fail to communicate during a random night encounter in the course of a return journey to their homeland, and they part in the darkness and far from home in mutual fear and mistrust as they oscillate between admitting or not admitting to authoring the stories of their crimes; overwhelmed by their power and the inexplicable (overdetermined) drives that underlie them, they show themselves to be the victims of compelling stories, unable to guarantee their correspondence to reality and unable to assume the responsibility for authoring them.

Whereas Nollas's heroes are invariably victimized in the multiplicity of incommensurate worlds revealed by the cross-cutting narratives that they are unable to control, Zyranna Zateli (b. 1951) seems to be making an altogether different point out of the same linguistic (self-)awareness. In her collection *Last Year's Fiancée*, which is almost a short-story cycle, the recurrent heroine-narrator masters successfully (and to her profit) the magical, supernatural elements that disturb the realist assumptions of the world she inhabits. Additionally, on another level, she grows out of the *Künstlerroman*-like structure of the first stories to become the self-conscious fully-grown author of the last ones, controlling both the fictional world of the book and the real world of the reader, who is invited to recognize her authorial accomplishment.

This collection would be most helpfully described in terms of magic realism, which involves the conflation of different ontological planes, as supernatural elements originating from the beliefs of traditional communities are seamlessly grafted onto realistic accounts. The first six interconnected stories of the collection make up a kind of saga where the supernatural constitutes a natural part of the heroine's childhood impressions, emerging normally from the trad-itions of an extended rural family that hosts the multiple individual worlds of its numerous members, including that of the dead. The vividness of the childhood impressions smoothes the ironic edge of the adult gaze of the average *Bildungsroman/Künstlerroman,* thus preserving the magic in a quite literal manner: in 'The Bewitched Cottage' the heroine's almost incestuous adolescent love affair with Stefanos is not only magically protected by being made literally invisible to everyone, but also bears fruit in the present, as his daughters (by different women) take after her. In the same context, the world of the dead is often presented as inextricably bound with that of the living, as in the case of the barber in the same story who dies soon after his remark that the dead Persephone might drag him down to the world of the dead to continue taking care of her there. Yet the coexistence of multiple worlds does leave space for a less lethal outlook. In 'Persephone and Another Story' the great-great-grandmother with the telling name of Persephone, 120 years old and situated between life and death, can foresee death and is presented as a privileged person, 'a witch', 'favoured by both life and death which confide their secrets to her'. A similar position is also gradually created for the heroine. The title story ('Last Year's Fiancée'), which appears first in the collection, takes the decisive step in establishing her cognitive superiority and mastery over both the world of the reader, who does not realize until the last word of the text that her fiancé Markos is a cat, and her own fictional environment, which in turn is unaware that the cat is her fiancé. The striking effect of this ruse, as well as its place at the outset, results in consolidating the heroine's ruling position over the two different ontological planes at every subsequent mention of Markos in the rest of the stories.

Grafted onto a large family and deprived of any one clear origin that would anchor her in a single world (her mother died moments after she gave birth and her father is 'as though he never existed'), the heroine seems to be hovering in a flickering ontological status resembling that of a witch. The traditional attributes of witchcraft, such as her engagement to a cat or her early love affair with a man with 'green cat's eyes [resembling] the eyes of a demon or someone possessed', soon give way to the manifestation of her crafting capacities as she self-consciously gives names to places and things, creating 'semi-fictional, semi-real' worlds such as that of Mygdonia in the story entitled 'Zina'. The pointed use of *mise-en-abyme* in 'Tornado' along with the literalization of similes, metaphors and metonymies, especially in 'The Birds' and 'Last Year's Fiancée', amounts to the same performative effect.

The earliest manifestation of the heroine's vocation lies in 'The Bewitched Cottage', where the story of her love affair with Stefanos is described in the summary of a twelve-page letter she sent him at the time, whereas the short story itself concludes with a (short) story she had composed in the same period. In explicitly and repeatedly thematizing her compulsive story-telling throughout the collection, the heroine-narrator inscribes her evolving literary activity in the tradition of the *Künstlerroman,* which generally involves the narrative of

progression towards artistic fulfilment while the same narrative constitutes the manifestation of its own completion. Yet in her case the last
three pieces of the collection, thematically differentiated from the saga
of the first six, stand as samples of her artistic development, not in the
fictional world built up by the first pieces, but in the world of the
reader, who is invited to attest to the heroine's authorial identity as
being on the same ontological level as his/her own. The heroine,
utterly enchanted by a deep assimilation of her multiple childhood
and adolescent worlds, comes to create artfully her own (authorial)
self, showing that to be a wizard one must first believe in magic.

Lastly, *New Athenian Stories* by Christos Vakalopoulos (1956–93)
moves the 'bucolic postmodernism'[7] that is magic realism to the urban
space of Athens and shows the fusion of natural and supernatural to
be the locus of both the dissolution of a stable self and the recovery of
the individual's innermost desires and a lost sense of community.

In those stories the multiplicity of worlds is revealed in sudden
illogical or magical disruptions of realistic landscapes such as Kalli-
dromiou Street being afflicted by a wave of incessant coughing and
babbling, with outbursts of honesty and sociability coming from every
direction as an old woman ventures to get hold of the last Monopoly
set in town in 'Go to Jail'. A similar disorder is apparent in 'The
Meaning of Life', in the disappearance of an old man from within a
jam-packed elevator that is stuck between floors as he whispers the
two-line poem of a girl in love. Similarly, in 'Heat-Wave Whirlpool',
the stagnant summer landscape of Athens is swept by a wave of petty
crimes following the radio broadcast of a café discussion where a deep
voice urges everyone to combat the excessive heat by releasing his or
her repressed desires. Likewise, in the story 'In the Grip of the
Nymph', a man finds himself caught in an unexpected quest for a
fairy, and, implausibly enough, every innocent bystander he happens
to come across comes to his assistance.

It is obvious that compulsive behaviour of various kinds and manifestations constitutes an invariable characteristic of these and other
instances, as the individuals are urged to involuntary actions that range
from the archetypal falling in love to stealing, coughing, talking about
their innermost fears and desires or giving information they did not
even know they possessed. In doing so they reveal their repressed or
unknown emotional or cognitive sides and lose control over their
assumed selfhood and customary self-images.

Interestingly enough, the suspension of their standard roles and the

disruption of their presumed individuality in those otherworldly inter-
ruptions is invariably connected to sound, music, spoken language. As
is most obvious in the case of the uncontrollable babble in 'Go to Jail'
and of the old man in 'The Meaning of Life' who disappears upon
uttering the two-line 'meaning of life' he once heard from a girl who
disappeared under identical circumstances, the dissolution of self
into language points to the twofold power of the public linguistic
medium in doing and undoing selfhood.

Yet it is this double bind that summarizes the redemptive power of
yielding to magic. In dissolving into the most pointedly social aspect
of language, which is orality, the various characters of the stories
generally seem to gain access to objects of deeper significance and
thought of as long perished: love, escape from loneliness and seclusion,
humanitarian missions, or indeed the meaning of life. Oral speech,
being the living conveyor of old communal practices and beliefs (both
magical and otherwise), allows the recovery of a lost sense of community
through its polyphonic potential for dissolving rigid structures and
promotes the renegotiation of the public space in favour of the lost
magic and bliss within the social bond. The outmoded goods that are
the reward of the protagonists who abandon themselves to the
unexpected quirks of polyphonic magic are thus shown to be the
products of the acceptance of multiplicity and diversification.

In this chapter I have attempted to trace the plurality of approaches
found in contemporary Greek short-story writers *vis-à-vis* the
subject of multiple worlds and their consequences for the individual.
From Agelaos's brave glimpse to the other heroes' increasingly positive
recognition of conflated multiple worlds, the challenges to unitary and
totalizing world-concepts share in common a deep concern for the
notion of selfhood and purposeful action. To suggest a progressive
movement from negative to affirmative, from existential angst to
polyphonic bliss, would be to use an obsolete vocabulary; hinting at
it is to recognize an old charm. But as the change in degree reaches
the critical point of marking a change in quality, contemporary Greek
authors testify to their own authorial identity by boldly entering a
global exchange of often incommensurate worlds.

## Notes to Chapter 9

1. As e.g. in the following collections: Pavlos Matesis, *Diigimata* (1978) and *Yli
   dasous* (1992), Zyranna Zateli, *Stin erimia me chari* (1986), Vasilis Gouroyannis,

*Diigiseis parafysikon fainomenon* (1990), Yorgos Skambardonis, *Mati fosforo koumanto gero* (1989), *I psicha tis metalavias* (1990), *I stenopos ton yfasmaton* (1992) and *Pali kentaei o stratigos* (1996), and Eva Karaïtidi, *Oneirevomai pos glytosa* (1996).

2. Cf. E. Ch. Gonatas, *I proetoimasia* (1991), 32: 'Don't despair. Your failed efforts most probably contain the seed of future success.'

3. Fragiski Abatzopoulou, 'I metamorfosi sto ergo tou E. Ch. Gonata', in *I grafi kai i vasanos*, 84–100, at 96.

4. On (self-)destruction as a major aspect of doubles see Carl F. Keppler, *The Literature of the Second Self*, 27–98.

5. Brian McHale, *Postmodernist Fiction*, 9, 16.

6. According to Hofstadter, 'the strange loop phenomenon occurs whenever, by moving upwards (or downwards) through the levels of some hierarchical system, we unexpectedly find ourselves right back where we started'. A system in which 'strange loops' occur is called 'tangled hierarchy' (Douglas R. Hofstadter, *Gödel, Eschel, Bach: An Eternal Golden Braid*, 10).

7. Wendy Faris, 'Scheherazade's children: magical realism and postmodern fiction', 182.

CHAPTER 10

❖

# Ideology's Discontents in Thanassis Valtinos's *Data from the Decade of the Sixties*

*Dimitris Païvanas*

So life was never better than / In nineteen sixty-three / [ ... ]
Between the end of the *Chatterley* ban / And the Beatles' first LP.
PHILIP LARKIN, 'Annus Mirabilis' (16 June 1967),
*Collected Poems*, Faber and Faber, London 1988

In Thanassis Valtinos's national-prize-winning novel *Data from the Decade of the Sixties*[1] Greece's transition from a traditional economy and ideologically introverted culture to a nation with a supranational outlook on the path to westernization and global capitalism is portrayed as particularly problematic. The novel's themes develop in the ideological climate of post-civil-war Greece and, at a global level, the Cold War, illustrating a collision between a timidly emerging egalitarianism and a patriarchal right-wing conservatism. This conflict leads to physical and psychological violence involving both men and women of different social strata, institutional involvement and political affiliation, and to a profound unhappiness in a scene of world developments that are encroaching on the Greeks and on Greece as a cultural and national entity. Shomit Dutta states in his review of the novel's English translation that '*Data from the Decade of the Sixties* is a moving portrait of a country and its people in a state of transition and crisis being dragged into a cosmopolitanism that is fundamentally alien, historically speaking, to the Greek psyche.'[2] How alien cosmopolitanism was to at least metropolitan Greek society in the 1960s is a moot point. However, it is difficult to disagree with the claim that it was a turbulent decade throughout social and political life in Greece,[3] as it was in other nations throughout Europe and the world. Valtinos (b. 1932) is a controversial author whose prose has more than once challenged narrative conventions in fiction and dominant views on Greek history, politics and culture. He belongs to what might be termed the second generation of Greek post-war fiction writers. He is best known for his detached matter-of-fact treatment of often risqué subject-matter through imitation of testimonial narratives or authentic documents and for an effacement of the implied author effected by these techniques. Indeed, some of his better-known works, including the novel under discussion, might be best described as works of 'faction' rather than fiction. His innovative techniques have influenced a number of younger authors, some of whose works have been described as products of a so-called 'Valtinos School'.

If, from the mid-1980s onwards, Greek fiction documents a disillusionment with political ideology, abandoning the latter in pursuit of a private or more global vision, in Valtinos's case we witness a proliferation of writings on the very theme of ideology as a hindrance to individual well-being. The dramatic tension in his work is mainly the result of an often violent encounter between national, cultural or ideological imperatives and individualistic pursuits. Ideology in Valtinos's fiction is a broad concept. Concomitantly, for the purposes of this chapter, ideology is defined broadly as a set of beliefs shared by groups of people or institutions which attempt to impose them on others by a variety of means. The term incorporates aspects of culture and the notion of 'myth' as an inflexible narrative about human conduct and perception that creates false consciousness.

Valtinos's preoccupation with an individual who is oppressed, disillusioned or (mis)led by ideology is not recent and is not simply the result of a 1980s discontent with politically tinted dogma. Arguably, it dates back to his first novella *The Descent of the Nine* (1963). Indeed in another of Valtinos's early works entitled *Three One-Act Plays* (1978), which can be considered as a precursor of *Data*, the transition from post-war Greece to democracy and capitalism is treated with savagely bitter irony. This is a short tripartite novel comprising the transcript of a post-civil-war court-martial trial, letters to a prisoner from his relatives and other characters, and a manual on how to get maximum benefit from a Kenwood mixer. The onslaught of capitalism as signified mainly by the discourse on an essentially absent kitchen appliance is ironically projected against a background of accusations amongst the 'victors' of the civil war, financial hardship, crime, crises in interpersonal relationships and social inequities. These themes, among others, and their ironic treatment, are also encountered in *Data* in different guises.

*Data* is not a narrative in the generally accepted sense. It is a complex concatenation of correspondence and other short texts supposedly quoted verbatim from the daily press and possibly other unspecified sources. The text is a quasi-epistolary novel combining a mélange of other documents and a list of annals. The documents referring to historical events of the 1960s make up the novel's rudimentary plot. The chronological arrangement of the subsidiary texts alludes to an orderly temporal sequence, yet the fragmented and diverse nature of the archive undermines such notions of uniform continuity. This 'anti-narrative' feature of the novel is significant because narrative is itself presented in the novel as one of the primary means of enforcing ideology.

The stringing together of documents without narratorial comment makes the reading of *Data* something like constant zapping through television channels for a dizzying viewing of a narrative pastiche. I hasten to qualify this simile with the reminder that the implied author is in charge of the remote control and that it is not viewing but reading that one is performing. Michel Grodent notes something similar in the preface to the novel's French translation, articulating what I consider an accurate short hand-description of the novel's effect: 'L'ouvrage de Valtinos pourrait [...] être décrit comme une caverne où les échos ne cessent de s'entrecroiser.'[4]

In spite of this vertiginous effect, the novel flirts with the idea of historical memory as a means to self-definition, both on a personal and on a national level. The late Spyros Tsaknias, for example, described the text as an 'identity novel'.[5] Contrarily, few commentators have stated that the 1960s as portrayed in the novel bear little resemblance to their own experience of the decade.[6] Such instances illustrate that personal readings may not necessarily be in full accord with 'nationally' inspired ones. Dutta, on the other hand, comments: 'Much of the book's art lies in the careful ordering of material, but we are made to ponder how far we ourselves project a pattern onto the data before us. There is perhaps an underlying sense that it is by creating fictional narratives, as authors or readers, that we gain our sense of history.'[7] To the extent that the author's selection and arrangement allow, it is the reader who has to narrativize the subsidiary texts by establishing connections between them. These connections are by no means monosemic, consistently obvious or straightforward. There is, therefore, an element of doubt about how judicious such interpretative acts might be. Interestingly enough, this last thought does not feature in the writings of the vast majority of Greek commentators on Valtinos's novel.[8]

Most critics generally agree that in *Data* the fragmented elements of a decade in Greece make up a mosaic or a collage which, in its totality, refers to an open national or historical wound. Dimitris Angelatos, for example, hastens to transform his perceived 'openness' of the novel's form into a reference to a historical wound.[9] However, even if the openness of the text's form refers to an unhealed national wound, it still refers to something. The interpretation and the perceived gaps in *Data* close themselves off neatly and the notion of 'openness' is contradicted. The novel's epigraph, 'Behold, I will overthrow the inhabitants of this land with affliction, that thy plague may be discovered', taken from the Septuagint version of Jeremiah (10: 18), is partly responsible for this interpretation, but the possessive pronoun need not be read as a synecdoche referring to everyone in the nation. It can also be read as the author's personal address to the female addressee of the book's dedication or to a reader who performs a more personal reading of the novel. Aristinos's interpretation of the novel is also contradictory. He argues that *Data* is a 'polyphonic' novel but eventually reduces it to no more than a single binary opposition.[10] What is therefore astonishing about the interpretative strategies employed by critics is that, even when the irony, polyphony, humour, parody, lacunae or 'openness' of the novel's form are perceived, an interpretative will to semantic stability yields comments that are fraught with ideas of totality and closure. Critics appear to reduce the formal features of *Data* to stylistic aspects of a superficial (post) modernity devoid of semantic consequences. Their readings betray an obvious ideological stance in relation to the novel's content, but they also render a great deal of it redundant.

To the extent that form and content can be separated, it is the general aim of this chapter to explore some of the consequences that the novel's form has for its content and to investigate the implications for its treatment as a kind of referential historiography. In doing so, I shall be commenting on some hitherto undiscussed aspects of the novel's themes, plot and character development, relating my observations to the issue of ideology.

## Narrative Progress: Reading for the Plot(s)

The novel's most prominent themes feature in two discernible groups of texts comprising its two main narrative axes, namely troubled inter-personal relations and Greek migration. The former theme is expressed mainly in letters written by women with multifarious problems confessing to and seeking advice from a phantom Kyria Mina, a radio agony aunt, whose advisory discourse is rarely and only indirectly witnessed by the reader. The second theme features mainly in letters addressed to DEME (Intergovernmental Committee for Emigration from Europe) by aspiring emigrants. Both character groups seek a thread that will allow them to continue their lives' narrative out of an emotional or financial labyrinth. In some bitterly humorous cases, the correspondents to DEME seek advice on how to return to Greece (277) or even to have their offspring returned to them (266). The sought thread appears to have led them to yet another impasse. This inconclusiveness of stagnant plot sequences in the lives of a plurality of characters is thematically related as it ag-glutinates to compound the reader's sense of a pinioning emotional malaise or fiscal quagmire.

Replies to such letters do not form part of the novel.[11] In the occasional instances where letters are composed by the same character, the correspondent usually evokes new complications that have arisen in the meantime. Therefore, the novel's two main narrative threads develop in undulatory rather than linear fashion, undermining any real plot or character development. This is intensified by the repetitiousness and a *déjà lu* quality in all documents. The repetition, however, is a repetition with a difference, and this being a broad definition of parody explains to an extent the parodic quality and ironic effect that most of these documents possess. One could also argue that the notion of lack of development is an irony resulting from the novel's implicit comparison with the novel tradition, which has relied for centuries on plot and character development to narrate a story.

In all the subsidiary documents of *Data* there are stated or implied narrative sequences. Their function is allegorical in the sense that what they signify almost annuls their sequential character. For example, the arrest, accusation, trial, sentence, appeal and subsequent release of a striptease artist ironically named Themis (= justice) signi-fies the tacit collaboration of the judiciary, the media and the church against the offensive of modern mores in an exercise of ideological control over erotically suggestive behaviour (168).

The single narrative sequence that unfolds across more than one document evokes the initially fairy-tale-like story of King Constantine's ascent to the throne, marriage and production of royal progeny, leading to the unceremonious denouement of his flight from Greece and abstinence from royal duties. This basic story-line contrasts ironically with incomplete, less uniform and more turbulent developments in the lives of other migrating characters.

The historical references contained in the novel conjure up historiographical discourse and establish the potential for creating a wholesale causative link between Sixties events and the private lives of the characters in the novel. Instead the novel illustrates a disparity between private and public life. It is also significant that, from a historiographical viewpoint, the conclusion of historical events occurring in the 1960s in Greece is traditionally placed in 1973–4. The novel concludes ironically in December 1969 with something between a bang and a whimper. Its final document reports that a very noisy explosive device detonated in front of the new law courts still under construction in Larissa, leaving no casualties and causing no damage. It is a rather non-dramatic ending that parodies de-dramatized novelistic endings, but appears to allude self-referentially to a reading that has been concluded, leaving its reader physically unscathed. It may also be argued that, in conjunction with another document (391), it alludes to the 1973 Polytechnic uprising in a kind of prolepsis or *prothysteron*. Indeed the novel's actual temporal frame of reference exceeds the boundaries of the decade in the title.[12] The second document in the novel refers to events in 1958 (13), and there are numerous apparently incidental references to the German Occupation, the ensuing civil war and a humorous allusion to the Turkish invasion of Cyprus in 1974 (166). This disparity between the claimed and the actual temporal frame of reference is ironic and forms part of a broader agenda involving irony.

## The Space of Irony

I am treating irony here as a rhetorical trope that is based on a discrepancy between the stated and the implied, the declared and the intended, the conjectured and the actual, or the content and the form of an utterance. This discrepancy involves the momentary displacement of apprehended meaning. I treat irony broadly as a figure that enforces the reappraisal of a meaning from an imposed spatiotemporal distance. This definition of irony is based on Paul de Man's posthumously published ideas on the trope, where he claims, among other things, that irony is reducible to 'a moment in the dialectic of the self'.[13] Indeed, while reading the novel, one gets the sense that one does not quite evade the space of this dialectic or the tropological space of irony.

Irony is omnipresent in Valtinos's novel first and foremost as a temporal incongruity. Documents of a past decade are read as present, many of the narrators' pleas for assistance are made in the 'now' of reading. This could, of course, be stated of every work of fiction. However, the historical component in *Data* and the putative authenticity of the documents create an illusion of a higher degree of referentiality than is generally expected of works of fiction. In *Data* the characters make pleas with a view to establishing interpersonal relationships, personal classifieds seeking partners and the letters to Mina among them. Given the established narrative pattern of 'plea followed by lack of response', the reading of *Data* takes place in the void of a temporal incongruity between the expectation of a discursive response to a document and the knowledge that such an expectation is destined to remain unfulfilled. This void is the space of irony.

When one reads, for example, an advertisement for seaside building plots available on the island of Salamis (35), the meaning of the subsidiary text is affected by other texts in the novel. The island, for instance, is associated with other islands off the coast of Attica where unrepentant communists were exiled and from which they returned with the 'peace-making measures' in the early part of the 1960s.[14] The previous document, a news item about the capture of two large sharks near the Attic coastline, is conducive to this interpretation, as the historically significant place names of Varkiza and Lavrion feature in it.[15] The rhetorical function of the de/recontextualized advertisement is both to advertise and to interact with other texts in the novel at the time of reading. It, like all the documents that precede and follow it, is both of the 1960s, in a referential sense, and not of the 1960s. One could almost say that it is addressed, both as an authentic document to a reader who is its contemporary and, as a recontextualized document, to a posthumous reader who might be something like a historian or social analyst. The novel's title and the supposed authenticity of each document enforce the former role, while the generic context of a novelistic fiction enforces the latter. It seems necessary for the actual reader of the novel to accept both roles, performing a kind of simultaneous double reading and accepting the ironic discrepancy that separates them. It may be that readers of novels, by definition, do not read the content literally, but the historiographical pretences of the novel undermine a purely metaphorical reading of its putatively authentic components. This type of double (ironic) reading is, in my view, what the reader is required to perform on every single document in the novel. The discussion of another example may help to further elucidate and expand the point.

In a letter to Mina in the second half of *Data* (327–9) a uniquely happy young woman expresses mixed sentiments about her forthcoming marriage to an apparently affluent older man. While claiming to have everything she could have wished for, she is still troubled by an inexplicable 'but' in her life ('ena anexigito "alla"'). An explanation is alluded to in the motives behind her marriage, but it is reinforced as a mystery for the entirety of the letter. In what can be described as an ironic moment in the dialectic of this reading subject's self, the next document forces a retrospective explanation of the 'but' as the general climate under dictatorship. The explanation is, of course, catachrestic in nature. The text that follows is a news item about King Constantine's allegedly unjustified abandonment of his duties and his replacement by the regent George Zoitakis (330). This does not change the catachrestic nature of the interpretation that public life affects the personal. In fact, the entire novel demonstrates 'under erasure' that this is actually the case. It does, however, draw attention to that link that I have just made as a tenuous one, as a link that is provisional, a kind of ghostly link that is both there and not there. It is the result of the contiguity of the two documents, of the arbitrariness of their juxtaposition, and forms a hint that the catachrestic connection is ideologically charged.

As I hope is evident from the examples discussed above, meaningful associations in the novel are subject to constant shifts, as they abscond the moment they appear. Meaning in the novel oscillates between what Roland Barthes has called *doxa* (the dominant ideology or common opinion)[16] and an exposure of its contrived or catachrestic nature. It is irony that is responsible for this exposure. In stating this, I am not privileging irony over other effects, but I am drawing attention to it as a fundamental feature of the novel that undermines the stability of other interpretations. It does not obliterate these interpretations in order to dominate, but subtly undermines them, introducing a doubt about their unquestionable validity. It is in this sense that the novel is, to use Mikhail Bakhtin's terminology, dialogical and polyphonic. As readers of *Data*, we are placed in the awkward position of reading an incomplete archive of putatively authentic documents not as history but as literature, and to accept all the consequences that this involves for historical memory, among other matters.

## From Occupation to Civil War and from Dictatorship to PASOK[17] Populism in the 80s

Valtinos's treatment of the Colonels' regime in *Data* is, perhaps unexpectedly, more playfully parodic than bitterly ironic, at times verging on sarcastic humour. The day of the coup, for example, is alluded to through reference to a kitsch performance of a nationalistic play celebrating the uprising against Ottoman rule in 1821 (308). Two pages later a weather report concludes allegorically with a blood bath effected by a pack of wolves attacking a flock of sheep and a herd of cows (310). Much later, in another potentially allegorical narrative, a swarm of internally migrating bees is reported to have escaped from a 'bee-yard' before being caught by its next owner (379). One may wonder why the author of much fiercer criticisms of the Colonels' regime in the short stories 'The Plaster Cast' and 'Peppers in the Flowerpot'[18] should adopt such obfuscating tactics to refer to the principles and practices of the military dictatorship.[19] The censorship usually associated with the Colonels' dictatorship during the Sixties is almost entirely absent from the novel (cf. 331). Instead it features in a letter dated 29 March 1961 (45–6), where a Cinderella-like correspondent to Mina considers herself a competent writer of short stories but has her manuscripts torn up by members of her family.[20] One may also be puzzled by the almost equal emphasis in the novel on both the practices of the regime and its public support from individuals, institutions and groups of the population.[21]

On the grounds of this and other textual evidence[22] as well as some secondary proof,[23] it is reasonable to argue that in *Data* there is an implicit criticism of PASOK's populism during the 1980s. PASOK appropriated the Left's claims to the 1973 events while cultivating a wholesale repugnance for the conservative right.[24] *Data* treats the period of the military junta more as an exaggerated farce evoking the buffoonery of its supporters and less as a tragedy. It could be argued that it does the same for PASOK's populism. However, in a semiosis that appears to occur independently from Valtinos's public views on populism, the novel performs a criticism of what I will term here a 'belatedness theory' of recent Greek history.[25] This theory asserts that while democracy had been put on its proper course prior to 1965, the events of that year led to the Colonels' dictatorship delaying democracy's natural progress until 1974, or, as PASOK's populists would have it, until 1977 or 1981. In other words, the 'belatedness theory' formulates a historiographic plot which treats the period from 1965 to 1974 as an extraneous narrative or parenthesis in the development of Greek history and Greece's eventual return to the path of parliamentary democracy.[26] That this is not the case in *Data* is amply demonstrated by the author's choice of temporal frame of reference, which exceeds the limits of the title's decade. This more extended period is treated as an uneven historical 'continuum', a headless and tailless narrative, which is fraught with numerous interweaving plots—both personal and public—contradictions, nebulous causes and narrative irregularities. The implication is that personal or national histories are far more complex than any ordinary narrative can capture. This is almost certainly one of the messages communicated by the novel's fragmented form and often vertiginous semiosis. One may ask where the search for the origins of this essentially historical discontent leads the reader of the novel.

*Data* points at two sources which run parallel to its two levels, namely the social and the historical or the private and the public. They are a conservative traditionalism in Greek culture and the German Occupation and Greek civil war.[27] The instances of characters succumbing to cultural myths or prejudices are numerous in the novel,[28] as there are several documents alluding to physical or psychological violence somehow connected with the civil war.[29] The prospects of a village lad migrating internally to Athens, for example, (66) are a far more attractive proposition than the rural environment where an ear-biting shepherd in the Arcadia region attacks a fellow-villager (67). The reason for this attack is the dubious victory of ERE in what were widely believed to be the rigged elections in 1961.[30] The text alludes proleptically to the 1964 victory of George Papandreou's Centre Union party, creating a historical irony at the expense of the squabbling villagers, but also conjures up all the ensuing events that led to the Colonels' military coup of 1967. It could also be argued, however, that the text describing the feud also alludes to the civil war as the source of the villagers' violent behaviour.

The ideological character of this narrativization evokes the fact that the problems of migration, both internal and external, of violence and political conservatism have their roots in previous historical periods and not exclusively in the turbulent 1960s. However, a causal relationship between acts of violence in the time of the novel and in its historical past is not explicitly drawn in *Data*.[31] In numerous documents violence is shown to be a pattern of behaviour within the family, but it is impossible to ascertain whether these patterns are replicated from public life, or whether public life replicates them. Thus the novel displays a resistance to becoming an ideological narrative, asserting itself instead as a dialogical narrative, illustrating a disparity between the public and the private. One could argue, as I do tentatively here, that the underlying narrative in the novel is the desire of the individual to pursue the path towards self-knowledge, personal freedom and happiness and the incessant postponement of this pursuit by contesting narratives or ideologies both cultural and political. Perhaps the underlying cause of all evils, public and private, in *Data* is an oppressive conservatism in Greek culture and its emphasis on dowry, social status, prudishness, marriage and procreation with a view to pursuing what approximates the capitalist dream. Again the suggestion here is that public discourse does affect the personal, but that link must be made with extreme caution, because there is no guarantee that the causal relationship between the two operates in one direction only. In addition, there are several references in the novel to the Cold War climate internationally while a number of documents mention ideological confrontations occurring in different social strata and other parts of the world.[32] In this sense, *Data* appears to present an argument against both a 'belatedness theory' and a theory of Hellenic isolation vis-à-vis world developments in the post-war period and becomes more universal than a strictly Hellenocentric reading would permit.

*Data* acknowledges but places itself at arm's length from the dominant historical discourse and forms an invitation to the reader to construct out of an archive of evidence a narrative that is apparently not guided by the authority of a god-like narrator. This is supported by the author's own claim that the historical events of the period are in need of a necessary re-examination and review.[33] It would be misleading to conclude, however, that the novel itself is devoid of an authoritative figure that possesses some sort of an ideological agenda that is itself historically defined.

## Self-Referentiality and the Resistance to Ideology

It is generally understood that historiography possesses a higher degree of referentiality as compared with realistic historical fiction. In *Data*, the differences between the two discourses are collapsed in a very threatening way by being established in a relationship of chiasmus. The same holds for the characters of the novel. The names of actual individuals coexist with those of invented ones, the former contributing to the verisimilitude of the latter. However, the reverse effect also occurs. In the fictional context, naming transforms all the characters into something like ghostly figures from the past. The word *stoicheía* (data) of the title (in unaccented capitals) almost gets transformed into *stoicheiá* (=spirits, ghosts). It is obvious that the title can also be interpreted as an ironic reference to 'elements', 'data', 'proof' or 'details' of the decade. However, it could also be read self-referentially as 'written characters' which are not necessarily 'about' but 'dedicated to' (*gia*) the Sixties. This latter sense introduces a doubt about a purely historiographic nature of the novel. So, in my view, there is an undecidable ambiguity in the title that is analogous to the effects of irony in the novel.

The notion of origins, of a transcendental source or beginning that will explain everything, is questioned in *Data*. Every one of its documents is an imitation of a type of document and a type of discourse that not only represents but is also represented. Indeed the notion of the object and its image is one of the novel's sub-themes, and much of the suffering experienced by the characters can be attributed to the confusion of the image with the object itself.[34] Moreover, the examples of despondent women in the novel are numerous, and a cultural discourse of prudishness conflicting with a typically 1960s promiscuity is often the cause of this unhappiness.[35] There are numerous instances in the novel where allusions are made to Greek and European novels and films,[36] as there are also excerpts from novel-like biographies. Aesthetics too is presented as part of ideology.[37] So in many of the documents it is suggested that life's content, structure and form are based on discursive principles. As one desperate correspondent to Mina puts it: 'I shall accept your *logos* [word or discourse], whatever it may be' (12). All this points to the ability of certain discourses (political, cultural, artistic and media ones alike) to transform words into action on the basis of ideology. The issue is not only life's imitation of a mythified reality, but also the individual's objectification through ideology and the subsequent personification of this object. It is in this sense that the characters in the novel are personified identities and their discourse and behaviour are parodies representative of contesting cultural and political discourses.[38]

Valtinos himself has described *Data* as being 'as imaginary as reality itself',[39] implying that reality is perceived through a language that fictionalizes and that fictionalization constructs our reality, so much so that we cannot tell the difference between the real and its narrativized form. This renders the difference between narrative and reality extremely difficult to discern. If personal or historical memory cannot be non-discursive, it would appear that we are not equipped to decide whether narrative observes life or vice versa.

*Data* effects a metonymic search for the origins of personal and national hardship, but this search does not really end with the discovery of a confidently demonstrable source, unless that source is thought to be, generally, ideology and narrative. The novel is an allegory of the inconclusiveness of interpretation or the allegory of life and the interpretation of history as an open-ended project, subject to an infinite set of narrativizations, some more harrowing and harmful than others. The novel's artistic counter-traditionalism is therefore thematically related. The selective memory represented in the novel results in a potentially ideologically charged narrative, but what the arrangement of texts illustrates is that the correlations or tropological links that can be drawn between them are historically defined, yet always provisional. That my own reading leads potentially to an ideological misreading of *Data* is an unavoidable historical contingency. Irony in the novel is the artistic effect of the fragmented presentation of recontextualized facts whose details and nature ultimately do not allow us to make interpretive decisions that could be called either judicious or just. It is the antipode of fixed and stable meaning, whether this meaning is treated as literary, historical or ideological. Irony is also, in my view, the characteristic of the work's literariness and one of the means of resistance to its own ideological force. This puts Valtinos, to my mind at least, in the select group of genuinely post-modernist fiction writers in Greece.

## Notes to Chapter 10

1. *Stoicheia gia ti dekaetia tou '60* (1989; 2nd edn. 1992); all references are to the second and definitive edition. Documents featuring on the same page are designated as 'a' or 'b' after the page number. The novel was awarded the Greek State Literature Prize for Best Novel in 1990.

2. Shomit Dutta, 'A disunited nation—Thanassis Valtinos'.

3. See e.g. K. Tsoukalas, *I elliniki tragodia: apo tin apeleftherosi os tous syntagmatarches* (1981), 153–93; R. Clogg, *A Short History of Modern Greece*, 177–95; and David H. Close, *Greece since 1945*, 44–123.

4. 'The work of Valtinos could be described as a grotto or cave where the echoes do not cease to overlap or interfere with each other': Michel Grodent, 'La décennie de tous les dangers', 8 (my translation).

5. Spyros Tsaknias, 'I peripeteia enos laou. Thanassis Valtinos: *Stoicheia gia ti dekaetia tou '60*'.

6. R.M., 'Stoicheia gia ti dekaetia tou 60 tou Thanassi Valtinou', and N. G. Davettas, 'Ena mythistorima-psifidoto tou Thanassi Valtinou'.

7. Dutta, 'Disunited nation'.

8. With the possible exception of Nikos Kasdaglis. See his 'Thanassis Valtinos'.

9. Dimitris Angelatos, *Logodeipnon*, 112. See also Pavlos Zannas, 'Tainies kai fototypies tou Thanassi Valtinou. Scholia sta *Stoicheia gia ti dekaetia tou '60*', in id., *Petrokalamithres*, 502.

10. Yorgos Aristinos, 'Me aformi tin periptosi tou Thanassi Valtinou', in id., *Dokimia gia to mythistorima kai ta logotechnika eidi*, 59.

11. With the notable exception of the letters on pp. 199, 205 and 207 which also form an inconclusive dialogue.

12. Two commentators have suggested that the novel also comments on the time of its publication. See E. Kotzia, 'Sti dekaetia tou 60', 24, and Kriton Chourmouziadis, review, 38–9.

13. Paul de Man, 'The concept of irony', in id., *Aesthetic Ideology*, 170. See also Hayden White, *Metahistory*, 37–8.

14. See pp. 147, 198.

15. The 'Varkiza Agreement' was signed in 1945 after the defeat of the Left in the so-called December events in Athens in the previous year. One of its main aims was the disarmament of ELAS, the military arm of the resistance organization EAM, set up under the leadership of the Greek Communist Party during the German Occupation. Lavrion alludes to the miners' strikes in 1896, which led to violent confrontations between miners and gendarmes.

16. R. Barthes, *The Pleasure of the Text*, 28–9.

17. PASOK is an abbreviation for the Panhellenic Socialist Party founded by Andreas Papandreou in 1974, which came to power in 1981.

18. Both stories are contained in the collection *Tha vreite ta osta mou ypo vrochin* (1992).

19. The 'Tarzan' excerpt (pp. 370–1) alluding to escapism and fantasy during the junta illustrates ironically that the *homme sauvage* uses logic to persuade an army general not to use violence against native tribes.

20. See also p. 356, where listening to the radio is forbidden to a young girl.

21. See pp. 359 and 360, 314 and 375, 335 and 366, and the tripartite, almost sarcastically sequenced, public requests for punishment of A. Panagoulis and S. Karagiorgas by professional associations (pp. 349, 374 and 379).
22. The novel contains a document on p. 218 mentioning the ASPIDA conspiracy along with a clandestine reference to Andreas Papandreou's suspected involvement in it. On ASPIDA see e.g. Tsoukalas, *Elliniki tragodia*, 176–7, 185–8.
23. Valtinos criticized PASOK's populism in three different interviews during the 80s. See Kostis Liontis, 'Ef' olis tis ylis'; Vangelis Raptopoulos, 'O Thanassis Valtinos milaei me ton Vangeli Raptopoulo'; and Katerina Schina, 'Zoume se mia epochi ekptosis ton panton'. In the last interview it is stated that Valtinos was amongst the 154 individuals who signed a petition against the PASOK government in 1989, almost replicating the gesture of the 18 in their 1970 declaration against the Colonels' censorship. Valtinos also mentions acts of censorship by PASOK followers.
24. Angelos Elefantis, in his vehement criticism of A. Papandreou's populism, claims that: 'The masses that turned towards PASOK as early as 1974 were not socialists in their ideology—unless one accepts as socialist the amalgam of populism, anti-Europeanism, antigovernmentalism, third-worldism, antijuntism, anti-Americanism, antidictatorism' ('Episis se o,ti afora tin oikonomiki domi eimaste sosialistes', 14).
25. See e.g. Elefantis's articulation of the 'belatedness theory', ibid. 10–11. The early Tsoukalas also describes aspects of the period in terms of a delay in the building of a democratic edifice (*Elliniki tragodia*, 178–9). See also Giorgos Margaritis, *Istoria tou Ellinikou Emfyliou Polemou 1946–1949*, i. 25, 26 and 29, and Angelos Elefantis, 'I "allagi" teleiose, zito i allagi', 15.
26. Elefantis describes the period between 1981 and 1989 as a continuation of the Greek historical tragedy initiated by the dictatorship and as a continuation of the country's deviation from the path to 'true democracy' since the equally tragic denouement of the Greek civil war (Angelos Elefantis, 'Ston asterismo tou laikismou', 35–6).
27. The latter was to be the topic of Valtinos's next 'affront' to the dominant ideologies and singular emplotments of Greek history during the 1980s and 1990s, in his novel *Orthokosta* (1994).
28. See the document on p. 13, the letters on pp. 40–1, 64, 77, 92, 163, 169–70, 176–7, 195–7, 209, 222, 232, 239, 249, 253, 274–5, 319–21 and 355–7, and the classifieds on pp. 30, 81, 87, 260 and 376.
29. See e.g. pp. 20, 25–7, 76, 103, 175, 198, 204b, 221b, 231, 257, 333a, 343–5 and 359–60.
30. Clogg, *Short History*, 178. ERE (National Radical Union) was the right-wing party led by Constantine Karamanlis. ERE was in power from 1955 to 1963.
31. The two documents that allude to a link between the two are connected with accidental explosions (pp. 20 and 366).
32. See e.g. pp. 62–3, pp. 85 and 91, pp. 150 and 338, pp. 94 and 393, p. 103 and pp. 132–3.
33. See e.g. Vangelis Hatzivassiliou, 'Thanassis Valtinos', 6.
34. See pp. 42–3, 82–4, 219 and 283.
35. See pp. 31–4, 49–50, 53–9, 62, 143–5, 182–4, 194a, 201–3, 214–16, 237, 254, 263, 270–3, 289–91, 292a, 301, 311–13, 354, 377–8 and 387.

36. See e.g. the allusion to Valtinos's own *Synaxari Antrea Kordopati: Ameriki* (1972; p. 22), to Melville's *Moby Dick* (p. 80), to Alexandros Papadiamantis's *I fonissa* (1903; pp. 250–1) and to the basic story line of Theo Angelopoulos's non-sequential film *Anaparastasi* [*Reconstruction*] (p. 292). Also pp. 39 and 358a.

37. See e.g. pp. 69, 85, 180b and 187.

38. See Elefantis's definition of populism: 'Populism [...] is the image that some people outside it [the 'people'] give it so that it can see itself [...]. Within populism the people must forget itself and come to resemble its distorted image, to imitate it. Just think of Andreas Papandreou dancing the *zeybekiko*' (Elefantis, 'Ston asterismo tou laikismou', 36).

39. Tina Politi, 'Dyo Ellines gia ta Nobel Evropis', 95.

# PART 5

❖

# New Treatments of Old Themes

# CHAPTER 11

❖

# The Portrait of the Artist in the Late Twentieth Century

*Angela Kastrinaki*

One of the most distinctive features of Greek fiction at the close of the twentieth century is the sudden proliferation of artists as the heroes of novels. Painters, poets, writers and musicians jostle for space on the pages of novels. This is an entirely new phenomenon of altogether cataclysmic proportions. Until recently one had to search painstakingly in the hope of finding some representative from the world of art among the peasants, petty-bourgeois and hobos that populated Greek fiction. Yet recently, over the past three or four years, the tide has turned: it is now difficult to find a novel that does not feature artists or at least intellectuals among its central heroes. Indeed, the hero's status as an artist is often his main trait—so much so that we can say the novel's theme concerns speculation about art itself.

The phenomenon in question had its beginnings around 1990. Before that, there were only a few *Bildungsromane*, and even fewer novels about artists. What is more, such works were among the least successful ever written by their authors, beginning with *Yperanthropos* [*Übermensch*] (1915) by Konstantinos Chatzopoulos and ending with *Six Nights on the Acropolis* (1974) by George Seferis, works in which their creators more or less settled scores with true-life contemporaries in the art world.

Yet all of a sudden everything has changed, not merely in terms of quantity, but also with regard to the way in which the hero is portrayed. The negative stereotype has given way to a positive one—black has become white. One does not have to go very far back in time to find an utterly negative caricature of the artist in Greek fiction: in 1985 Kapandais, the protagonist of *The Fantastic Adventure* by Alexandros Kotzias, gave a triumphant centre-stage performance as the epitome of the ridiculous hero. Kotzias's artist is a mere nobody in artistic terms, but he is also a traitor to friendship, an opportunist and a liar, and, ultimately, a peacock and a self-congratulatory waste of space, yet one who sweeps the board of all the prizes and honours offered by the Greek state. Exactly the same is true of the hero in Kostas Chatziargyris's novel *Road to Glory* (1958): he is a novelist who sells out his art so as to embrace the general public, money and fame. Through a series of manoeuvres he gains positions of high office granted by the state, which is of course in the habit of conferring honours on those least worthy of them.[1]

In Kotzias and Chatziargyris, truly worthy people are marginal figures both in life and in the pages of the narrative. They are presented as foils, occupying minimal yet ideologically significant space. In *Road to Glory* the worthy artist is another novelist who chooses to sell lemons to make a living, while printing his works on a duplicating machine so as to make no concessions to popular taste. In *The Fantastic Adventure* the positive counterpart of the protagonist bears the real author's name, Alexandros Kotzias: he is an unassuming author full of doubts about his work, in stark contrast to Alexandros Kapandais, the self-congratulatory nobody.[2]

Both works lash out at public figures and institutions. Chatziargyris attacks writers and critics of the 'Generation of 1930',[3] along with their institutions, such as the Academy of Athens. Kotzias lashes out by name at well-known university professors, the radio, the Academy of Athens and state prizes. 'As for the sum total of the University—a few personal exceptions don't save it—I couldn't give a shit for it',[4] concludes the fictional Alexandros Kotzias, having denounced almost all official institutions. It is obvious that both authors feel brushed aside by the state apparatus and its official systems of recognition.[5] Yet *The Fantastic Adventure* went on to win the First State Prize for the Novel in 1986, a fact which to my mind has a great deal to do with the change in the course of things over the following years. First, there is the increasingly important role played by artists in modern social institutions, together with the proliferation of awards conferred by these same institutions—in other words, their participation in the contest for power. Added to this is the proliferation of universities and, consequently, greater access to them. All of these factors have contributed to the transformation of the accusatory narrative into its exact opposite.

The exact opposite is the narrative of self-praise. Perhaps the best example of this is Menis Koumandareas's novel *Twice Greek* (2001). In this case the hero is an altogether positive figure, an acclaimed author, hugely popular with young people, who are mad keen to get close to him:

'You know, they read you, they would be delighted if...'
'If what?'
'If they could get to know you at first hand.'
'Aren't they afraid of being disappointed?'
'Don't say that. You're not that kind of person. We think of you as one of us.'[6]

The author is quite clearly pleased with himself and his popularity, and makes no secret of it. If the novel does contain some criticism of social institutions, and of the universities in particular, by this stage it is a pale reflection of the past. Almost the same is true in Petros Abatzoglou's novel *In the Silence of Love* (1997), except that in his case self-praise is filtered through humour. Whatever the case may be, here again young people are presented as reading Abatzoglou and holding him in high regard, while the self-acclaim is vindicated on the theoretical level through the reflections of the young protagonist, who is a novelist:

But I differ from ordinary people, because I am compelled and fated to admire my work, to argue that it is worthwhile, in the face of all those who ignore or slight it. Have you any idea how very hard you have to work at admiring yourself, especially when you're no fool, and how difficult it is to try and keep some measure of control?[7]

Apart from the humour, we see here an entirely new sense of ease, an exoneration of the status of artist exuded by the text. The self-adulatory stance we saw portrayed as reprehensible in Kotzias has now become acceptable, albeit within the limits of self-awareness.

Throughout the 1990s, positive artist heroes have become the rule. Apart from the examples mentioned above, Rhea Galanaki's Eleni Altamura, Alexis Panselinos's Andreas Roilos and the young author in Kostas Kontodimos's humorous narrative entitled *The Author and the Cover* (1991) are just a few examples of engaging or admirable protagonists.[8]

When true-life historical individuals lie behind these fictional characters, and we know the details of their lives, in some cases we can talk of idealization. In *Eleni, or Nobody* (1998), Rhea Galanaki makes a very likeable woman of Eleni Boukoura; the slightest hint that, for example, at the time of her marriage to Saverio Altamura she was an unpleasantly dreary partner appears in the pages of the novel only to be refuted as the opinion of a man who cannot understand another person's character. Here we might also take the idealization of the book's cover into account: Eleni, depicted on the front cover dressed as a young man, has been drastically altered when compared with the somewhat ugly original persona.[9]

The same can be said of Alexis Panselinos's Roilos in *Zaida, or The Camel in the Snow* (1996), who is to a great extent a mask for the poet Dionysios Solomos. The protagonist is graced with the rarest of attributes: a noble, radiant, almost divine countenance,[10] a keen eye for politics, a revolutionary conscience and even a subversive attitude towards social hierarchy. As for his erotic misdemeanours, they are depicted with the utmost delicacy and are moreover absolved by the monk who keeps him company for a while. Panselinos's other artist-hero, the mask for Mozart, is also engaging, though slightly inferior on account of being a 'Westerner': for all his wantonness and sadistic tendencies, he is vindicated both as an artist and as a human being. Furthermore, even the artist in Takis Theodoropoulos's *The Unimaginable Landscape* (1991), despite his association with the Colonels' junta, is at bottom presented as another positive figure.[11]

The trend is obvious: if authors tended at one time to present a negative caricature of themselves, they now tend to present an entirely positive one, a protagonist behind whose guise readers can trace the writer him- or herself.

That said, authors still abstain from autobiographical writing in the narrower sense of the term. With the possible exception of Yannis Kiourtsakis, who in *Like a Novel* (1995) attempts an in-depth investigation of how his ideas are formed (yet not exactly of his literary incarnation), all other authors prefer to project their status as artists onto an objective veneer. This has everything to do with a time-honoured Greek prohibition. 'Not—in God's name—a pretext for autobiography', wrote Angelos Terzakis in 1945, in the foreword to his nonetheless autobiographical short-story collection entitled *April*.[12] Rhea Galanaki was to repeat the same idea in gentler terms in 1998, through her heroine: 'I have not striven to put my life down in writing, so as to justify my actions on that pretext.'[13]

So it is that autobiography remains a proscribed genre in Greece. Why is this? It is, among other things, because the weight of what is collective, a poorly developed culture of the ego and a vacillating bourgeois consciousness continue to define the artistic scene.[14] And despite the waning of the collective and the waxing of individualism over the last few years, tendencies have not been overturned altogether. The presence of the artist as hero signals the release of egotistical forces, yet at the same time inhibition in the face of true autobiography remains, like some powerful vestige of the past.

By contrast, we can perceive the insistent presence of history in Greek narrative, above all in that written by the older generation of prose writers. Thus Koumandareas makes his hero Angelos Angelidis about five years older than himself, so as to enable him to experience history in the form of political exile on the island of Makronisos during and after the Civil War in the 1940s. So it is that this plainly autobiographical hero is endowed with a few crucial years of Greek history and with a characteristic gravity greater than that of his creator.

For her part, Rhea Galanaki stresses the relationship between her heroine and the Greek Revolution of 1821 to the greatest possible extent. The novel states that Eleni (a real historical figure) became an artist thanks to the revolution, having been born—by pure chance, of course—in that crucial year. The revolution and Eleni's secret spiritual relationship with the war heroine Bouboulina (who came from the same island of Spetses) teach her the love of freedom, a prerequisite for artistic creation. Panselinos involves Solomos-Roilos in various historical and political adventures, though not in the revolution of 1821. In *The Wedding Present* (1995), a novella about the liberation of a woman from the stagnation of married life towards the creativity of art, Victoria Theodorou deems it appropriate to root the narrative in recent history by beginning it in the prisons and exile of the post-Civil War period.[15]

In this regard, authors at the very end of the twentieth century do not differ in essence from their predecessors—from Yorgos Theotokas, when he invested *Leonis* (1940) with the historical weight of the First World War, to Kotzias, who covered the entire length of Greek history from the German Occupation onwards so as to talk about the artist.

This presence of history is of course a collective counterbalance to the individualistic subject of the artist. In the authors' consciousness, the egotistical novel with leanings towards autobiography should be countered by a sufficient quantity of situations that surpass the individual and embrace the collective. Yet all of this ceases to apply to younger writers: Amanda Michalopoulou, Alexis Stamatis, Nikos

Panayotopoulos, and even Evgenia Fakinou, who is fifteen to twenty years their senior, no longer think of how to link their heroes to history. Indeed, history ultimately appears almost as a parody, in the form of a political demonstration, in Abatzoglou's *Silence of Love*, a tale almost exclusively of love and art set in the present. Yet at the very last moment, the author introduces a political demonstration at which the heroes' paths cross, as a final obstacle before they are united for the last time. By this stage history has degenerated into a weary demonstration with worn-out slogans, or a backdrop for a lovers' tryst: 'They reached the park and sat down on a bench, to the left and right of the revolutionary heroes of 1821. Busts and heads, without arms, body or legs' (232). The heroes of 1821 are mere disembodied statues and the demonstrations the tattered remains of past struggles. This may provoke a degree of sadness, yet is at the same time liberating. The status of the artist no longer requires politics or history as an alibi; it now appears to have gained its independence, brimming with buoyant and playful confidence.

At the same time, we come across another type of aggressive use of history in Takis Theodoropoulos's novel *The Unimaginable Landscape*. The author has his hero participate in history, going as far as to embroil him in one of the most unpleasant episodes in recent times— the dictatorship of the military junta in 1967–74. The author does this so as to illustrate precisely how insignificant politics and history are when compared to art, given that the latter is great. The fictional biographer of the hero (an artist who collaborated with the junta) is attracted by the idea of provoking those around him by elevating the artist's stature, at the expense of those who reject him on account of his political judgement.[16]

In the works of some more recent authors, history has given way to contemporaneity, their heroes being caught up in journeys the length and breadth of Europe. In other cases, a curious substitution is made: it is not history but freak weather conditions that give rise to action and reaction in the novel. Thus stifling heat features in *The Sleep-Walker* (1985) by Margarita Karapanou and flash flooding in the height of summer in *Filthy Weather* (2000) by Amanda Michalopoulou. As the latter aptly puts it in her novel: 'Freak weather conditions are the moral equivalent of war. Of a symbolic war, without casualties.'[17] The only objection here is that if history was a collective counterbalance, floods and heat-waves are nothing more than substitutes for underdeveloped introversion.

In a highly typical way, both of the above novels are set on an island. Almost half a century ago, Stratis Tsirkas set the action of his short story 'For a Pair of Roses' (1947) on an island so as to illustrate the deplorable distance kept by the painter-hero from politics and history.[18] Now that politics and history are absent, authors place their artistic communities on islands as a matter of course. What once symbolized a reprehensible tendency towards isolationism ('insularity'!) is now triumphant autonomy.

Taken as a class, artists really have won their autonomy; they have formed themselves into a self-contained entity with its own attributes and have attained the critical mass necessary for becoming a suitable subject for *ithografia* (the realistic presentation of traditional Greek life), as peasants and the petty bourgeoisie once were. If we compare the novels written in the year 2000 and set on an island with their predecessor, *The Sleep-Walker*, we can detect an important change in the identity of the artists; in *The Sleep-Walker*, the artists were almost exclusively foreigners, whereas in present-day novels Greeks are clearly in the majority. The correlation with social reality is plain to see; the growth of the artistic class in Greece over the last few years has resulted in their being represented in the world of fictional heroes.

Let us now move on and look at how present-day works deal with the theme, or rather dilemma, which is as old as the novel on artists itself: the dilemma between art and life. Is it worth the artist's while to sacrifice his or her life, relationships with others, and love for the sake of art? Or is life itself, in all its various manifestations, whether as love, childbearing or even as a social or national struggle, ultimately placed above all other values, even for creators, that special category of people?

Both the question and the answer to it are often explicitly expressed in Greek novels, while in a number of cases they can be inferred from what unfolds in the narrative. Alexis Panselinos gives us an explicit, categorical answer: 'Anyone who puts art in the place of life commits the same sin as someone who forgets people in the name of God,' says Roilos-Solomos (456), and the author with him. Indeed, in *Zaida*, works of art really are presented as the means for achieving ends that clearly surpass aesthetics. The liberation of a woman from a dark dungeon, or of Greece from slavery, are the goals that make irresolute artists rediscover their artistic inspiration.

Abatzoglou also appears to say the same thing, in a mild manner and without the weighty intellectual baggage carried by Panselinos; according to him, books are there to help us in life and love.[19] On the other hand, Faidon Tamvakakis's hero in *The Landscapes of Philomela* (1988) prefers to live 'above the incomprehensible land of Philomela' inhabited by the gifted young pianist, since when all is said and done it is absurd 'to talk to your lover instead of giving her a thousand kisses'.[20]

Yet in Rhea Galanaki's work matters are more complicated. The beginning of the novel comes out reasonably clearly in favour of acquiring art, even if this involves loss of erotic identity; Eleni becomes 'Nobody' and renounces her body in order to become an artist. The fact that she identifies with Bouboulina, who fought for the liberation of Greece just as she struggles to free herself from the limitations of her gender, shows how much the author has invested in the value of the struggle for art, a struggle definitely worth some sacrifices, including the renunciation of the body. All the same, the end of the novel turns these views on their head; Chapter Omega excludes 'a woman's love' which 'lives what is dead alongside what is living'. And with the phrase 'this love is the only resurrection granted' as a concluding observation, the author in essence rejects the 'immortality' provided by art. As far as the contrast between life and art is concerned, the scales are now quite categorically tipped in favour of life, love and survival through the memory of others rather than through a work of art.

A similar vacillation between life and art is also to be found in Victoria Theodorou's novella *The Wedding Present*. In this case the heroine escapes from the conventionality of married life and isolates herself in a house near the sea (almost on an island). She does this so as to create: 'that too is a kind of immortality', as she says (95). Immediately afterwards she rejects this immortality in favour of human contact: 'Love, at the end of the day, is the perpetuation of "living selves". It is worth more than posthumous fame' (102). This unexplained volte-face, ending precisely where love is, just as in Galanaki, is not illustrative of an equilibrium or a new synthesis of art and life, but rather of ambivalence.

To a great extent Evgenia Fakinou also appears to side with art in *Blind-Man's Buff* (1999). Her artist Simos, a mild version of Van Gogh with self-destructive tendencies when he cannot paint, torments his wife with a string of affairs that supply him with the necessary creative impulse. The fact that his good wife accepts his immoderate character and acquiesces to his peculiar rights as an artist is at the very least a partial recognition of the rights of art over life.

When compared with Panselinos's categorical bid in favour of 'life', also advocated by the other two male authors, the three women writers appear highly ambivalent. Could this view perhaps be peculiar to women? Such a hypothesis seems logical enough; it stands to reason that precisely those people who have to struggle to gain a particular status and position should appreciate it more. While the status of the artist is taken for granted by men, for women it remains ground to be gained.

What is more, the work of fiction most heavily influenced by aesthetics in the past few years was the product of someone who had suffered repression, not on account of his gender, but because of his involvement in politics. In his 1976 story 'Murder by Isabella Molnar', Dimitris Hatzis was to vindicate a woman artist who murdered her husband when she saw herself losing her art on account of the good life she had attained within her marriage. Hatzis extols this state of affairs as a 'profound object lesson', a 'symbol of devotion, con- scientiousness and responsibility'.[21] Such a view of art could not come into being in any other way than as an outburst following severe repression. And so it was: Hatzis had only just returned to Greece from exile in Hungary and was finally in a position to overturn the dogmas (chiefly socialist realism) that had repressed him for so many years.

It thus appears that aesthetic tendencies, which have been very limited over the last few years, find fertile ground among those most repressed; the value of art is more emphatically promoted precisely in places where artistic power labours hardest to find expression. That said, Amanda Michalopoulou, a contemporary woman author born at least twenty years after Galanaki, Theodorou and Fakinou, argues just as categorically as the men in favour of promoting life over art.[22] At least from a feminist point of view, this most probably represents a consolatory levelling of the playing-field; the right to artistic creativity is ground that has now been won by modern women.

Last of all, one feature highly characteristic of the major difference that has arisen between novels written over the past few years and those of the past is the denouement. In the few post-war texts featuring artists as heroes, the denouement involved the death of the artist, and a dramatic and painful death at that. In Stratis Tsirkas's short story 'For a Pair of Roses' (1947), the artist was to choose suicide in despair over his inability to create. In M. Karagatsis's novel *The Yellow File* (1965), the novelist suffered a violent death at the hand of a murderer. Hatzis led his heroine to madness and death, and Kotzias led his hero to a massive heart attack. Chatziargyris may not have chosen death, but he did inflict upon his hero terrible nightmares of impending death. In contrast, heroes of the last few years do not die. They live on and continue to create, whether more or less satisfied with their life and art.

We do have two exceptions, both of which would seem to prove the rule: Yorgos Galanos, the artist in Takis Theodoropoulos's *The Unimaginable Landscape*, who dies of cancer, and Koumandareas's hero Angelos Angelidis. The cancer suffered by the former is the last violent death of an artist in Modern Greek fiction. The fact that the hero collaborated with the military junta—albeit ingenuously—may well justify his end. On the other hand, Angelidis's death is more like a peaceful sleep than death, a painless extirpation constituting an intermediary link between the violent deaths of former times and the unimpeded survival of present-day heroes.

Murderous intentions directed against artists occasionally appear in contemporary works, yet only so as to be ridiculed. In Evgenia Fakinou's *Blind-Man's Buff* the hero is so unbearable in his private life that his wife, together with his housekeeper, who is also in love with him, considers murdering him for his string of affairs. This idea is nevertheless rejected; the entire conversation between the two women sounds to the reader like nothing more than a parody of talk about death.[23] The artist is destined to live on, enjoying wife and lovers while applying himself to the noble struggle for his art. The novel's closing scene has him talking to his wife and housekeeper about their favourite kinds of food.

In contrast to the fatal denouement of earlier works, novels of the 1990s feature two cases of resurrection from the dead. While Rhea Galanaki narrates the death of her heroine, in the final chapter she offers her a kind of resurrection on Easter Sunday, when—perhaps as a spirit—Eleni appears at her relatives' Paschal feast. A kind of resurrection also features in Panselinos's novel; he depicts Mozart's death as a carefully fabricated manoeuvre so as to allow the high-spirited composer to dispense with his former identity and continue his life on new terms. In other words, though Mozart died in 1791, Panselinos extends his fictional life by several years, so as to lead him on to new adventures and discoveries. In leaving him alive at the end of the novel, the author grants him a kind of continuity in the future.

What was once violent death has thus given way to the uninterrupted continuation of life or to resurrection. Yet death is punishment, whether inflicted by others or by oneself. The problematic artists of the post-war world are punished for their arrogance, for their mistaken choices or for their ill-deserved glory. At times they may be punished for epitomizing aspects of their creator which he or she does not dare to legitimize, in which case we are dealing with self-inflicted punishment.[24] But there is no reason for today's artists to be punished. Whether more or less perfect, they achieve either immortality or, at the very least, a place in our everyday lives.

## Notes to Chapter 11

1. The similarity between the two heroes was observed by I. K. Papadimitrako-poulos, 'Kostas Chatziargyris: parousiasi-anthologisi', 135.
2. Alexandros Kotzias, *Fantastiki peripeteia* (1985), 136–43.
3. The Generation of 1930 was a group of Greek writers, artists and critcs, including the poet and essayist George Seferis, who first came to prominence in the 1930s. Their mildly modernist aesthetic influenced Greek literature and art until the late 20th c.
4. Ibid. 43.
5. Cf. the way in which Kotzias described the status of the author in Greece in 1986: 'The social status of authors here is zero. Unless they are "someone" in some other profession, unless they have other "resources" in their life—either from inheritance or dowry—authors are "nothing", they are totally marginal': interview with Vena Georgakopoulou, *I Aristera simera* 15 (Jan.–Feb. 1986), 59.
6. Menis Koumandareas, *Dyo fores Ellinas* (2001), 663.
7. Petros Abatzoglou, *Sti siopi tou erota* (1997), 84.
8. Rhea Galanaki, *Eleni, i o Kanenas* (1998), Alexis Panselinos, *Zaida, i i kamila sta chionia* (1996), Kostas Kontodimos, *O syngrafeas kai to exofyllo* (1991).
9. A photograph of the artist can be seen in the biography of her by Athina Tarsouli, *Eleni Altamoura* (1934), as well as in the periodical *O Politis* 42 (Nov. 1997), 32.
10. Roilos is described by Chrysostomos (Mozart) as follows: 'the other man's [Roilos's] high forehead and shock of hair, which stood out like a halo around his noble, radiant face, with its gentle eyes and austere mouth. Had he seen him before? Or was he remembering some picture, some painting, or perhaps some statue? "A god", he thought.' (Panselinos, *Zaida*, 186–7).
11. See the closing phrase in Takis Theodoropoulos's novel: 'Yet the die was cast. And the author [the artist's biographer] could not ignore the fact that all the same, the *Unimaginable Landscape* had existed and still did so—the impression of this indescribable painting, which for better or worse, or at least naïvely, constituted the hallmark of authenticity in its own right' (*To adianoito topio* (1991), 278). Thus, despite certain reservations, what remains as the highest possible praise is 'authenticity'.
12. Angelos Terzakis, *Aprilis* (Athens: Oi filoi tou vivliou, 1946), 9.
13. Galanaki, *Eleni*, 172.
14. Angela Kastrinaki, 'Nearoi kallitechnes stin elliniki pezografia'.
15. Victoria Theodorou, *Gamilio doro* (1995), written 1984–5.

16. Theodoropoulos, *Unimaginable Landscape*, 231–2.
17. Amanda Michalopoulou, *Paliokairos* (2001), 287.
18. Stratis Tsirkas, 'Gia 'na zevgari roda', in *Diigimata* (1978), 268–77 [written in 1947 and first published in the collection entitled *O ypnos tou theristi* (1954)].
19. The following exchange takes place between the young author Michalis Zakynthinos and the (fictional) Abatzoglou in the Kedros publishing office: '"I have read you," Michalis said, "and actually, you were the pretext for my getting to know a girl." "How did that happen?" "I was waiting for a friend in the café at the French Institute and a girl at the table next to me was reading *Strange and Terrible Things*. I'm rather ashamed to say so, but because I had read and liked it, I used it to get into conversation with her. I really liked the girl too, you see." "There's nothing wrong in that", Abatzoglou said. "As a matter of fact, I also write books to get into conversation with strangers"' (Abatzoglou, *Sti siopi tou erota*, 198–9).
20. Faidon Tamvakakis, *Ta topia tis Filomilas* (1988), 221, 223.
21. Dimitris Hatzis, 'To foniko tis Izabelas Molnar', in *Spoudes* (1976), 56.
22. See the conversation between Victoria, the heroine, and Otto, in Michalopoulou, *Paliokairos*, 340–1.
23. '"What if we didn't give him any food, only water?" "How long for? Two or three days. Longer's not right. It's punishment we're after, not a crime." The word was said by chance, not consciously, but its weight made them silent. Anna saw a corpse lying in the atelier, a corpse with a knife sticking out of its chest, a corpse they didn't know what to do with' (Evgenia Fakinou, *Tyflomyga* (2000), 282–5).
24. In my view this applies to Manos Tasakos in Karagatsis's *O kitrinos fakelos* (1956) and to Isabella in Hatzis's 'To foniko tis Izabelas Molnar'. The second case is more complex, since the sculptress's death is both a 'punishment' for having murdered and a 'beatification', given that she is represented as a 'martyr' for art.

❖

# CHAPTER 12

# Angels in the Storm:
# The Portrait of the Woman Writer
# in Three Contemporary Novels
# by Women

*Argiro Mantoglou*

Simone de Beauvoir's renowned saying that 'one is not born a woman but rather becomes one', implies a more complicated 'becoming', as far as the formation of the woman writer is concerned. Such a formation signifies a shift towards a more complex transformation: the process of becoming involves a number of exclusions for this woman, and her writing marks a new type that includes new notions of female subjectivity, as well as new ways of expression—ways that usually, among other properties, tend to subvert the traditional stereotypes, even if this is not the main aim. Attempting to shed some light on the complex process through which the female writer is formed, we come up with an issue that concerns not only the biological formation of the body and its cultural connotations but also the way a woman expresses herself. However, psychoanalysis has revealed that we cannot be preoccupied with the body as such, but rather as something that precedes and then enters the field of language.

In any case, the transformation of a woman into a writer becomes more complicated because the task of a 'true' writer implies assertion, whereas a 'true' woman has traditionally implied submission. Through a series of practices, the heroines of the novels that will be discussed here break through the tradition that has shaped the discourse they are using, together with the models of femininity that have depicted them as culturally and intellectually inferior, or even as products of male desire. The writers offer new modes of representation, often celebrating femininity as a position in which new subversive texts can be produced. They offer new ways of 'escaping' traditional femininity, although their narrative practices signify that the process of rupture often coincides with the affirmation of the old dichotomies and prejudices. At the same time, new inventions and new forms of ignorance are revealed that go hand in hand with the radical ways of coping with the fragmented self as well as the otherness within or outside the self.

## The Unwritten Page

In the novels discussed here, one can find alternative depictions of the woman writer, that is portraits that embody some of the key issues of the genesis, transformation and assertion of the writing subject, a subject that reveals the numerous and divergent tropes of writing as a woman in the male-orientated and patriarchal culture of Greece. These depictions take various forms: there is the young girl Nina in Ersi Sotiropoulou's prize-winning novel *Zig-Zag through the Orange Trees* (1999), who wants to rearrange the world around her and finds a radical way to express and describe her impulses and impressions; there is Sofia Mahtou in Maria Gavala's novel *In the Dew of my Gardens* (2001), who is a woman writer trying to come to terms with the traumatic experiences of her past by writing a novel entitled 'The Woman Bled'; in this novel-within-a-novel the creation of the writer is viewed as a way of coping with a disturbed and feminine sexuality, her trauma being turned into a point of departure for artistic creation; finally, there is Victoria Louka, the heroine of the latest novel by Amanda Michalopoulou, *Filthy Weather*, who is depicted as a thief, a mimic and a travesty of femininity. Two of the central themes of the book are her promotion from poet (subjective) to novelist (objective) and her relation with other writers, mainly with writers from another tradition; writing here is presented as a performance produced through her interaction with her male and female predecessors.

In these three different approaches to the issue of female writing, the entrance of a woman into writing, the 'attempt of the pen', to use Susan Gubar's expression, is depicted as problematic. The transformation of their experiences into words seems to be closely related to their experience of becoming unified subjects as well as to their sexuality, which is revealed particularly in the act of naming, which has been a male prerogative. Experiencing her gender as a 'painful obstacle', the woman writer inscribes her own sickness, bleeding, paralysis, agoraphobia, or the fear of otherness in her texts.

There are certain and distinctive features in these texts. First, there is a general feeling of discomfort about being a woman writer: one of the main characteristics of all the heroines in the novels under examination is the fact that they are depicted as victims of a system of conventions, even when they are trying to subvert this very system through revision, appropriation or incorporation. This attempt at subversion constitutes the main issue of these books, although it becomes more than obvious that the female talent and preoccupation with writing translates sexual difference into difference in the plot and narrative voice, which is not assertive, but mainly personal and confessional. On the other hand, despite their painful experiences, women are not depicted as passive victims of male desire; rather, in their own idiosyncratic way, they appear powerful and more complex entities than their male counterparts in male-oriented novels. They are presented as women in search of a truth, even if their texts are written to appropriate their difference which has been silenced through the centuries. Since there is no alternative discourse, the woman writer has to describe her disaffection either through deliberate mimicry, imitation or even parody, and these practices lead to innumerable alternatives. Using the politics of parody to undermine the discourse as well as subversive narrative strategies, the metaphors of female desire focus on depictions of the woman as a figure in resistance, who is learning to use new tools other than those that have been used by her male predecessors.

Second, silence is a central theme and a recurrent motif in women's writings: while male writers explore their creative dilemmas through the trope of conquering the blank page, female authors explore them in order to expose how women have symbolically been identified with this blank page, have been defined by patriarchy as being a *tabula rasa*, a lack, a negation, an absence. Susan Gubar's study of the sexual metaphors involved in the literary creativity in her essay entitled 'The blank page' documents the association of the female body with the 'empty page' that awaits the male author's pen and the impact of this association on the female imagination.[1] By keeping all this in mind, we can find a recurrent imagery of confinement, alienation, and typical metaphors that involve bodily transformation, lack, absence and a sense of loss, as well as a strong awareness of their gender, sexuality and physicality which have been subjected to deformation. The scar is the metaphor used by the French writer Hélène Cixous in her writing: 'The wound is what I sense. The wound is a strange thing: either I die, or a kind of work takes place, mysterious, that will reassemble the edges of the wound. The wound is also an alteration [...] and there is also a scar. I like the scar, the story.'[2]

Finally, another central feature of female creativity is the eccentric ways through which women experience their creativity; this is mainly inspired after an injury of the female body. The inspiration of Gavala's heroine, Sofia, starts after excessive bleeding, while for Sotiropoulou's Nina creation starts after a deliberate mark on her body (she carves a cross on her knee), and for Michalopoulou's Victoria, it comes after plastic surgery. 'Because of the forms of self expression inherited by women, artistic creation often feels like violation', claims Susan Gubar, '[...] rather than possessing and controlling.'[3] This violation is mainly acted by the 'other within'. Women violate themselves, and the act seems to imply that writing is the result of the painful wounding of a passive self whose boundaries have been violated. 'Someone has placed an icon on her writing. A hand has placed an icon on her body. The ink has melted with her blood', writes Gavala (408). Later, having reworked her experience, she declares: 'Sofia Mahtou was writing something about haemorrhage, both that of her soul and that of the inside of her stomach' (401).

The continuity of life and art, biography and text, experience and writing, becoming a woman and becoming a writer and the recurrent identification of writing with violation, with the process of 'bleeding into print', as Gubar puts it,[4] reflect the woman writer's awareness that her body and her text are mysteriously connected. Gubar declares that 'many women experience their own bodies as the only medium for their art, with the result that the distance between the woman artist and her art is often radically diminished. [...] [O]ne of the primary and most resonant metaphors provided by the female body is blood and cultural forms of creativity are often experienced as a painful wounding.'[5] It is clearly revealed that a woman artist who experiences herself as killed into art may also experience herself as 'bleeding into print'. The stains of the vaginal imagery, the centrality of blood as a symbol furnished by the female body is revealed in Maria Gavala's novel-within-a-novel. While in prison, her heroine, Sofia, suffers from menstrual pains and at the same time she hears the cries of someone being tortured in the next cell. It is exactly then that for the first time she conceives the title of her book, 'The Woman Bled'. Blood is symbolically connected with ink, recalling the tragic associations of sacrifice for women writers. The blood of menstruation certifies impurity, guilt and difference and implies that the connotations of blood are a way of understanding the nature of female creativity, that is creativity loaded with guilt, difference and deviation:

The first time she felt the desire to write a novel was when she was pushed violently—almost thrown—inside the office of the chief of police. She wasn't sure about the title, but she would like to start with the image of the pure snow, or why not start with the image of marble? She had at least found out how to start the novel, the novel she would write sometime in the future, when she would find a way to escape from here (281).

The alternating image of purity and impurity, the purity of the snow associated with the blank page and the unwritten body, calls to mind the body of the heroine/writer and its manipulation, and signifies something more than a mere metaphor.

## The Marked Body

In an article on cyberbodies, Rosi Braidotti has declared that the 'artificially constructed face'—post-human, as she calls it—'is a crossroad of intensive forces, it is a surface of inscriptions of social codes'.[6]

The heroine of Michalopoulou's novel declares at the end of her book that her novel was written in two different stages, 'One before the plastic surgery and one after'. Plastic surgery is liberating for the heroine/writer, who bears the name Victoria, a name with numerous associations. The new nose offers a new face that leads to more objective writing. She states that after altering her nose the pain of her psyche is more sophisticated and acceptable:

I've been straining my ears to listen to you. You say I nibble instead of biting. I stand for common sense instead of my own ideas. Right, besides talent, poetry needs courage, to be myself nonstop, not to work so hard for the ghost's shake. Maybe that is why I started writing a novel—it is a safe area for the scared. I play the brave, the wise, the incompatible. I play the patient, the realist. The girl with the brand-new nose but with the old head (188).

Poetry is identified with the old face, the genuine, the untouched yet subjective, whereas novel-writing appears to be more like a construction, an ambitious attempt that coincides with the physical alteration of the woman writer.

In Sotiripoulou's novel, the prominent writer, Nina, puts her arms around the fridge and talks to it as if to a lover, and in an act of frustration she carves the mark of a cross on her knee.

'I love you', Nina said, putting her arms round the fridge. It was about her own height. The fridge quivered and let out a short moan before falling silent once again. She held her breath in sympathy. 'I love you', she repeated, stroking the cold surface. There was a knife hanging from a hook, it was used for slicing watermelons. In the dark she fumbled for the handle and held it tight. Then she slid her finger gently along the blade. They'll be sorry, she thought. They'll all be sorry, she whispered. She heard soft steps approaching. 'Black...', she whispered. She knelt in front of the fridge door. 'Black, come to me...' She took the puppy in her arms and held him tight. Then with her free hand she carved a cross on her knee. I swear I will love you for ever, she said to herself... (80)

## The Mythic Woman

Virginia Woolf's famous injunction that the creative woman needs to 'kill the angel in the house' that inhabits the most ancient layers of her identity is quite relevant here. In the novels examined, it is the image of the caring, nurturing, self-sacrificing, soft female that stands in the way of self-realization; on the other hand, the exploration of a dispersed/relational/collective concept of identity becomes a weapon for 'killing the angel in the house'. The writer-heroines seek to become aware of the paralysing and alienating determinations of the myth of Woman, but equally to avoid embracing an identity articulated through an ideal of a coherent subjectivity which for them would represent the dominant cultural form of masculinity.

In this light, the contemporary woman writer could be described as 'the angel in the storm'—a storm of references, both cultural and personal, a storm of contradictions and dilemmas, as well as of power relations. Although she keeps hurting herself and doing violence to her own body, there seem to be many ways in which this process is not so destructive after all.

Much of women's writing, claims Patricia Waugh, can in fact be seen not as 'an attempt to define an isolated ego but to discover a collective concept of subjectivity which foregrounds the construction of identity, enabling women to shift away from the personal.'[7] If women have traditionally been positioned in terms of 'otherness', then the desire to become subjects is likely to be stronger than the desire to deconstruct, decentre or fragment subjectivity. Especially in Sotiropoulou's novel, through the brave heroine Nina, alternative ways of conceiving subjectivity are revealed. Her way of expressing herself is not dependent on others or on the maintenance of boundaries and distance, nor upon the definitions those others have to offer. She struggles to become a subject, a writing subject, using her own tools, which in her case offer her distance from given truths and doctrines as well as a critical stance towards the clichés that seem to dominate the world around her. She needs to assert her own gaze on things, redefine and reshape the world so that she can find her own position in it. Becoming a 'person' involves being stripped of these roles and struggling to discover the 'inner essence' within the existing patterns of culture.

Idiots, Nina thought. They wanted to rearrange her life. They wanted to make her be like them. Her eyes were wet. She tried to keep calm but she couldn't. She turned, grasped the fridge with both hands and shook it: 'Listen, you idiots,' she whispered, 'I hate you, I hate you.' Out on the balcony they were laughing louder and louder. Write about beauty. Write something beautiful. Write! Rage, anger were growing inside her. Write something real! Write about the sunset! Write! Nina kicked the fridge ferociously. (226)

She confesses her love to the fridge, though she kicks it when she is strong enough to discover her own identity.

Nina cannot describe reality, because 'reality has no synonyms', as Hélène Cixous puts it; she cannot write about sunsets and the sea. She needs to detach herself, 'visualizing her private desert' where she would be walking alone, keeping her 'perfect balance'.

The metaphor of the fridge, which Nina treats like a living creature, is a perfect example of what external reality means to her. It is unreal, hard, frozen, mysterious. By talking to it and holding it in her arms, she tries to make it softer, to make it be like her, she tries to create a bridge between herself and others, between the present and the future, between frozen reality and her burning fantasy. She is possessed by words that keep returning to her mind and forming new sentences. She wishes to write what is not expected of her. Nina 'plays with sounds and words, not so much with their meaning but with their flesh and taste on her tongue' (260). She describes the 'perfect sense of emptiness' that she achieves at times when she enters the world of writing.

Women writers have been described as 'thieves of language', to use Claudine Hermann's phrase, through having been culturally and intellectually inferior, since they speak a language that has been an encoding of male privilege. The identification of the woman writer with a thief is celebrated by Amanda's Michalopoulou's heroine, Victoria, who steals in order to be familiar with what is unattainable, that is the thoughts, secrets and experiences of others. Reading other people's diaries is a necessary stage for her before she starts describing the world, before she starts claiming objectivity. She writes:

An objective novel can be written only by stealing their thoughts. You have to steal their poem to see what's in their heads, to read their diaries or a postcard that was written in rage [...] The writing of this book is my only brave act. I keep notes, although they are all watching me suspiciously and keep talking about me. I can hear their accusations: Victoria Louka is a thief. (342)

The twentieth-century stereotype of an anxious traumatic experience as a result of being possessed and wounded that saturates Sylvia Plath's poetry is repeated in the heroine of *Filthy Weather*, who bears the same name as the heroine of Plath's *The Bell Jar*.

Contemporary writers in Greece are still struggling to define and express themselves by coming to terms with their past experiences. Although they have started showing less concern with the fragmentation and disintegration of the subject, they now concentrate more on merging and connecting, having already described the feeling of being split and on the fringe. Today, much of women's writing can in fact be seen as an attempt not so much to define an isolated individual ego as to discover a collective concept of subjectivity which foregrounds the construction of identity in relation to the world and offers a positive affirmation of femininity. The metaphors described above, that is those of the thief, the bleeding woman, the woman whose body and face are altered through the creation or removal of markings, indicate a woman writer that traverses and redirects herself, who, apart from her defences, has also discovered new patterns of incorporating language and culture.

By the end of Sotiropoulou's novel, when Nina leaves behind the place of her girlhood, she has already made up her mind about what to write and how; having discovered 'a perfect sense of balance inside her', the mark on her knee fades. She doesn't have to be reminded of her isolation, she has enough confidence to be able to write as she likes, and this coincides with the liberating departure from the familiar, the known and the trivial (people, places, ways of expression), and she is heading for the freedom of the unknown, where she will be free to practise her own way of transforming the world into writing:

The mark on her knee had faded. The cross could no longer be seen with the naked eye. She looked out of the window and saw the village houses becoming a narrow line before they disappeared from sight. Entering the highway, the bus speeded up.
I am on the bus. And I keep a balance inside me. A straight, heaven-sent journey. All the others are stupid idiots because they cannot see it. A bit to the left, a bit to the right. I can go wherever I like. I keep a fine balance and I move on. The bus slides along the glistening highway. It turns. It stops. It starts again. It turns abruptly. It brakes. The bus runs along the silver asphalt, it runs and disappears. I don't care. I keep a balance. My mind helps. Paliovouna disappears. I can write whatever I like. (261–2)

## Notes to Chapter 12

1. Susan Gubar, 'The blank page and the issues of female creativity', 78.
2. Hélène Cixous and Mireille Calle-Gruber, *Rootprints*, 16.
3. Gubar, 'The blank page', 86.
4. Ibid. 78.
5. Ibid. 86.
6. Rosi Braidotti, 'Cyberfeminism with a difference', 3.
7. Patricia Waugh, *Feminine Fictions*, 17.

CHAPTER 13

❖

# The Disunification of the Nation: Contemporary Greek Historical Fiction and Collective Identities

*Konstantinos Kosmas*

In a number of Greek novels with historical content written since the 1980s, the way in which collective identities are described rejects the traditional tools of religion, language and past that make up the modern mythical nationality of historicism. Among the most significant examples of historiographic metafiction[1] in Greek literature are *The History of a Vendetta* by Yorgis Yatromanolakis, *The Life of Ismail Ferik Pasha* by Rhea Galanaki, *The Statue, The Message* and *The Façade* by Philippos Drakontaeidis, *Data from the Decade of the Sixties* by Thanassis Valtinos, *The Silver-Grass is Blooming* by Vasilis Gouroyannis, *The Audio-Novel of Captain Agras* and *What that Chamaedracon Held in Store* by Panos Theodoridis and *Zaida, or The Camel in the Snow* by Alexis Panselinos. In these novels, new forms of collective identities unite people in groups that are opposed to the terms of traditional nationalism.

The mythical models proposed by historiographic metafiction are put forward with the help of contrastive pairs that move and coexist in parallel, reflecting the postcolonial model of the 'divided nation' that is contrasted to the modern homogeneous nation.[2] Thus, for example, Yatromanolakis's *The History of a Vendetta* contrasts the way of life and the ideology of the Dikeakis and Zervos families, while Galanaki's *The Life of Ismail Ferik Pasha* contrasts the 'traitor' Ismail with his 'patriotic' brother Antonis.

The Greek historiographic metafiction that has just been mentioned deconstructs specific national myths that have been cultivated by more traditional forms of the novel. I will mention just a few examples: Eleftherios Venizelos as the Greek statesman *par excellence* in *The History of a Vendetta*; the supposed categorical difference between Greeks and Ottoman Muslims in *The Life of Ismail Ferik Pasha* and in Theodoros Grigoriadis's *The Waters of the Peninsula*; the decade of the 1960s as idealized chiefly by the left-wing intelligentsia in *Data from the Decade of the Sixties*; the supposedly homogeneous Greek language in *The Silver-Grass is Blooming*; western European rationalism as the basic structural feature of the modern Greek nation and as the image of civilization in *Zaida, or The Camel in the Snow*; and the natural and unquestioned Greekness of Macedonia in *The Audio-Novel of Captain Agras*. Nevertheless, the rational deconstruction of national myths in historiographic metafiction would be of severely limited interest and, moreover, would have very little efficacy if it were confined to this role, since the rational project loses its prestige as soon as it is proved false or disappointing. The innate need for collective identity leads once again necessarily to myth, in other words to a transcendent essence that is valid beyond rationally comprehended reality. The human tendency to seek a common 'we' explains the contemporary rekindling of nationalisms precisely at the time when the two most significant rational and secular challenges to the mythical systems of nation and religion are crumbling, namely the Enlightenment and Communism. In this chapter, through an analysis of Panos Theodoridis's novel *The Audio-Novel of Captain Agras* (1994), I shall present a brief example of a text that deconstructs a national myth and replaces it with another equally mythical model, stealing the language of myths, as Roland Barthes has put it.[3]

## The 'Macedonian Question'

For the whole of the twentieth century the so-called 'Macedonian struggle' remained one of the most central Greek national myths, which was rekindled with particular fanaticism at the beginning of the 1990s, when the Republic of Macedonia, declaring its independence, provoked exaggerated fears and nationalist reactions in the Greek mass media, political parties and public opinion, because of the Republic's use of the name Macedonia, a name that also denotes the greater part of northern Greece. The prevailing national myth presupposes not only the self-evident fact that the geographical region of Greek Macedonia belongs to the Greek state, but that historically, culturally and racially it belongs to the Greek nation.

Nevertheless, the scholarly community now accepts that the Macedonian struggle was an attempt by the young nation-states of Greece and Bulgaria, and secondarily of Serbia and Romania, to appropriate the populations that inhabited Macedonia with the aim of eventually incorporating them into the corresponding state territories.[4] The Macedonian populations were linguistically mixed and in any case lacked any national consciousness, at least in places where Greek or Bulgarian propaganda had not penetrated.[5] The Greek national narrative glorified the Macedonian struggle and the 'Makedonomachoi' (armed nationalist guerrillas who were active against the corresponding Bulgarian gangs and the regular Ottoman army, at the same time terrorizing the villagers), with the result that the policy of the time was transformed into a national myth, in which the reality of a culturally and linguistically heterogeneous population was obscured by the idea of a national-popular struggle.

In these circumstances, the young nation-states of Greece and Bulgaria, which were the chief rivals for Macedonia, had to develop mechanisms for the construction of the Other, since the mixed Macedonian population did not permit self-evident divisions. According to this process, mentally constructed stereotypes of self-definition and of definition by the Other were used, which functioned as evaluative criteria and helped to create the total picture of the values and obligations of the community.[6] A basic ingredient of this image is the historical model of individuals and social groups that emerges from the processing of various experiences from the past; as Bhabha puts it, the process by which the terms 'race', 'gender', etc. are differentiated is the moment that defines colonial discourse.[7]

Pinelopi Delta's *In the Secret Places of the Marsh* (1937) is a novel with an exciting plot and inexhaustible imagination. Despite the repulsive scenes of violence that it contains, it is considered to be a children's novel and continues to be published as such. Delta's text is yet another 'exercise in programmatic mythology', as Hobsbawm puts it,[8] adapting colonial discourse[9] to the service of the Greek national myth in its approach to the Macedonian problem and its construction of the Other.

## Macedonia in National Myth and in *The Audio-Novel of Captain Agras*

In her last and most popular novel, which functions as Theodoridis's sub-text,[10] Pinelopi Delta describes the adventures and the armed struggle waged by Greeks in and around the now drained marsh of Yannitsa, which is situated a few kilometres north-west of Salonica and was one of the most important sites of military activity between 1904 and 1908.

Delta's novel employs a realistic presentation, treating the Other as an already known object, the result of the subject's pre-existing knowledge—a characteristic technique of colonial ideology. The West, represented by the Greeks and synonymous with its civilization, legitimates its dominance not through material dominance but through cultural superiority, which is based on the axiom that the ruler knows perfectly well what the ruled is.[11] In this particular novel it is implied that the 'Bulgarophones' were originally Greeks who were 'Bulgarized',[12] most probably by force. At the same time, the armed Bulgarian nationalists are likened to 'monsters', or to the cannibals that the fictional *makedonomachos* Gregos had previously annihilated in Uganda in collaboration with the British colonial forces. The supposed national differentiation among the inhabitants of Macedonia culminates in the presentation of the distinctive biological characteristics that define the Slav 'Bulgarophones' and the Greeks and which stem from the pseudo-empiricism of racism.

Theodoridis's novel, by means of a decentred narration and various intertextual references, systematically displays its inability to voice an authoritative opinion about the events that it wants to describe. In this way it distances itself both from the desire to exercise power through the claim to the possession of knowledge and from the western colonial gaze. Nevertheless, *The Audio-Novel* does not confine itself to thematizing its distance from hegemonic Orientalism. At the same time it directly thematizes the colonial framework in which the narrative of the Macedonian struggle has been placed. Theodoridis's text uses the colonial gaze in Macedonia as a counterpoint to the hybrid figure of Captain Agras, which it proposes in place of the idealized version of this historical personage that is embodied in Delta's novel.

The national narrative represents the conviction that Greek national interests are genuine and that Greek nationalism thus differs from the corresponding manifestations of nationalism in Europe.[13] On the contrary, *The Audio-Novel* places the Macedonian problem within a framework of international nationalisms and political interests that are characterized by the gaze of the colonial West. *The Audio-Novel* begins with the scene of the landing by Captain Agras[14] at the Yannitsa marshes, which is accompanied by the narrator's comment that Agras had no idea about the 'railways the French are building in Indochina';[15] the construction of railways and other works of technical infrastructure in the colonies was the indispensable means that assisted the French and British colonialists in imposing themselves on the colonies as audacious and enterprising forces.[16] The link between the colonialist activities of the time and Agras's landing in Macedonia gives rise to analogous associations.

In Delta's novel, the fortification of the Kounga hut renders it so high that it becomes impossible to defend. The narrator of *The Audio-Novel* employs a characteristic simile for the same event: the Kounga hut is likened to a fortress occupied by colonial forces:

As soon as he [Agras] left, those who remained behind in the Kounga sought to fortify the hut in the best way. They erected a huge fortification wall, which was so tall that it stood out above the reeds for a large distance. The organizers had forgotten that these huts were the lairs of wild animals, hide-outs that had to remain unseen and unrecognized and not to project out of the reeds *like the sharp-pointed battlements erected in Africa during Napoleonic times to chasten the natives.* (86: my italics)

In *The Audio-Novel of Captain Agras* it is repeatedly stressed that all those who voice an opinion about places and situations in which they do not live simply repeat stereotypes that restrict the image of reality to the discourse of authority. The Athenian state official points out that people in the West only know the share-prices of Greek com-panies and that 'there is a widespread view that we wear skirts' (35); the Ottoman governor protests that the West is ignorant of the modern technical infrastructure of the empire and that it treats the Ottomans as 'lascivious orientals' (64), while, despite the fact that the French minister of foreign affairs is unaware of the political circumstances of the Bulgarian organizations in Macedonia, he behaves with the arrogance of omniscience (42).

If, however, the West and Pinelopi Delta—and even the narrator of *The Audio-Novel*—restrict the image of reality to stereotypes or fragments of the truth, those who were responsible for the policy on Macedonia in Athens are presented as being out of touch with the local situation. In the following dialogue two characters discuss the death of a *makedonomachos* who is not of Macedonian origin:

'Her husband went up to Macedonia as a guerrilla leader with twenty men. He was sent to... hold on, what's it called?... Chalkida... Chalkidiki... They went out with weapons and baggage, like an army, without guides and

without any knowledge of the terrain. They were ambushed in a pass. Only one of them escaped.'
'How come they send people there like sheep to the slaughter?'
'They don't know the terrain.'
'And they won't admit it.' (27–8)

Despite the ignorance of local conditions and against the advice of many *makedonomachoi*, the government in Athens insists on running the Macedonian Struggle itself. A significant part of *The Audio-Novel* is devoted to describing the disagreements between Captain Agras and the central authorities. The dispute about whether strategic decisions should be made locally or in Athens was one of the most crucial points in the Macedonian struggle,[17] without being exclusive to it: western colonialist policy had already faced the same dilemma, and the arguments and the results were similar. Central authority was imposed systematically at the expense of local organization, the essential motive being to control knowledge and direct it according to the specific interests of colonialist Orientalism.[18] The dispute between the central authorities in Athens and the local participants is presented in a stage-managed dialogue between an anonymous representative of Athenian policy and a supporter of the self-government of Macedonia and is condensed in the metaphor of the wood and the trees. The Athenian states that 'We look forward to the eventual union of our beloved Macedonia with the body of our nation. Let us leave bully-boy tactics aside. It is the wood that interests us, not the trees. [...] We have a specific target in view: the fulfilment of our national aims' (35–6).

The language of power is imprinted not only in its form (the above quotation is in *katharevousa*, the official language of Greece at the time) but in its essence: the 'national aim' has absolute priority. Agras's predecessor, Panagiotis Papatzaneteas, is presented as a good patriot who follows the orders of the central authorities in Athens.[19] His tactics are those that were pursued by patriotic *makedonomachoi*: 'the bloody tactics of terrorizing villages, burning crops, expelling those farmers who had an unstable national consciousness, and threatening villages headmen and aghas' (58)—generally speaking, activities that the rest of the guerrilla leaders described as 'prudence-instilling campaigns'.

The victims of these murderous attacks and those from the Bulgarian side, were not, as the Greek national myth likes to claim, respectively 'fanatical *komitadjis*' or 'innocent Greeks', but innocent peasants who were compelled to align themselves with one or other of the two camps, according to circumstances.[20] The 'patriots' are not represented as idealists inspired by justice, but as a timeless category of people who are driven not by national but by psychological motives, which are always similar, irrespective of nationality and historical period.

Renowned patriots, no matter whose standard they fought under, say farewell to their wives and children and with their axes in their hands set forth to expel the tyrant, whoever this may be. On the way they learn that gangs of partisans have burnt their homes, seized their children and pinned their wives' shoulders to the ground with their boots. Thus they return, immature wolves, not knowing what they are avenging, and thus they turn into nocturnal birds that croak during the magical evenings, not under the moon but under the neon lights of cafeterias. (26)

'The Ballad of Henry Ford' sings that the telegraph-poles of Macedonia were festooned with 'the heads of murdered annihilated Turks Greeks Bulgars Romanian-sympathizers Jews and other peoples' (29), and the Turkish landowner protests at the damage inflicted on his cotton-fields as a result of the indiscriminate terrorist activities of the nationalists: 'How are we to harvest [the cotton]? My farm is on the way. Gangs come and go... the peasants get scared and don't work... now they pay for the Patriarch [the Greek Orthodox Patriarch of Constantinople], now for the [Bulgarian] Exarch—we've gone crazy...' (30).

At the other extreme from those who, from a distance, see to it that the central authorities in Athens maintain control of the situation are those who seek to prioritize not the wood but the trees, not the 'national aim' but the individuals whom the national aim claims to be trying to protect, namely the peasants of Macedonia. The Athenian who expresses his indifference towards the trees in favour of the wood is interested not in the fate of the peasants but in the victory of Athenian policy. It is characteristic that the historian Konstantinos Vakalopoulos writes that Papatzaneteas set off 'with six men and five peasants';[21] it is obvious that by 'men' he means conscripted guerrillas, but the use of the words 'man' and 'peasant' is not devoid of evaluative criteria, which here favour the guerrillas over the peasants. The ideology of nationalism assigns the positive label 'man' not to the anonymous civilian, but to the armed nationalist who is conscripted by the state, even though the nationalist warrior was, as Vakalopoulos himself comments, a 'brigand from Phthiotis' who was completely ignorant of the problems of Macedonia.[22]

### The Antithesis of the Colonialist Gaze, or Why did Agras Die?

Captain Agras pursues a particular policy towards the Macedonian question, which in principle consists in approaching the rival Bulgarians with the aim of forging an alliance with them. Indeed, the historical figure of Captain Agras pursued such an independent policy, yet what is interesting is the way this policy is presented and interpreted: both in Delta's novel and in the contemporary sources Agras is presented as a fearless 'nobleman' who was interested in bridging 'the gap between the Christians'.[23] The motives attributed in such cases are those of the colonialist gaze: natural nobility and Christian faith against un-Christian barbarism. Thus Agras's insubordinate policy is brought into harmony with the discourse of power.

A different Agras emerges from between the lines of *The Audio-Novel*. The information he receives concerning the situation of the Macedonian conflict makes no mention of Greece's supposedly age-old claims on Macedonia, but states that it is a clash of interests, primarily between Greece, Bulgaria, Serbia and the Ottoman Empire, and secondarily between the other neighbouring and 'great' powers. 'The last people who have a say in the matter are the populations who live here,' 2nd Lt. Nikolaos Rokas tells Agras (45). This judgement would have been inconceivable and quite unrealistic in the mouth of a volunteer *makedonomachos* in 1906; an officer in the Greek army like Rokas would be bound to think that the *makedonomachoi* were fighting for the rights of the supposedly authentic Greek population of Macedonia. This inconceivable phrase is thus aesthetically distanced from the reader. It is not simply the view of a fictional character but a position which the text, in its desire to highlight it, renders remarkably unrealistic. Similarly unrealistic are Agras's plans: the narrator supposes that Agras was dreaming of rallying the Christian populations together against the Ottoman Empire— something that the Bulgarians seemed to want (100)—but he hastens to make clear that 'Agras's thought was like the United Nations resolutions on Cyprus: foreign troops should leave, the introduction of colonizers into the northern region should stop, and the rival sides should come to an agreement through dialogue. If this was unattainable in 1987, you can understand how unfeasible it would have been in 1907' (96).

'Foreign troops' in this case are the Bulgarians, the Turks and of course the Greeks; the three national armies are foreign to the local populations that interest Agras, contrary to the policy of Athens. One of the reasons why the collaboration between the local populations was not feasible, quite apart from the neighbouring national armies, was the Greek national policy. The state official who represents the nationalist central authorities comments that '*Balkan sobranie* [Balkan collaboration] may be an excellent make of tobacco, but it's not a reasonable way of dealing with history' (35). The colonialist gaze in Macedonia had constructed, in the person of the non-Greek-speaking Exarchists,[24] the stereotypical image of the Other, and any policy of collaboration would have refuted this. Naturally, in the novel, all the other representatives of national armies are presented as also being against Agras's initiatives; the Young Turk Hilmi Pasha, commander of the local military units, is alarmed, and the 'Romanian sympathizers' betray the meeting between Agras and Zlatan,[25] as do Zlatan's Bulgarian superiors.

The narrator comments that he would have preferred it if the central character of the novel, Captain Agras, had not become a distinguished army officer but a simple migrant who with other individuals from the Balkans and Italy had gone to America and worked alongside blacks on the margins of society (97). Thus, the centre of gravity is transferred from the central authorities in Athens and the 'heroic' *makedonomachoi*, not only to the local Macedonian populations, but to an anonymous and undefined subaltern mass of people who are systematically squeezed into the margins of history. The Macedonian problem itself, or even its possible solution, cannot be focused upon in *The Audio-Novel*, because the text is not interested in politics as it is understood by traditional history.

The most significant event in Agras's biography in Macedonia is his meeting with Zlatan. The novel uses this meeting as an opportunity to suggest that it is not isolating the Macedonian struggle as a distinct event of historical significance, but is placing it within the inter-national context of an arrogant, superficial, petty-bourgeois and profiteering West. At the same time, the meeting between Agras and Zlatan is not situated at some realistic point in time during the Macedonian struggle, but in an undefined, timeless context, in which the centre of attention is scattered and distributed among the diachronically anonymous people of history:

What day is it? What time is it? In Europe offices have shut and underground trains spew forth slightly used human beings into their dark neighbourhoods, where they will eat potatoes and cabbage with pork-fat and then give themselves over to sleep, while those who go out and enjoy themselves see fast-moving films, and the opera-houses are ready to receive the luxurious crowds. [...] In other cities of Europe, Asia and South America, smartly dressed ministers and provincial governors throw ornamented switches that bring electric light to the prosperous neighbourhoods, while in India and Africa the lives of thousands of starving people are extinguished with the light of day. In other places people dream of becoming more important, financially independent, marrying Claudette, killing their rival, doubling their productivity, putting grandma in an old people's home, curing their flu, and being looked at through flower-bedecked windows by hysterical Neapolitan goddesses. But now that Agras is walking to the north of Naousa to meet Zlatan, I'm not interested in all this. I'm interested in the Italians migrating to America outside Naples harbour, when the waters are shining in the sea's mirror and the divine moon's haze, as I sense them walking on the oily deck with the slightly sour smell of vomit, well-dressed and dirty, tearing up the fullness of time as bankrupts tear up cheques.

'Addio mia terra Napoli' (105–6).

The Greek national narrative, as it is presented in historiography or in historical novels like Delta's, approaches the concept 'Macedonia' from the viewpoint of western colonialism. In Theodoridis's text this perspective is replaced by a subversive subalternity, by way of an un-focalized gaze that is directed either towards the anonymous peasants of Macedonia who suffered from both Greek and Bulgarian armed nationalists, or towards people on the margins, workers in big cities and immigrants. Agras's meeting with Zlatan 'doesn't interest' the narrator as a theme. The text's gaze displaces the figure of Agras from the context of the nationally emotive Macedonian struggle towards the nationally insignificant story of people on the margins; in the end, those who interest the narrator in this novel that promises to thema-tize a phase of the Macedonian struggle are not the *makedonomachoi* but the peasants who 'now pay for the Patriarch, now for the Exarch', or 'the blacks on the margins of society who play the trumpet' (97).

The change of perspective with regard to Macedonia and the Macedonian problem also entails a change in the approach to the meaning of 'homeland': in *The Audio-Novel*, homeland is identified with the anonymous peasants who move between the national camps according to political compulsion, and the marginal immigrants who move between states according to economic compulsion. It is a homeland without a centre, which continually postpones definition.

The novel ends with a long monologue by Captain Agras, who

disappears like a ghost, and more precisely with a question: 'I'm not complaining. I know why I died. But do you know? What do you know?' (149). Captain Agras was killed in possession of a vision. Not only that, but Agras himself appears in *The Audio-Novel* like a vision when, during one of his various appearances among the living, he confesses that he was fortunate to have died, because as a military man he did not want to be exploited by state interests.

The reason why Theodoridis's text is called *Audio-Novel* is clearly that it wants to be considered as halfway between a radio broadcast and a novel. In the final chapter the most important character appears as a ghost in front of his comrades-in-arms, who happen to have found themselves near his hide-out, but also in front of the makers of the radio programme. Agras's name is isolated in an intermediate space between life and death, natural existence and non-existence. Agras does not remain in the underworld, but returns as a ghost, clearly attempting to attract attention: he asks the makers of the broadcast—and in a way the narrator—to convey 'to those who should hear it that Agras is still alone and isolated, even in the Lower World. Those who snubbed him in life are continuing to snub him after death' (149). Agras wants to convey the message that, both dead and alive, he is ignored by those who are in power. He appears in the nine chapters of the novel as a realistic figure, but the novel closes with him returning from the dead and giving an account of himself; it seems that Agras had to die in order to be able to give an account of himself as a vision, asking us the question 'what do we know?' Agras does not exist as a physical being because he appears as 'ultra-sound and meta-matter' (147), yet he possesses a discourse that is directed straight to the reader, who will remove him from the ignorance that he complains about. Appearing as a vision and conveying a vision, he turns our attention to a space between two worlds, a utopia.

The appearance of the ghost in Theodoridis's novel is presented with self-irony and results in Agras's being powerfully distanced from any reader. Thus one's attention turns to the signifier, to the text that contravenes realistic conventions and is fragmented by the signified, the text's 'content'. As a realistic physical being, the *makedonomachos* Captain Agras embodies the model of the patriot who is inspired by the ideals of a culture superior to that of his adversaries. An indispensable precondition for the national narrative to be capable of conveying the symbolism of the national hero effectively is that Agras must be dead, that is, finished, without the possibility of being altered, like a stone memorial. Agras's image can be given national significance as a hero or a martyr only as a finite, dead form, which can be represented in the form of a bust or in a historical text with claims to truth. At the beginning of her book, Pinelopi Delta dedicates it 'to the memory of the ideal hero Telos Agapinos, Captain Agras'. Her text is thus to be taken as the signifier of Captain Agras's memory, in the belief that in this way he will be placed and preservēd within the national memory. The same claim was made by Theuth when he offered the art of writing to King Thamus as a *pharmakon* for memory.[26] At the same time, however, *pharmakon* means the poison that can kill memory; writing, *typos*, the sign of discourse, imprisons memory and leads to oblivion:

Confiante dans la permanence et l'indépendance de ses *types (tupoi)*, la mémoire s'endormira, ne se tiendra plus, ne tiendra plus à se tenir tendue, au plus proche de la vérité des étants. Médusée par ses gardiens, par ses propres signes, par les types commis à la garde et surveillance du savoir, elle se laissera engloutir par *Léthé*, envahir par l'oubli et le non-savoir.[27]

Writing, in other words the attribution of meaning to memory, leads to the oblivion of its signified, which is imprisoned in the signs of the words that guard it. In Theodoridis's text oblivion is a yellow dust: those who had retired from the Macedonian struggle 'used to gather together, until they were all overtaken by a yellow dust that optimists call oblivion and pessimists death' (144).

Oblivion is presented in *The Audio-Novel* as synonymous with death. Delta's writing attributes meaning to Captain Agras as 'an ideal [national] hero', as the author herself stresses by killing him. Only in death can Captain Agras become a national hero and only as a monumentalized dead point can he constitute part of the national narrative. The model of the dead hero in the guise of national martyr corresponds to the model of traditional nationalism, which presents the nation as a homogeneous and unchangeable entity.

To the question 'why did Captain Agras die?' we can provide the following answer: he died as a traditional image of the nation in order to return in resurrected form as an intermediate state, as his utopian vision. Agras's vision at the end of *The Audio-Novel* is not made of matter and therefore cannot be given meaning by being included in a finite monument, that is, he cannot be presented as a truth. Since he returns from the dead, in other words from the situation of the definitive attribution of meaning, Agras is able to claim that the narrator has no idea about his biography.[28] He is a ghost that exists between two spaces or centres, namely life and death, Earth and Hades. In addition, however, just as the marginal masses whom the narrator prefers are situated outside the epicentre of history and consequently cannot be categorized according to criteria of nationality, the two centres between which Agras is situated could be the two national centres that defined the history of Macedonia and the Macedonian question, namely Greece and Bulgaria. Agras, like the anonymous masses that interest the narrator, exists beyond the known national categories; he is the *différance* between the Greek and the Bulgarian (and later the Macedonian) national identity that was imposed by the nation-states on the local populations of Macedonia.[29]

## Conclusions

In the novel *The World's Fair* by E. L. Doctorow, the author of what is in a sense the manifesto of historiographic metafiction,[30] the administration of the 1939 World Trade Fair in New York decides to include the image of his age in the form of a number of objects, which will be placed in a huge, secure time capsule, which will then be buried, to be opened several millennia later as a historic monument of its time. Everyday industrial products, commonly used chemical substances, the Lord's Prayer in many languages, commercial art as well as details of the economy, military history and high politics are buried at an official ceremony. In the time capsule are placed symbolic products that represent the culture of the capitalist economy, industrial production, military and political power, and entertainment. At the end of the novel the central hero of the novel, little Edgar, together with a school-friend, hides his own collection, as the antithesis of the official version: his own subaltern version includes a school essay, broken toys, a second-hand harmonica, worn-out clothes and broken spectacles. The alternative proposed by the boys, who are ignored by official history and politics, consists of cheap, second-hand fragments. Nevertheless, Doctorow's novel assigns special value to these objects, since the whole novel ends with a description of them. Contrary to the official objects that represent a generalized and abstract image of a culture that is presented as unified, the selection put together by Edgar and his friend consists of specific objects belonging to specific people, and their heterogeneity does not allow a schematic, generalized image of a culture to be formed; Edgar's battered toys, his brother's old harmonica, his mother's laddered stockings, Arnold's old broken glasses—the objects they choose do not have any abstract content, and consequently they cannot symbolize anything beyond the specific function they once had.

The generalized model, constructing abstract totalities and giving them the identity of a uniform collectivity, such as the concepts 'nation', 'western civilization' or 'Orient', can be described by Bhabha's term 'the many as one'.[31] Such models of collective identity stress the homogeneity of the community, presenting it as a subject with unitary characteristics which is represented by theories that treat concepts such as class, gender and race as social categories.

Greek historiographic metafiction systematically presents an opposing model, either through historical anachronisms or through split, hybrid forms of identity, a model that could be described as 'out of the many one'. This is the most interesting way in which post-colonial society opposes the validity of the traditional idea of the nation,[32] viewing itself as everyday practice rather than thinking of itself as unitary subject, cultural heritage or national memory.

In the novels that have been mentioned—very briefly in view of restrictions of space—traditional forms of identity are combined with strange hybrid ones into a single whole: in Galanaki's *The Life of Ismail Ferik Pasha*, the patriot and national benefactor Antonis Papadakis coexists with the split personality of the 'abject' Ismail; in Yatromanolakis's *History of a Vendetta* the 'marginal' Dikeakis family coexists with the 'successful' Zervos clan; in Panselinos's *Zaida, or The Camel in the Snow*, the reader's pre-established knowledge of Mozart coexists with the paradoxical Crisostomo Masarini; and in Theodoridis's *The Audio-Novel of Captain Agras*, national heroes of the Macedonian struggle coexist with anonymous migrants, constituting a hybrid culture made up of internal discontinuities, dissimilarities and differences. These paradoxical hybrid models actively work towards a redefinition of society and create new collective identities. At the same time, they create a new tradition based on internal differences rather than on the past, and by constructing a new paradoxical past they introduce inconceivable concepts of temporality into a tradition that denies access to primordial or authoritative identities. In postcolonial society, the idea of the collective national community can be inscribed only in discontinuous, heterogeneous and fragmentary intermediate spaces.

Homelands are also constantly transitional in these novels, and the heroes seek them in vain: the 'waters' that are sought for by the sexually and nationally indeterminate figures in Grigoriadis's novel *The Waters of the Peninsula*, the content of the message and the place towards its bearer directs himself in Drakontaeidis's *The Message*, the vagueness and liminality of space and language in Gouroyannis's *The Silver-Grass is Blooming*, the house containing the ghosts of past and present to which Ismail returns, the carobs on the boundaries and the unhomely homes of the Dikeakis family, the non-existent fairytale Orient of *Zaida* that Panselinos's heroes are seeking in their endless eastward journey, the aesthetically alienated Macedonia and the homeless subaltern migrants of *The Audio-Novel*, or the invisible, demythologized Greece that disappears behind the mass of false documents in Valtinos's *Data from the Decade of the Sixties*.

Such texts make it clear that they are participating in the 'war of symbols', as Vasilis Lambropoulos has put it: in the postmodern age of virtual reality, it is not enough to reveal the constructed nature of myths and symbols; alternative, hybrid symbols must be constructed, which will be 'dynamic, rich, open and susceptible of multiple creative interpretations'.[33] The supplementary spaces created by the paradoxical heroes of the novels I have been discussing give rise to alternative proposals for collective identities, replacing the traditional ones that have been established since the time of the western Enlightenment, which invented the concept of 'national community'.

*Translated by Peter Mackridge*

## Notes to Chapter 13

1. The term 'metafiction' was used for the first time by William Gass to describe fictional texts in which 'the forms of fiction [serve] as the material upon which further forms can be imposed' (William H. Gass, *Fiction and the Figures of Life*, 25). These texts comment in a peculiarly intense way on their own fictionality; this phenomenon was first described in 1967 by the fiction-writer and theorist John Barth ('The literature of exhaustion'), who had in mind writers such as Beckett and Borges (and of course himself). There is an exceptionally extensive bibliography on historiographic metafiction, from which one can select the following indicative works: Robert Scholes, *Fabulation and Metafiction*; Raymond A. Mazurek, 'Metafiction, the historical novel and Coover's *The Public Burning*'; Patricia Waugh, *Metafiction*; Linda Hutcheon, *Narcissistic Narrative*; ead., *A Poetics of Postmodernism*; ead., *The Politics of Postmodernism*; Brian McHale, *Postmodernist Fiction*; Elisabeth Wesseling, *Writing History as a Prophet*; Susana Onega, 'British historiographic metafiction'; Ansgar Nünning, *Von historischer Fiktion zu historiographischer Metafiktion*, i; Thomas Irmer, *Metafiction, Moving Pictures, Moving Histories*. See also n. 30.

2. 'The boundary that marks the nation's selfhood interrupts the self-generating time of national production and disrupts the signification of the people as homogeneous. The problem is not simply the "selfhood" of the nation as opposed to the otherness of other nations. We are confronted with the nation split within itself, articulating the heterogeneity of its population' (Homi K. Bhabha, *The Location of Culture*, 148).

3. 'A vrai dire, la meilleure arme contre le mythe, c'est peut-être de le mythifier à son tour, c'est de produire un mythe artificiel: et ce mythe reconstitué sera une véritable mythologie. Puisque le mythe vole du langage, pourquoi ne pas voler le mythe?' (Roland Barthes, *Mythologies*, 222).

4. 'The Macedonian question in the second half of the nineteenth century essentially involved the conflicts generated by the frantic attempts of the new national states to incorporate local ethnic groups into the "imagined communities" they represented in order to lay claim to the territories these groups inhabited' (Paschalis Kitromilides, *Enlightment, Nationalism, Orthodoxy*, XI: 169).

5. The following quotation from Henry Noel Brailsford, written in 1906, is characteristic: 'One hundred years ago it would have been hard to find a central Macedonian who could have answered with any intelligence the question whether he were Servian or Bulgarian by race. The memory of the past had vanished utterly and nothing remained save a vague tradition among the peasants that their forefathers had once been free. I questioned some boys from a remote mountain village near Ohrida which had neither teacher nor resident priest, and where not a single inhabitant was able to read, in order to discover what amount of traditional knowledge they possessed. I took them up to the ruins of the Bulgarian Tsar's fortress which dominates the lake and the plain from the summit of an abrupt and curiously rounded hill. "Who built this place?" I asked them. The answer was significant: "The free men." "And who were they?" "Our grandfathers." "Yes, but were they Serbs or Bulgarians or Greeks or Turks?" "They weren't Turks, they were Christians." And this seemed to be about the measure of their knowledge' (Henry Noel Brailsford, *Macedonia: Its Races and Their Future*, 99). It is generally accepted that until the Macedonian struggle 'the inhabitants of Macedonia, in fact, did not constitute a single ethnic group but were rather composed of several distinct populations' (Anastasia N. Karakasidou, *Fields of Wheat, Hills of Blood*, 278 n. 19).

6. Arnold Suppan, 'Einleitung: Identitäten und Stereotypen in multiethnischen europäischen Regionen', 15.

7. Bhabha, *Location*, 67.

8. Eric Hobsbawm, *Nations and Nationalism since 1780*, 101.

9. This term should be understood to suggest that Macedonia was a Greek colony, as Popov and Radin put it (Chris Popov and Michael Radin, 'An analysis of current Greek government policy on the Macedonian issue' cited in Victor Roudometof, 'Nationalism and identity politics in the Balkans', 269), and that the Greek national narratives used the colonial gaze to construct the Other in the still-contested Macedonia. It is perhaps not insignificant that Pinelopi Delta was born and raised in Egypt at the time when it was a British colony.

10. See Terry Eagleton, *Literary Theory*, 178.

11. Edward W. Said, *Orientalism*, 32.

12. Peter Mackridge, 'Macedonia and Macedonians', 49–50.
13. See Konstantinos Th. Dimaras, *Neoellinikos Romantismos*, 363: 'The terms in which [the phrase 'national unity'] is presented in the Greek consciousness possess such a sufficient inherent rationale that it is unnecessary to examine them in comparison with Italy, Germany, the Slav nations and Romania.'
14. Captain Agras was the *nom de guerre* of Sarandos Agapinos. He volunteered for service in Macedonia immediately after his graduation from the Athens Military Academy; in 1906 he was promoted to the position of corps commander in the Vermio region. Captain Agras is one of the best-known *makedonomachoi*, thanks chiefly to Pinelopi Delta's novel.
15. Panos Theodoridis, *To ichomythistorima tou Kapetan Agra* (1994), 9.
16. Said, *Orientalism*, 88–92.
17. See Konstantinos Vakalopoulos, *O enoplos agonas sti Makedonia (1904–1908)*, 20–6.
18. 'But how did and does Orientalism work? How can one describe it all together as a historical phenomenon, a way of thought, a contemporary problem and a material reality? [Cromer in 'The Government of Subject Races'] envisions a seat of power in the West, and radiating out from it towards the East a great embracing machine, sustaining the central authority yet commanded by it' (Said, *Orientalism,* 44).
19. Cf. Vakalopoulos, *O enoplos agonas*, 168–74.
20. Karakasidou, *Fields of Wheat*, 103–4.
21. Vakalopoulos, *O enoplos agonas*, 174.
22. Ibid. 172.
23. See the telegram from Koromilas, Greek consul in Salonica, mentioned ibid. 194–6.
24. This term referred to the Christians who pledged their allegiance to the autocephalous Bulgarian church (Exarchate) rather than to the Patriarchate of Constantinople. The allegiance to one or other of the churches was, together with language, one of the most significant criteria used by the interested parties to distinguish racially between the inhabitants of Macedonia.
25. Before his planned departure from the contested territories for health reasons, the real-life Captain Agras attempted to arrange a meeting in a neutral zone with the commanders of the Bulgarian guerrilla groups, Kazapsev and Zlatan, with the aim either of buying them off or of acting in concert with them against the Ottoman army. The meeting failed to take place, and Agras and his companion were captured by Bulgarian guerrillas and hanged.
26. Plato, *Phaedrus*, 274 D–275 A.
27. Jacques Derrida, *La Dissémination*, 119–20.
28. 'I listened to you carefully and I confess I liked some things... the little song I keep singing, for instance. Indeed, I used to sing a little song, though not of course the one you make me sing... it was another one... otherwise I don't have any demands. You know very little about what it means to be a soldier... as for my wit, you've understood it as much as Mrs Delta, that is, not at all! [...] and so you've viewed me as it suited you...' (Theodoridis, *Ichomythistorima*, 148).
29. For the development of Greek national consciousness in the Greek portion of Macedonia see Peter Mackridge and Eleni Yannakakis (eds.), *Ourselves and Others*.

30. E. L. Doctorow, 'False documents'; Doctorow does not, however, use the term
'historiographic metafiction'.
31. Bhabha, *The Location of Culture*, 142.
32. Ibid.
33. Vasilis Lambropoulos, 'I diekdikisi ton eikonon se mia eikoniki epochi', *To Vima
tis Kyriakis*, 7 Jan. 2001.

# BIBLIOGRAPHY

❖

## Note

The bibliography is divided into two parts. The first includes all the works of Greek fiction published since 1974 and mentioned in this volume; each is given by its Greek title—if the work has not been published in English—followed by a literal English translation of the title in square brackets. In the case of works published in English translation, bibliographical details of the translation are provided in square brackets after details of the Greek original. Since this volume focuses on Greek fiction published since 1974, details of Greek fictional works published before that date are not provided. All secondary works mentioned in the volume are also listed below.

## Works of Greek Fiction

ABATZOGLOU, PETROS, *Sti siopi tou erota* [*In the Silence of Love*] (Athens: Kedros, 1997).

AKRIVOS, KOSTAS, *Kitrino rosiko keri* [*Yellow Russian Candle*] (Athens: Kedros, 2001).

ALEXANDROPOULOS, MITSOS, *Mikro organo gia ton epanapatrismo* [*A Brief Manual for Homecoming*] (Athens: Kedros, 1980).

ALEXANDROU, ARIS, *To kivotio* (Athens: Kedros, 1975) [*Mission Box*, trans. Robert Crist (Athens: Kedros, 1996)].

ANASTASEA, NIKI, *Afti i argi mera prochorouse* [*This Slow Day was Progressing*] (Athens: Polis, 1998).

AXIOTIS, DIAMANTIS, *To elachiston tis zois tou* [*The Least of his Life*] (Athens: Kedros, 1999).

BAKOLAS, NIKOS, *I megali plateia* (Athens: Kedros, 1987) [*Crossroads*, trans. Caroline Harbouri (Athens: Kedros, 1997)].

CHATZITATSIS, TASOS, *San spasmena ftera* [*Like Broken Wings*] (Athens: Polis 2003).

CHEIMONAS, THANASIS, *Ramon* (Athens: Kedros, 1998).

—— *Spasmena ellinika* [*Broken Greek*] (Athens: Kedros, 2000).

CHOURMOUZIADOU, ELIANA, *I idiaitera* [*The Private Secretary*] (Athens: Kedros, 1998).

DIMITRAKAKI, ANGELA, *Antarktiki* [*Antarctica*] (Athens: Oxy, 1997).

DIMITRIOU, SOTIRIS, *Djallth im Christaki* [*Christaki, my Little Boy*] (Athens: Ypsilon, 1987).

—— *N' akouo kala t' onoma sou* (Athens: Kedros, 1993) [*May Your Name be Blessed*, trans. Leo Marshall, introd. by Dimitris Tziovas (Birmingham: Centre for Byzantine, Ottoman and Modern Greek Studies, 2000)].

—— *I fleva tou laimou* [*The Vein in the Neck*] (Athens: Patakis, 1998).

—— *Ena paidi ap' ti Thessaloniki* [*A Boy from Thessaloniki*] (Athens: Kedros, 1989).

—— *I vradyporia tou kalou* [*The Tardiness of Good*] (Athens: Patakis, 2001).

—— *Tous ta leei o Theos* [*God Tells Them*] (Athens: Metaichmio, 2002).

DOUKA, MARO, *I archaia skouria* (Athens: Kedros: 1979) [*Fool's Gold*, trans. Roderick Beaton (Athens: Kedros, 1991)].

—— *Enas skoufos apo porfyra* (Athens: Kedros, 1995) [*Come Forth, King*, trans. David Connolly (Athens: Kedros, 2003)].

—— *Ourania michaniki* [*Heavenly Mechanics*] (Athens: Kedros, 1999).

DOXIADIS, APOSTOLOS, *O theios Petros kai i eikasia tou Goldbach* (Athens: Kastaniotis, 1992; rev. edn. 2000) [*Uncle Peter and Goldbach's Conjecture*, (London: Faber and Faber and Bloomsbury, 2000)].

—— *Ta tria anthropakia* [*The Three Manikins*] (Athens: Kastaniotis, 1997).

DRAKONTAEIDIS, FILIPPOS, *To agalma* [*The Statue*] (Athens: Syntechnia, 1984).

—— *I prosopsi* [*The Façade*] (Athens: Estia, 1992).

—— *Sinaisthimatiko taxidi* [*Sentimental Journey*] (Athens: Nea Synora, 1998).

—— *To minyma* [*The Message*] (Athens: Estia, 1999).

EFSTATHIADIS, YANNIS, *Me gemato stoma* [*With your Mouth Full*] (Athens: Ypsilon, 2002).

EFTHYMIADI, NENI, *I poli ton glaron* [*The City of Seagulls*] (Athens: Kastaniotis, 1997).

FAIS, MICHEL, *Aftoviografia enos vivliou* (Athens: Kastaniotis, 1994) [*Autobiography of a Book* (excerpt), trans. Yiorgios Anagnostu, in Leontis, *Greece*, 186–203].

—— *Ap' to idio potiri kai alles istories* [*From the Same Glass and Other Stories*] (Athens: Kastaniotis, 1999).

—— *Aegypius monachus* (Athens: Kastaniotis, 2001).

FAKINOS, ARIS, *To oneiro tou protomastora Nikita* [*The Dream of Master Builder Nikitas*] (Athens: Kedros, 1998).

FAKINOU, EVGENIA, *Astradeni* (Athens: Kedros, 1982) [*Astradeni*, trans. H. E. Criton (Athens: Kedros, 1999)].

—— *Tyflomyga* [*Blind-Man's Buff*] (Athens: Kastaniotis, 2000).

—— *Poios skotose ton Moby Dick?* [*Who Killed Moby Dick?*] (Athens: Kastaniotis, 2001).

GALANAKI, RHEA, *Tria omokentra diigimata* [*Three Concentric Tales*] (Athens: Agra, 1986).

—— *O vios tou Ismail Ferik Pasa* (Athens: Agra 1989) [*The Life of Ismail Ferik Pasha*, trans. Kay Cicellis (London: Peter Owen, 1996)].

—— *Tha ypografo Loui* (Athens: Agra, 1993) [*I Shall Sign as Loui*, trans. David Connolly (Evanston, IL: Northwestern University Press, 2000)].

—— *Eleni, i o Kanenas* (Athens: Agra, 1998) [*Eleni, or Nobody*, trans. David Connolly (Evanston, IL: Northwestern University Press, 2003)].

—— *O aionas ton lavyrinthon* [*The Century of Labyrinths*] (Athens: Kastaniotis, 2002).

GAVALA, MARIA, *Sti drosia ton kipon mou* [*In the Dew of my Gardens*] (Athens: Estia, 2001).

GONATAS, E. CH., *I proetoimasia* [*The Preparation*] (Athens: Stigmi, 1991).

GOUROYANNIS, VASILIS, *Diigiseis parafysikon fenomenon* [*Accounts of Paranormal Phenomena*] (Athens: Kastaniotis, 1990).

—— *To asimochorto anthizei* [*The Silver-Grass is Blooming*] (Athens: Kastaniotis, 1992).

GRIGORIADIS, THEODOROS, *Ta nera tis chersonisou* [*The Waters of the Peninsula*] (Athens: Kedros, 1998).

HARITOPOULOS, DIONYSIS, *Apo do perase o Kilroy* [*Kilroy was Here*] (Athens: Kastaniotis, 1992).

HATZIS, DIMITRIS, *Spoudes* [*Studies*] (Athens: Keimena, 1976).

—— *To diplo vivlio* [*The Double Book*] (Athens: Exantas, 1976).

KAPPA, VASSILIKI, *I diaita tis yainas* [*The Hyena's Diet*] (Athens: Kastaniotis, 2000).

KARAÏTIDI, EVA, *Oneirevomai pos glytosa* [*I Dream that I've Survived*] (Athens: Alexandreia, 1996).

KARAPANOU, MARGARITA, *O ypnovatis* [*The Sleep-Walker*] (Athens: Ermis, 1985).

KARYSTIANI, IOANNA, *Mikra Anglia* [*Little England*] (Athens: Kastaniotis, 1999).

—— *Koustoumi sto choma* [*A Suit in the Earth*] (Athens: Kastaniotis, 2000).

KIOURTSAKIS, YANNIS, *San mythistorima* [*Like a Novel*] (Athens: Kedros, 1995).

—— *Emeis oi alloi* [*We the Others*] (Athens: Kedros, 2000).

KOLLIAKOU, DIMITRA, *To mageio* [*The Magic Hole*] (Athens: Estia, 1999).

KONTODIMOS, KOSTAS, *O syngrafeas kai to exofyllo* [*The Author and the Cover*] (Athens: Thema, 1991).

KOTZIAS, ALEXANDROS, *Fantastiki peripeteia* [*The Fantastic Adventure*] (Athens: Kedros, 1985).

KOUMANDAREAS, MENIS, *I myrodia tous me kanei na klaio* [*Their Smell Makes Me Want to Cry*] (Athens: Kedros, 1996) ['The Romanian Kid', trans. by Patricia Felisa Barbeito and Vangelis Calotychos, *Mondo greco*, 5 (Spring 2001), 29–47].

—— *Dyo fores Ellinas* [*Twice Greek*] (Athens: Kedros, 2001).

KOURTOVIK, DIMOSTHENIS, *I nostalgia ton drakon* [*The Nostalgia of the Dragons*] (Athens: Estia, 2000).

194    BIBLIOGRAPHY

MANTOGLOU, ARGIRO, *Virginia Woolf Café* (Athens: Apopeira, 1999).
MARANGOPOULOS, ARIS, *Oi oraies imeres tou Veniamin Sanidopoulou* [*The Beautiful Days of Benjamin Sanidopoulos*] (Athens: Kedros, 1998).
MATESIS, PAVLOS, *Diigimata* [*Short Stories*] (Athens: Kedros, 1978).
——— *Yli dasous* [*Forest Matter*] (Athens: Kastaniotis, 1992).
MESKOS, MARKOS, *Muharrem* (Athens: Nefeli, 1999).
MICHAILIDIS, MICHALIS, *I skyla kai to koutavi* [*The Bitch and the Puppy*] (Athens: Kastaniotis, 2002).
MICHALOPOULOU, AMANDA, *Yantes* [*Wishbone*] (Athens: Kastaniotis, 1996).
——— *Oses fores antexeis* [*As Many Times as You Can Stand It*] (Athens: Kastaniotis, 1998).
——— *Paliokairos* [*Filthy Weather*] (Athens: Kastaniotis, 2001).
MILIONIS, CHRISTOFOROS, *Dytiki synoikia* [*Western District*] (Athens: Kedros, 1980).
NOLLAS, DIMITRIS, *To tryfero derma* [*Tender Skin*] (Athens: Kastaniotis, 1982).
——— *Oneirevomai tous filous mou* [*I Dream of my Friends*] (Athens: Kastaniotis, 1990).
——— *O tymvos konta sti thalassa* [*The Tomb by the Sea*] (Athens: Kastaniotis, 1991).
——— *Foteini magiki* [*Magical Fotini*] (Athens: Kedros, 2000).
PAMPOUDI, PAVLINA, *Chartini zoi* [*Paper Life*] (Athens: Roes, 2003).
PANAYOTOPOULOS, NIKOS, *To gonidio tis amfivolias* [*The Gene of Doubt*] (Athens: Polis, 1999).
PANOU, YANNIS, *Apo to stoma tis palias Remington* [*From the Mouth of the Old Remington*] (Thessaloniki: Trilofo, 1981).
——— *I istoria ton metamorfoseon* [*The History of Transformations*] (Athens: Kastaniotis, 1998).
PANSELINOS, ALEXIS, *Zaida, i i kamila sta chionia* [*Zaida, or The Camel in the Snow*] (Athens: Kastaniotis, 1996).
PAPAGEORGIOU, FANI, *To miden kai to ena* [*The Zero and the One*] (Athens: Kedros, 2000).
POLITOPOULOU, MARILENA, *Oikos enochis* [*House of Guilt*] (Athens: Kedros, 2002).
ROUSOS, TASOS, *O kairos tis Lize* [*Lize's Time*] (Athens: Kastaniotis, 1993).
ROUSSOU, NICOLE, *Stoichimata me tous theous* [*Betting with the Gods*] (Athens: Alexandreia, 2000).
SIOTIS, DINOS, *Deka chronia kapou* [*Ten Years Somewhere*] (Athens: Kastaniotis, 1995).
SKAMBARDONIS, YORGOS, *Mati fosforo koumanto gero* [*Phosphorus Eye, Firm Control*] (Athens: Kastaniotis, 1989).
——— *I psicha tis metalavias* [*The Bread of Communion*] (Thessaloniki: Ta Tramakia, 1990).
——— *I stenopos ton yfasmaton* [*The Bottleneck of Fabrics*] (Athens: Kastaniotis, 1992).

—— *Pali kentaei o stratigos* [*The General is Embroidering Again*] (Athens: Kastaniotis, 1996).

—— *Gernao epitychos* [*I Grow Old Successfully*] (Athens: Kastaniotis, 2000).

SKASSIS, THOMAS, *Elliniko stavrolexo* [*Greek Crossword*] (Athens: Polis, 2000).

SOTIROPOULOU, ERSI, *Zig-zag stis nerantzies* [*Zig-zag through the Orange Trees*] (Athens: Kedros, 1999).

SOUROUNIS, ANTONIS, *Meronychta Frankfourtis* [*Days and Nights in Frankfurt*] (Athens: Ypsilon, 1982).

—— *Mison aiona anthropos* [*Human for Half a Century*] (Athens: Kastaniotis, 1992).

—— *Gas o gangster* [*Gus the Gangster*] (Athens: Kastaniotis, 2000).

STAIKOS, ANDREAS, *Epikindynes mageirikes* (Athens: Ypsilon, 1997) [*Les Liaisons culinaires*, trans. Anne-Marie Stanton-Ife (London: Harvill, 2000)].

STAMATIS, ALEXIS, *Bar Flober* (Athens: Kedros, 2000).

SYMBARDIS, YORGOS, *O achristos Dimitris* [*Useless Dimitris*] (Athens: Kedros, 1998).

TAMVAKAKIS, FAIDON, *Ta topia tis Filomilas* [*The Landscapes of Philomela*] (Athens: Estia, 1988).

—— *Oi navagoi tis Pasifais* [*The Castaways of the Pasiphae*] (Athens: Estia, 1997).

TASSOPOULOS, STEFANOS, *Iliako orologio* [*Sundial*] (Athens: Kedros, 1988).

THEMELIS, NIKOS, *I anazitisi* [*The Quest*] (Athens: Kedros, 1998).

—— *I anatropi* [*The Overthrow*] (Athens: Kedros, 2000).

—— *I analampi* [*The Gleam*] (Athens: Kedros, 2002).

THEODORIDIS, PANOS, *To ichomythistorima tou Kapetan Agra* [*The Audio-Novel of Captain Agras*] (Athens: Kedros, 1994).

—— *Ti efylage aftos o chamaidrakon* [*What that Chamaedracon Held in Store*] (Athens: Kedros, 1996).

THEODOROPOULOS, TAKIS, *To adianoito topio* [*The Unimaginable Landscape*] (Athens: Estia, 1991).

THEODOROU, VICTORIA, *Gamilio doro* [*Wedding Present*] (Athens: Gnosi, 1995).

TRIANTAFYLLOU, SOTI, *Savvato vrady stin akri tis polis* [*Saturday Night at the Edge of the City*] (Athens: Polis, 1995).

—— *Avrio mia alli chora* [*Tomorrow Another Country*] (Athens: Polis, 1997).

—— *Ypogeios ouranos* [*Underground Heaven*] (Athens: Polis, 1998).

—— *To ergostasio ton molyvion* [*The Pencil Factory*] (Athens: Patakis, 2000).

TSIAMBOUSIS, VASILIS, *I glykeia Bonora* [*Sweet Bonora*] (Athens: Kedros, 2000).

TSIRKAS, STRATIS, *I chameni anoixi* [*The Lost Spring*] (Athens: Kedros, 1976).

VAKALOPOULOS, CHRISTOS, *Nees athinaikes istories* [*New Athenian Stories*] (Athens: Estia, 1989).

VALTINOS, THANASIS, *Tria ellinika monoprakta* [*Three One-Act Plays*] (Athens: Kedros, 1978).

—— *Stoicheia gia ti dekaetia tou '60* (Athens: Stigmi, 1989; 2nd edn., Athens: Agra, 1992, repr. Okeanida, 2001) [*Data from the Decade of the Sixties*, trans. Jane Assimakopoulos and Stavros Deligiorgis (Evanston, IL: Northwestern University Press, 2000)].

—— *Tha vreite ta osta mou ypo vrochin* [*You'll Find my Bones in the Rain*] (Athens: Agra, 1992).

—— *Orthokosta* (Athens: Agra, 1994).

—— *Imerologio 1836–2011* [*Diary 1836–2011*] (Athens: Okeanida, 2001).

VOULGARIS, KOSTIS, *Sto oneiro panta i Peloponniso* [*Peloponnese Forever in a Dream*] (Athens: Gavriilidis, 2001).

VOUPOURAS, CHRISTOS, and KORRAS, YORGOS, *Mirupafsim tha pei: kali antamosi* [*Mirupafshim Means Till we Meet Again*] (Athens: Estia, 2000).

YANNAKAKI, ELENI, *Peri orexeos kai allon deinon* [*On Taste and other Horrors*] (Athens: Estia, 2001).

YATROMANOLAKIS, YORGIS, *Leimonario* (Athens: Kalvos, 1974).

—— *I arravoniastikia* [*The Fiancée*] (Athens: Kedros, 1979).

—— *Istoria* (Athens: Kedros, 1982) [*The History of a Vendetta*, trans. Helen Cavanagh (Sawtry: Dedalus, 1991)].

—— *Anofeles diigima* (Athens: Kedros, 1993) [*A Report of a Murder*, trans. Helen Cavanagh (Sawtry: Dedalus, 1995)].

—— *Erotikon* (Athens: Kedros, 1995) [*Eroticon*, trans. David Connolly (Sawtry: Dedalus, 1999)].

—— *Stin koilada ton Athinon* [*In the Valley of Athens*] (Athens: Kedros, 2000).

ZATELI, ZYRANNA, *Persini arravoniastikia* [*Last Year's Fiancée*] (Athens: Sigaretta, 1984).

—— *Stin erimia me chari* [*In the Wilderness with Charm*] (Athens: Kastaniotis, 1986).

—— *Kai me to fos tou lykou epanerchontai* [*And at Wolf-Light they Return*] (Athens: Kastaniotis, 1993).

ZEI, ALKI, *I arravoniastikia tou Achillea* (Athens: Kedros, 1987) [*Achilles' Fiancée*, trans. Gail Holst-Warhaft (Athens: Kedros, 1991)].

## Secondary Material

ABATZOPOULOU, FRAGISKI, *I grafi kai i vasanos: zitimata logotechnikis anaparastasis* (Athens: Patakis, 2000).

ANGELATOS, DIMITRIS, 'I ek-plixi tis pezografias kai ton apokliseon: i periptosi tou "Dialith' im Christaki" tou Sotiri Dimitriou', *Tetramina*, 39–40 (Summer 1989), 2609–16.

—— *Logodeipnon: parathematikes praktikes sto mythistorima* (Athens: Smili, 1993).

APPADURAI, ARJUN, *Modernity at Large: Cultural Dimensions of Globalization* (Minneapolis: University of Minnesota Press, 1996).

ARISTINOS, YORGOS, 'Stoicheia gia tin periptosi tou Thanassi Valtinou: mia "parametriki" kritiki', *Anti*, 428 (9 Feb. 1990), 58–62.
—— *Dokimia gia to mythistorima kai ta logotechnika eidi* (Athens: Smili, 1991).
ASHCROFT, BILL, et al. (eds.), *The Post-Colonial Studies Reader* (London and New York: Routledge, 1995).
BAKHTIN, MIKHAIL, *The Dialogic Imagination*, ed. Michael Holquist, trans. Caryl Emerson and Michael Holquist (Austin: University of Texas Press, 1981).
—— *Problems of Dostoyevsky's Poetics*, ed. and trans. Caryl Emerson, introd. Wayne Booth (Minneapolis: University of Minnesota Press, 1984).
BARTH, JOHN, 'The literature of exhaustion', in Currie, *Metafiction*, 161–72 [first publ. 1967].
BARTHES, ROLAND, *Mythologies* (Paris: Éditions du Seuil, 1957).
—— *The Pleasure of the Text*, trans. Richard Miller (New York: Hill and Wang, 1975).
BEATON, RODERICK, *An Introduction to Modern Greek Literature* (Oxford: Clarendon Press, 1994).
—— 'Land without novels? Occupation and civil war: the midwives of Greek fiction', *Times Literary Supplement*, 12 Oct. 2001.
BHABHA, HOMI K. (ed.), *Nation and Narration* (London and New York: Routledge, 1990).
—— 'Interrogating identity: the post-colonial prerogative', in D. T. Goldberg (ed.), *Anatomy of Racism* (Minneapolis: University of Minnesota Press, 1990), 188–209.
—— *The Location of Culture* (London and New York: Routledge, 1994).
BIENCZYK, MAREK, 'Metaxy alligorias kai alligorias', *Atelier du Roman*, 2 (special edition in Greek: 'Metaxy geografias kai istorias: to mythistorima stin epochi tis pankosmiopoiisis', Thessaloniki, 2001), 32–41.
BOOTH, WAYNE, *The Rhetoric of Fiction* (Chicago and London: University of Chicago Press, 1983).
BOYM, SVETLANA, *The Future of Nostalgia* (New York, Basic Books, 2001).
BRAIDOTTI, ROSI, 'Cyberfeminism with a difference', http://www.let.uu.nl/womensstudies/rosi/cyberfem.htm.
BRAILSFORD, HENRY NOEL, *Macedonia: Its Races and Their Future* (London: Methuen, 1906).
BRAY, JOE, 'Embedded quotations in eighteenth-century fiction: journalism and the early novel', *Journal of Literary Semantics*, 31/1 (2002), 61–75.
BRENNAN, TIMOTHY, 'The national longing for form', in Bhabha, *Nation and Narration*, 44–70.
BRUNER, JEROME, *Actual Minds, Possible Worlds* (Cambridge, MA: Harvard University Press, 1986).
—— 'The narrative construction of reality', *Critical Inquiry*, 18 (1991), 1–21.
CASTELLS, MANUEL, *End of Millennium* (Information Age, 3; Oxford: Blackwell, 1998).

CAVAFY, C. P., *Collected Poems*, trans. Edmund Keeley and Philip Sherrard (Princeton: Princeton University Press, 1992).

CHOULIARAS, YORGOS, 'Greek culture in the New Europe', in Psomiades and Thomadakis, *Greece, the New Europe*, 79–122.

CHOURMOUZIADIS, KRITON, review of Thanassis Valtinos, *Stoicheia gia ti dekaetia tou '60'*, *Grammata kai Technes* 59 (Sept.–Dec. 1989), 38–9.

CIXOUS, HÉLÈNE, and CALLE-GRUBER, MIREILLE, *Rootprints* (London: Routledge, 1997).

CLOGG, RICHARD, *A Short History of Modern Greece* (Cambridge: Cambridge University Press, 1979).

CLOSE, DAVID H., *Greece since 1945* (London: Longman, 2002).

CROSS, DONNA WOOLFOLK, *Pope Joan* (New York: Ballantine Books, 1996).

CURRIE, MARK (ed.), *Metafiction* (London and New York: Longman, 1995).

DALLAS, GIANNIS, 'Metapolemiki pezografia kai mikro-istoria', in *Istoriki pragmatikotita*, 81–98.

DAVETTAS, N. G., 'Ena mythistorima-psifidoto tou Thanassi Valtinou' (photocopy of a book-review published in the Greek press from Valtinos's personal archives).

DE MAN, PAUL, *Aesthetic Ideology*, ed. Andrzej Warminski (Minneapolis and London: University of Minnesota Press, 1996).

DERRIDA, JACQUES, *La Dissémination* (Paris: Éditions du Seuil, 1972).

DIJK, TEUN VAN, 'Discourse semantics and ideology', *Discourse and Society*, 6/2 (1995), 243–89.

DIMARAS, KONSTANTINOS TH., *Neoellinikos Romantismos* (Athens: Ermis, 1982).

DIMITRIOU, SOTIRIS, 'Kinitra grafis', *Entefktirio*, 33 (Winter 1995–6), 54–5.

—— interview with Michel Fais, *Diavazo*, 399 (Sept. 1999), 50–4.

—— 'Anikoume ston koino paronomasti tou agnostou', interview with Sotiris Letsios, *Anti*, 752 (14 Dec. 2001), 46–7.

—— 'Itan pio eleftheroi apo mas, gematoi ormi kai zoi', interview in *Kathimerini*, 20 Apr. 2003.

DIRLIK, ARIF, 'The Global in the Local', in Wilson and Dissanayake, *Global/Local*, 22–45.

DOCTOROW, E. L., 'False documents', *American Review: The Magazine of New Writing*, 26 (1977), 215–32.

DUTTA, SHOMIT, 'A disunited nation—Thanassis Valtinos: *Data from the Decade of the Sixties*', *Times Literary Supplement*, 12 Jan. 2001.

EAGLETON TERRY, *Literary Theory: An Introduction* (Oxford: Blackwell, 1995 [1st edn. 1983]).

—— *The Idea of Culture* (Oxford: Blackwell, 2000).

ELEFANTIS, ANGELOS, 'Episis se o,ti afora tin oikonomiki domi eimaste sosialistes', *O politis*, 42 (Apr.–May 1981), 6–15.

—— 'I "allagi" teleiose, zito i allagi', *O politis*, 96 (Dec. 1988), 13–17.

—— 'Ston asterismo tou laikismou', *O politis*, 100 (Aug. 1989), 28–37.

FAIS, MICHEL, 'I grafi tis exorias', *Entefktirio*, 33 (Winter 1995–6), 51–3.

FANON, FRANZ, *The Wretched of the Earth* (Harmondsworth: Penguin, 1967).

FARINOU-MALAMATARI, GEORGIA, 'The representation of the Balkans in Modern Greek fiction of the 1990s', in Tziovas, *Greece and the Balkans*, 249–61.

FARIS, WENDY, 1995, 'Scheherazade's children: magical realism and postmodern fiction', in Lois Parkinson Zamora and Wendy B. Faris (eds.), *Magical Realism: History, Theory, Community* (Durham, NC, and London: Duke University Press, 1995), 163–90.

FEATHERSTONE, MIKE, *Postmodernism: Theory, Culture and Society* (London: Sage, 1988).

—— *Undoing Culture: Globalization, Postmodernism and Identity* (London: Sage, 1995).

—— et al. (eds.), *Global Modernities* (London: Sage, 1995).

FOUCAULT, MICHEL, 'Questions on geography', in id., *Power/Knowledge*, trans. Colin Gordon (Brighton: The Harvester Press, 1980), 63–77.

GABARDI, WAYNE, *Negotiating Postmodernism* (Minneapolis: University of Minnesota Press, 2000).

GALANAKI, RHEA, 'Topos, mia speira atermoni (i peri entopiotitas, ethnikou, Anatolis, Dysis)', *Simeio-fylladio*, 1 (Nicosia, 2000), 5–25.

GASS, WILLIAM H., *Fiction and the Figures of Life* (New York: Knopf, 1970).

GELLNER, ERNEST, *Nations and Nationalism* (Oxford: Basil Blackwell, 1983).

GENETTE, GÉRARD, *Seuils* (Paris: Éditions du Seuil 1987).

GRODENT, MICHEL, 'La décennie de tous les dangers', introduction to Thanassis Valtinos, *Éléments pour les années soixante*, trans. Michel Saunier (Institut Français d'Athènes/Actes Sud, Arles 1995).

GUBAR, SUSAN, 'The blank page and the issues of female creativity', in Elizabeth Abel (ed.), *Writing and Sexual Difference* (Brighton: Harvester, 1982), 73–93.

HÄGG, TOMAS, *The Novel in Antiquity* (Oxford: Blackwell, 1983).

HALL, STUART, 'The local and the global: globalization and ethnicity', in King, *Culture, Globalization and the World-System*, 19–39.

—— 'Who needs identity?', in Stuart Hall and Paul du Gay (eds.), *Questions of Cultural Identity* (London: Sage, 1996), 1–17.

HANNERZ, ULF, 'Cosmopolitans and locals in world culture', in Mike Featherstone (ed.), *Global Culture: Nationalism, Globalization and Modernity* (London: Sage, 1990), 237–51.

—— 'Stockholm: doubly creolizing', in A. Daun et al. (eds.), *To Make the World Safe for Diversity: Towards an Understanding of Multicultural Societies* (Stockholm: Swedish Immigration Institute, 1992).

—— *Transnational Connections* (London: Routledge, 1996).

HATZIS, DIMITRIS, 'O syngrafeas brosta sti sychroni elliniki pragmatikotita', in id., *To prosopo tou neou Ellinismou: anekdotes dialexeis kai dokimia*, ed. Venetia Apostolidou (Athens: Rodakio, 2003), 349–68.

HATZIVASSILIOU, VANGELIS, 'Thanassis Valtinos: i logotechnia den grafetai me aisthimata', *O kosmos tou vivliou* 1 (July 1989), 3–7.

―― 'Sti skia tis istorias', *Eleftherotypia*, 7 Aug. 1998.

―― 'I elliniki logotechnia meta to '74: sygkliseis kai apokliseis', *Anti*, 688 (1999), 36–8.

―― 'From modernism to post-modern?: Changes in Greek fiction (1975–2001)', *Ithaca*, 18 (Sept. 2002), 9–15.

―― [Vanguelis Jatsivasiliu], 'Nuevos caminos de la narrativa griega', *Ithaca (Books from Greece)*, Edición especial, Septiembre 2003, 4–9.

HIRSCHON, RENÉE (ed.), *Crossing the Aegean: An Appraisal of the 1923 Compulsory Population Exchange between Greece and Turkey* (New York and Oxford: Berghahn, 2003).

HOBSBAWM, ERIC, *Nations and Nationalism since 1780: Programme, Myth, Reality* (Cambridge: Cambridge University Press, 1990).

HOFSTADTER, DOUGLAS R., *Gödel, Escher, Bach: An Eternal Golden Braid* (Hassocks: Harvester, 1979).

HUTCHEON, LINDA, *Narcissistic Narrative: The Metafictional Paradox* (London and New York: Methuen, 1984 [1st edn.1980]).

―― *A Theory of Parody: The Teachings of Twentieth-Century Art Forms* (New York and London: Methuen, 1985).

―― *A Poetics of Postmodernism* (London and New York: Routledge, 1988).

―― *The Politics of Postmodernism* (London and New York: Routledge, 1989).

HUYSSEN ANDREAS, *After the Great Divide: Modernism, Mass Culture, Post-modernism* (Bloomington: Indiana University Press, 1986).

IGGERS, GEORG, *Historiography in the Twentieth Century* (Hanover and London: Wesleyan University Press, 1996).

IRMER, THOMAS, *Metafiction, Moving Pictures, Moving Histories: Der historische Roman in der Literatur der amerikanischen Postmoderne* (Tübingen: Günter Narr Verlag, 1995).

*Istoriki pragmatikotita kai neoelliniki pezografia (1945–1995)* (Athens: Etaireia Spoudon Neoellinikou Politismou kai Genikis Paideias, 1997).

JAMESON, FREDRIC, 'Third-world literature in the era of multinational capitalism', *Social Text*, 15 (1986), 65–88.

―― 'On "Cultural Studies"', *Social Text*, 34 (1993), 17–52.

KAKAVOULIA, MARIA, 'On reported discourse: recording speech and thought in modern Greek literary and press narrative', in Christos Clairis (ed.), *Recherches en linguistique grecque*, i (Paris: L'Harmattan, 2002), 251–4.

KAPLAN, CAREN, *Questions of Travel: Postmodern Discourses of Displacement* (Durham, NC, and London: Duke University Press, 1996).

KARAKASIDOU, ANASTASIA N., *Fields of Wheat, Hills of Blood: Passages to Nation-hood in Greek Macedonia 1870–1990* (Chicago and London: University of Chicago Press, 1997).

KASDAGLIS, NIKOS, 'Thanassis Valtinos', *To tram*, triti diadromi, 13–14 (June 1990), 75–84.

KASTRINAKI, ANGELA, 'Nearoi kallitechnes stin elliniki pezografia: i koultoura tou egotismou kai kapoies "elleipseis"', *Oi chronoi tis istorias: gia mia istoria tis paidikis logotechnias kai tis neotitas* (Athens: Geniki Grammateia Neas Genias, 1998), 253–63.

KEPPLER, CARL F., *The Literature of the Second Self* (Tucson: University of Arizona Press, 1972).

KEZA, LAURIE, 'Ena simeioma tis Loris Keza', *Na ena milo*, 1 (Dec. 2002), 5–6.

KING, ANTHONY D. (ed.), *Culture, Globalization and the World-System: Contemporary Conditions for the Representation of Identity* (London: Macmillan, 1991).

KITROMILIDES, PASCHALIS, *Enlightment, Nationalism, Orthodoxy: Studies in the Culture and Political Thought of South-Eastern Europe* (Aldershot: Variorum, 1994).

KOKORIS, DIMITRIS, 'Apo ti Valeria ston Spetim: logotechnika prosopa tou Sotiri Dimitriou', *O politis dekapenthimeros*, 11 (29 Sept. 1995), 46–9.

KOTZIA, ELISAVET, 'Sti dekaetia tou 60', *Kathimerini*, 10 Sept. 1989, 24.

—— review of Rhea Galanaki, *Eleni, i o Kanenas*, in *Kathimerini*, 6 Sept. 1998.

—— 'To ergo ton metapolemikon pezografon sti metadiktatoriki periodo', *Anti*, 688 (June 1999), 32–5.

—— 'Elliniki pezografia 1930–1999: ithika prostagmata i evzoia?', *Vivliothiki* (*Eleftherotypia*), 118 (1 Sept. 2000), 9–10.

—— 'Mystikos, zontanos kosmos', *Kathimerini*, 4 Nov. 2001.

—— 'Elliniki pezografia kai kosmopolitismos 1930–2000', *K* 1 (Mar. 2003), 57–65.

KOTZIAS, ALEXANDROS, interview with Vena Georgakopoulou, *I Aristera simera*, 15 (Jan.–Feb. 1986), 59.

KOURTOVIK, DIMOSTHENIS, *Imedapi exoria: keimena gia tin elliniki logotechnia 1986–91* (Athens: Opera, 1991).

—— 'I nostalgia gia ton Kanena', *Ta Nea*, 12 June 1999.

—— 'Ena dilimma choris noima', *Vivliothiki* (*Eleftherotypia*), 118 (1 Sept. 2000), 14–15.

LAMBROPOULOS, VASILIS, 'I diekdikisi ton eikonon se mia eikoniki epochi', *To Vima tis Kyriakis*, 7 Jan. 2001.

LARKIN, PHILIP, *Collected Poems* (London: Faber and Faber, 1988).

LEE, ALISON, *Realism and Power: Postmodern British Fiction* (London: Routledge, 1990).

LEONTIS, ARTEMIS (ed.), *Greece: A Traveler's Literary Companion* (San Francisco: Whereabouts Press, 1997).

—— 'Primordial home, elusive home', *Thesis Eleven*, 59 (1999), 1–16.

—— 'In the eyes of strangers', *Ithaca* 9 (May–June 2001), 11–14.

LEVI, GIOVANNI, 'On microhistory', in Peter Burke (ed.), *New Perspectives on Historical Writing* (University Park, PA: Pennsylvania State University Press/Cambridge: Polity Press, 1991), 93–113.

LIONTIS, KOSTIS, 'Ef' olis tis ylis: mia syzitisi me ton Thanassi Valtino (4.5.1984)', *I Aristera simera*, 7 (July 1984), 50–4.

LODGE, DAVID, *Small World* (London: Secker and Warburg, 1975).

MCHALE, BRIAN, *Postmodernist Fiction* (London and New York: Methuen, 1987).

MACKRIDGE, PETER, 'The two-fold nostalgia: Lost homeland and lost time in the work of G. Theotokas, E. Venezis and K. Politis', *Journal of Modern Greek Studies*, 4 (1986), 75–83.

—— 'Macedonia and Macedonians in *Sta mystika tou valtou* (1937) by P. S. Delta', *Dialogos: Hellenic Studies Review*, 7 (2000), 41–55.

—— 'The myth of Asia Minor in Greek fiction', in Hirschon, *Crossing the Aegean*, 235–46.

—— and YANNAKAKIS, ELENI (eds.), *Ourselves and Others: The Development of a Greek Macedonian Cultural Identity since 1912* (Oxford and New York: Berg, 1997).

MARGARITIS, GIORGOS, *Istoria tou Ellinikou Emfyliou Polemou 1946–1949*, vol. i (Athens: Vivliorama, 2001).

MARONITIS, D. N., 'Paramethorios pezografia: to paradeigma tou Sotiri Dimitriou', *Entefktirio*, 33 (Winter 1995–6), 47–50.

MASSON, JEAN-YVES, 'I idea tis pankosmias logotechnias os antidoto stin pankosmiopoiisi', *Atelier du Roman*, 2 (special edition in Greek: 'Metaxy geografias kai istorias: to mythistorima stin epochi tis pankosmiopoiisis', Thessaloniki, 2001), 18–31.

MAZUREK, RAYMOND A., 'Metafiction, the historical novel and Coover's *The Public Burning*', *Critique: Studies in Modern Fiction*, 23/3 (1982), 29–42.

MOUZELIS, NIKOS, 'The concept of modernization: Its relevance for Greece', *Journal of Modern Greek Studies*, 14 (1996), 215–27.

MURSHED, MANSOOB, *Globalization, Marginalization and Development* (London: Routledge, 2002).

NAYYAR, DEEPAK (ed.), *Governing Globalization: Issues and Institutions* (Oxford: Oxford University Press, 2002).

NÜNNING, ANSGAR, *Von historischer Fiktion zu historiographischer Metafiktion. Band I: Theorie, Typologie und Poetik des historischen Romans* (Trier: Wissenschaftlicher Verlag Trier, 1995).

ONEGA, SUSANA, 'British historiographic metafiction', in Currie, *Metafiction*, 92–103.

PANSELINOS, ALEXIS, 'Ta vivlia einai viomata', interview with Olga Sella, *Anti*, 636 (6 June 1997), 56–8.

PAPACHELAS, ALEXIS, *O viasmos tis ellinikis dimokratias: o amerikanikos paragon, 1947–1967* (Athens: Estia, 1997).

PAPADIMITRAKOPOULOS, I. K., 'Kostas Chatziargyris: parousiasi-anthologisi', in *I metapolemiki mas pezografia*, viii (Athens: Sokolis, 1988), 126–71.

POLITI, TINA, 'Dyo ellines gia ta Nobel Evropis', *E*, Nov. 1991, 94–6.

POPOV, CHRIS, and RADIN, MICHAEL, 'An analysis of current Greek government policy on the Macedonian issue', *Macedonian Review*, 19 (2–3) (1989), 177–99.

PSOMIADES, HARRY, and THOMADAKIS, STAVROS (eds.), *Greece, the New Europe and the Changing Order* (New York: Pella, 1993).

RAPTOPOULOS, VANGELIS, 'O Thanassis Valtinos milaei me ton Vangeli Raptopoulo', *Anti*, 294 (5 July 1985).

R.M., 'Stoicheia gia ti dekaetia tou 60 tou Thanassi Valtinou', *Odigitis*, 20 July 1989.

ROBERTSON, ROLAND, *Globalization: Social Theory and Global Culture* (London: Sage, 1992).

ROUDOMETOF, VICTOR, 'Nationalism and identity politics in the Balkans: Greece and the Macedonian Question', *Journal of Modern Greek Studies*, 14 (1996), 253–301.

SAID, EDWARD W., *Orientalism* (New York: Vintage Books, 1979).

SCHINA, KATERINA, 'Zoume se mia epochi ekptosis ton panton', *Kathimerini*, 4 June 1989.

SCHOLES, ROBERT, *Fabulation and Metafiction* (Urbana: University of Illinois Press, 1979).

SHORT, MICK, MARTIN, WYNNE, and SEMINO, ELENA, 'Reading reports: Discourse presentation in a corpus of narratives, with special reference to news reports', in H.-J. Diller and E. O. G. Stratman (eds.), *English via Various Media* (Heidelberg: Universitätsverlag C. Winter, 1999), 39–66.

SUPPAN, ARNOLD, 'Einleitung: Identitäten und Stereotypen in multiethnischen europäischen Regionen', in Valeria Heuberger et al. (eds.), *Das Bild vom Anderen: Identitäten, Mentalitäten, Mythen und Stereotypen in multiethnischen europäischen Regionen* (Frankfurt am Main and Berlin: Peter Lang, 1999), 9–20.

TANNEN, DEBORAH, *Talking Voices: Repetition, Dialogue and Imagery in Conversational Discourse* (Cambridge: Cambridge University Press, 1989).

TARSOULI, ATHINA, *Eleni Altamoura* (Athens: Dimitrakos, 1934).

TODOROV, TZVETAN, *Mikhail Bakhtin: The Dialogical Principle*, trans. Wlad Godzich (Manchester: Manchester University Press, 1984).

TSAKNIAS, SPYROS, 'I peripeteia enos laou: Thanassis Valtinos, *Stoicheia gia ti dekaetia tou '60*', *To Vima*, 3 Sept. 1989.

—— 'O Kafka kai oi alloi', *To Vima–Vivlia*, 10 Jan. 1999.

TSOUKALAS, CONSTANTINE, *I elliniki tragodia: apo tin apeleftherosi os tous syntagmatarches* (Athens: Nea Synora, 1981) (first publ. in English by Penguin, 1969).

—— 'Greek national identity in an integrated Europe and a changing world order', in Psomiades and Thomadakis, *Greece, the New Europe*, 57–78.

TZIOVAS, DIMITRIS, 'Residual orality and belated textuality in Modern Greek literature and culture', *Journal of Modern Greek Studies*, 7 (1989), 321–35.

—— *The Other Self: Selfhood and Society in Modern Greek Fiction* (Lanham, MD: Lexington Books, 2003).

—— (ed.), *Greece and the Balkans: Identities, Perceptions and Cultural Encounters since the Enlightenment* (Aldershot: Ashgate, 2003).

VAKALOPOULOS, CONSTANTINE, *O enoplos agonas sti Makedonia (1904–1908): O Makedonikos Agonas* (Athens: Irodotos, 1999).

VITTI, MARIO, *I Genia tou Trianta: ideologia kai morfi* (Athens: Ermis, 1982).

VOLOŠINOV, V. N., *Marxism and the Philosophy of Language*, trans. Ladislav Matejka and I. R. Titunik (New York and London: Seminar Press, 1973).

—— *Freudianism: A Marxist Critique*, trans. I. R. Titunik (New York: Academic Press, 1976).

WALLERSTEIN, IMMANUEL, 'The national and the universal: can there be such a thing as world culture?', in King, *Culture, Globalization and the World-System*, 91–105.

WAUGH, PATRICIA, *Metafiction: The Theory and Practice of Self-Conscious Fiction* (London and New York: Methuen, 1984).

—— *Feminine Fictions: Revisiting the Postmodern* (London: Routledge, 1997).

WESSELING, ELISABETH, *Writing History as a Prophet: Postmodernist Innovations of the Historical Novel* (Amsterdam and Philadelphia: John Benjamins, 1991).

WHITE, HAYDEN, *Metahistory: The Historical Imagination in Nineteenth-Century Europe* (Baltimore and London: Johns Hopkins University Press, 1973).

—— *Tropics of Discourse: Essays in Cultural Criticism* (Baltimore and London: Johns Hopkins University Press, 1978).

—— *The Content of the Form: Narrative Discourse and Historical Representation* (Baltimore and London: Johns Hopkins University Press, 1987).

WILSON, ROB, 'Goodbye paradise: global/localism in the American Pacific', in Wilson and Dissanayake, *Global/Local*, 312–36.

—— and DISSANAYAKE, WIMAL (eds.), *Global/Local: Cultural Production and the Transnational Imaginary* (Durham, NC, and London: Duke University Press, 1996).

YUVAL-DAVIS, NINA, *Gender and Nation* (London: Sage, 1997).

ZANNAS, PAVLOS, *Petrokalamithres: dokimia kai alla 1960–1989* (Athens: Diatton, 1990).

ZENAKOS, LEONIDAS, 'Melpo Axioti: '"To spiti mou"', *O Tachydromos*, 652 (8 Oct. 1966), 62.

ZIRAS, ALEXIS, 'Synyfansi paradosiakou kai monternou kai krisi tis monternikotitas stin elliniki pezografia 1980–1995', in *Istoriki pragmatikotita*, 193–211.

# INDEX

❖